# PRAISE FOR _3...2...1... WE'RE ON THE AIR_

"Every good television sports presentation requires the talent and hard work of those who are never seen or heard on the air and whose names don't always appear near the top of the credits. This is especially true at the Olympics where thousands such people are perhaps unheralded but certainly indispensable. Bob Steinfeld has been part of significant productions—local, national, and international. Here are his stories of decades in sports television."

> —**Bob Costas,** Sportscaster for NBC Sports (1980-2019) and Prime-Time Host of 12 Olympic Games

"I have known Bob for almost thirty-five years as a decorated sports television producer. He made an immediate impression on me with his steady hand, gracious personality, and a keen sense of how to navigate a large crew through a broadcast. _3 . . . 2 . . . 1 . . ._ takes us into the production truck for an authentic look at how it all comes together. Just writing that title gets my energy and excitement up—I just wish it was more frequently Bob's voice that was counting down into my headset! Nothing but respect!"

> —**Jim Nantz,** Sportscaster for CBS Sports

"I stepped into the booth for my first CFB broadcast having no idea what I was doing. Thankfully the voice in my headset was the Dr. himself Bob Steinfeld! Bob's level of preparation and leadership is top-notch and continues to drive me to this day. Reading _3 . . . 2 . . . 1 . . . We're On The Air_ brought me back to that day with the rush of excitement I felt then. This peek behind the production curtain is a must for anyone that enjoys watching their favorite sports on TV."

> —**Joel Klatt,** Lead College Football Analyst for Fox Sports

"I first met Bob Steinfeld when he was a young man, and I was still thin and had hair. We shared a couple of adventures back then. He's had a terrific career in sports television production. I know you will enjoy reading his stories and listening to his advice."

> —**Verne Lundquist,** Sportscaster for CBS Sports (1982-2024)

"Great Spurs chapter! I began my now twenty-year broadcasting career under Bob's tutelage and owe much of my success to Bob. His meticulous production skills set a high bar for sports television. By the way, as you'll read in the book, don't ever buy Bob a PB&J sandwich on the golf course!"

> —**Sean Elliott,** San Antonio Spurs 1999 NBA Champion and 2-Time NBA All-Star; 1989 AP College Basketball Player of the Year & John R. Wooden Award Winner

"Bob Steinfeld was one of my first producers. His guidance helped shape my career, and our time together coincided with the rise of the San Antonio Spurs dynasty. Many of those David Robinson, Tim Duncan, and Gregg Popovich moments are included in this book. They are treasured memories for me, and I know you'll enjoy reading about them. Great stories and great lessons both in life and broadcasting for announcers, producers, and sports television fans."

—**Brian Anderson,** Play-by-Play Announcer for MLB, NBA, NCAA Turner/ CBS, & Milwaukee Brewers

"Bob shares an incredible behind the scenes experience from the elite level of journalism and broadcasting. He captures the challenges and true struggles that go into producing the best of the best from professional sports to the Olympic Games. The book captivates our hearts and minds as it shares in the journey for excellence. I appreciate Bob fighting for increasing national television exposure and reach for elite women's athletics. His stance for adding coverage for the 1996 USA Softball team in their quest for the Olympic gold medal is honorable, and you will read many more inside stories of what goes into producing some of the most memorable moments in sports."

—**Dot Richardson,** MD, Olympic Gold Medalist ('96 & '00)

"A wonderful read. Bob gives you insight behind-the-scenes with legendary sports stories and sports icons."

—**Ann Meyers Drysdale,** Naismith Memorial Basketball Hall of Famer, Network Sportscaster, and VP of Phoenix Mercury and Phoenix Suns

"Bob has been on the inside as a television producer who has worked across the landscape of sports, and he has so many wonderful stories to tell. Not to give too much away, but the Cal Ripken story is particularly fun. You'll enjoy this a lot."

—**Joe Posnanski,** NY Times Best-Selling Author of Paterno, The Baseball 100, and Why We Love Baseball: A History in 50 Moments; Co-Host of The PosCast; Writer at JoeBlogs

"Very much enjoyed reading it. . . . One of the good guys, Bob has had a front-row seat to both the evolution and revolution of sports television over the last forty years. From the nascent days of sports on cable television to the heights of the Olympic Games, Bob has lived every sports junkie's dream."

—**Keith Samples,** Filmmaker, Television Director/Producer, and former Syndication Executive with Warner Brothers, Walt Disney, and Lorimar-Telepictures; Founder of Rysher Entertainment

"What great memories! What a career! Really enjoyed it!"

　　—**Ron Thulin,** Commentator for WNBA and College Basketball & Football

"I thoroughly enjoyed it!"

　　—**Mike Martin,** Associate Professor of Professional Practice, Bob Schieffer College of Communication, TCU

"If you want a front row seat into the adventurous odyssey of becoming a sports television producer, here's your VIP admission ticket. In *3 . . . 2 . . . 1 . . . We're on the Air,* Bob generously takes us by the hand and walks us through the corridors of his early internships, cub reporter roles, and finally his high-octane television producing career—a world bursting with ambition, high stakes, home runs, air balls, penalties, and ultimately championships.

　　I found myself smiling at the pages as Bob described his fumbles and faux pas, because I know the delicate balance we creatives attempt to strike when voicing our opinions while still maintaining our professionalism. You want the job, but not at the expense of your personal dignity. I also know that the worlds Bob has traveled in his five-decade career are universes that millions might watch on TV, but will never actually have a 'view from the truck.' And that privilege alone is worth the price of admission."

　　—**Fran Harris,** Television Personality, MVP of 1986 Texas Longhorns NCAA Championship Team, and Member of 1997 WNBA Champion Houston Comets

"Outstanding! Dr. Robert Steinfeld is truly a television legend who brought creativity and fun to every show. Plus, unlike the rest of us in the truck, he's a snappy dresser! I can't wait to read the rest of his memoir."

　　—**Scott Johnson,** ESPN Director

"Bob Steinfeld tells fascinating stories from his career producing the widest possible range of television sports across the past four decades. His experience and insights will undoubtedly be helpful for young professionals just embarking on their careers."

　　—**Dennis Deninger** - Professor Emeritus, Syracuse University; Emmy Award–winning 25-year ESPN veteran

"What a career you had! I wish I could have been a fly on the wall for some of these stories. Loved the interaction with Timmy [Duncan]."

　　—**Sheryl Beesley,** Associate Producer, CBSSN and ESPN

"Oh, the places I've been telecasting sporting events with Robert Steinfeld designing the coverage. Hundreds of them, maybe thousands. Everything from Nolan Ryan's 5,000th strikeout game to indoor soccer championships to Texas-Oklahoma football to boxing matches held at the Fort Worth stockyards. He always came so prepared, so focused. For Robert, any event became an opportunity to craft another story, whatever that story might be. All of us who worked with him over the years feel privileged to have been at his side. *3 . . . 2 . . . 1 . . .* I miss those years.

> —**Norm Hitzges,** Sports Broadcaster/Commentator, Author, and Texas Radio Hall of Fame Inductee

"Bob Steinfeld is one of the most talented people in the sports television industry . . . Full Stop! His ability to lead a production and technical team through a live sports television event is similar to a conductor with an orchestra—on point and brilliant."

> —**Tim Scanlan,** VP Sports Broadcast & Media at Octagon, ESPN VP/Talent Planning, & Development and Coordinating Producer MLB

"Appreciate your expertise in leading the broadcast!"

> —**Dawn Staley,** Head Coach University of South Carolina Women's Basketball; Head Coach 2020 USA Basketball National Team (Gold Medal), and Commentator for 2022 WNBA Commissioner's Cup Championship

"You do a terrific job producing our philosophy and making it come to life. The Cotton Bowl is very fortunate to have you on our team."

> —**Rick Baker,** President/Chief Executive Officer Goodyear Cotton Bowl

"A special tip of the hat to our Executive Producer Bob Steinfeld for his commitment and dedication to producing a best-of-class show. Thank you, Bob."

> —**Greg Bibb,** President & CEO, Dallas Wings

"I worked with [Bob] on many mainline sports telecasts of baseball, basketball, and football. . . . I never ever worked with a producer more fully prepared to do his job in prepping for a telecast . . . from "minor" sports to the majors."

> —**Greg Lucas,** Sports Broadcaster and Author

"Bob's career spans decades over time and is a great resource for learning what this crazy TV business is all about. You see Bob walking the hallways or coming to the broadcast table to say hello and you smile. His passion is contagious!"

> —**Lisa Byington,** Play-by-Play Announcer for the Milwaukee Bucks, Chicago Sky, CBS March Madness NCAA Tournament, and the 2021 and 2024 WNBA Commissioner's Cup Championship

**3...2...1...**
# WE'RE ON THE AIR

As Tim Duncan told me,
"You gotta dominate
where you can, man."

ENJOY!

# 3...2...1...
# WE'RE ON
# THE AIR

*An Inside Look at Sports Television,
Journalism, and Gender Equity*

ROBERT STEINFELD

FORT WORTH, TEXAS

Library of Congress Cataloging-in-Publication Data

Names: Steinfeld, Robert Howard, 1955- author.
Title: 3 ... 2 ... 1 ... we're on the air! : an inside look at sports television, journalism, and
    gender equity / Robert Steinfeld.
Other titles: Three ... two ... one ... we are on the air!
Description: Fort Worth, Texas : TCU Press, 2024. | Summary: "Imagine what it's like
    to make hundreds of decisions in just two hours on "live" network television with
    your work seen by millions of people. That's what a sports television producer
    does each time they sit in "the big chair." In 3...2...1... We're on the Air, Emmy
    Award-Winning Producer Robert Steinfeld takes readers inside the world of
    sports television through his career producing some of the biggest sporting events,
    such as the Summer Olympics, the NBA and WNBA, the MLB, and the FIFA
    World Cup. Along the way he crossed paths with athletic stars like Cal Ripken,
    Alex Rodriguez, Nolan Ryan, Nancy Lieberman, Tim Duncan, David Robinson,
    Bill Walton and announcers Bob Costas, Jim Nantz, and Robin Roberts. Join
    Robert Steinfeld on his path from eager, ambitious teenage journalist to ultimately
    realizing his dream producing major sporting events. So, "3...2...1...We're On the
    Air!""-- Provided by publisher.
Identifiers: LCCN 2024032996 (print) | LCCN 2024032997 (ebook) | ISBN
    9780875658803 (cloth) | ISBN 9780875658971 (ebook)
Subjects: LCSH: Television broadcasting of sports. | Television--Production and direc-
    tion. | Television and sports. | Mass media and sports. | Equality.
Classification: LCC GV742.3 .A15 2024  (print) | LCC GV742.3  (ebook) | DDC
    070.4/49796--dc23/eng/20240724
LC record available at https://lccn.loc.gov/2024032996
LC ebook record available at https://lccn.loc.gov/2024032997

TCU Box 298300
Fort Worth, Texas 76129
www.tcupress.com

Design by Preston Thomas, Cadence Design Studio

# DEDICATION

*For Sarah, the love of my life,* who inspired me to pen my memoir to keep me out of her hair when there were no games to produce during the COVID pandemic. We've been married since 1981. As a friend and associate once said, I certainly outkicked my coverage. He was correct.

Well, Sarah encouraged me to document my career and share with others. I could not have worked more than five decades in this business without her support. She basically raised our children while I was producing telecasts in Dallas, Arlington, San Antonio, New Orleans and on the road with my teams and varying national networks, which is the major reason our children, Elaine and Leon, turned out to be so successful in their personal and professional lives.

# CONTENTS

# CONTENTS

# ACKNOWLEDGMENTS

*There are many people I want to thank* for supporting me along the way, all of whom believed in me.

My late parents, Elaine and Fred Steinfeld. They always encouraged me to pursue my passion.

My wife, Sarah. She always dealt with my traveling and my late night games, nursing my sports injuries (just a few), and helping me recover from my cardiac event in New Orleans and the ensuing bypass surgery and recovery back home in Dallas. It would have been impossible without her love and support.

My late father-in-law and mother-in-law, Leon and Farida Esquenazi, for understanding my career and love for their daughter.

My children, Elaine and Leon, for always being a fan of the team I was producing. They respected the fact that I was busy working when they were growing up, but I trusted they knew my heart was always with them. I hope they learned from my work ethic, persistence, and love of my job. I trust they are passing those values on to their spouses, Mike and Rebecca, and to our grandchildren, Ellory and Remi.

My brother, Jay, for letting me tag along to sporting events. He taught me dice baseball, *Sports Illustrated* baseball, wiffleball, stickball, hardball, how to shoot rockets, and how to collect baseball cards during our childhood in New Jersey and Dallas. I admire the career he built for himself and his family, and I've learned a lot from him.

My aunt Carol, who has been like a second mother to me after my mom passed away. And late uncle Arthur Edelman, for always welcoming me when visiting Princeton, and for allowing me to stay with the family for a few months after college.

My first cousins, Nancy Frank Cook and Seth Frank, for their love since we were kids.

My best friends since I moved to Dallas when I was nine years old: Ted Tobolowsky and the late Mark Bodzin and Steve Saltzman.

Professionally, Liberty Sports president/CEO Ed Frazier; Liberty Sports COO Joe King; Liberty Sports VP Jack Stanfield; ON TV/HSE program director/executive producer Glenn Gurgiolo; Fox Sports Net executives Roy Hamilton, Gary Garcia, Bill Borson, Doug Levy, Ron Gralnik, George Greenberg, the late Doug Sellars, and many others in Los Angeles; Fox Sports SW general manager Jon Heidtke; Fox Sports SW executive producer Mike Anastassiou; Fox Sports SW coordinating producer Ed Pete; San Antonio Spurs Sports and Entertainment executive vice president Lawrence Payne and president and CEO Russ Bookbinder; San Antonio Spurs director Mike Kickirillo; Dallas Mavericks broadcaster Allen Stone; director Dave Burchett; and my high school journalism teacher, the late Julia Caroline "Judy" Jeffress.

I appreciate the editorial assessment and developmental editing by longtime professional journalist and author Joseph Dionisio as well as freelance editor and University of Kentucky Graduate Instructor Alex Gergely for his copyediting. The student beta readers from the "Remote Sports Production" and "Producing Live Sports Event" classes taught by Mike Martin—TCU's associate professor of professional practice in film, television and digital media—also proved invaluable to this book.

Further thanks to University of North Texas adjunct instructor Hank Dickenson and his Sports Broadcasting class. The advice and feedback I received from Dennis Deninger—one of my former coordinating producers at ESPN, and currently a journalism professor at Syracuse University—were also gratifying.

I enjoyed and appreciated the collaboration with TCU Press Director Dan Williams and staff. Guiding me along the initial publishing road was Joel Pitney and his group at Launch My Book. Publicity for the book launch was professionally guided by Sharon Bially and her staff at BookSavvy.

The Cotton Bowl Athletic Association is run by an accomplished group of dedicated and loyal professionals. Rick Baker guides the team, working with Marty McInnis on the business side; Michael Konradi on marketing and sponsorships; Lisa Fortenberry on pageantry and game presentation (specifically the bands, drill teams, anthem and Kilgore Rangerette performances); Charlie Fiss and Scottie Rodgers on history and media relations; plus recently retired Nancy Mills, vice president of executive services, who makes my job easy. Everyone knows their roles and where to go to ensure a quality bowl game. These people and the board of directors and chairpersons made the Cotton Bowl what it is: a game that every team, coach, and fan wants to attend because of the way they are treated and how the game and activities are handled. I am fortunate to be a small part of that esteemed group.

During those Fox Sports football years, I forged many fond memories and friendships, especially with directors Kenny Miller and Phil Mollica, associate directors Amanda Bowditch and Daniel Ashcraft (who produces Spurs, too), and replay operator Nathan Beck.

Special shoutout to Jeff Hunt's public relations class at the University of Texas-Austin, my alma mater, for their help designing a social media campaign for this book.

Thank you to the many other friends and business associates who have and will continue to stand by me throughout my career and personal life. I hope I have lived up to your expectations as a professional, business associate, friend, and most importantly, family member.

I hope you enjoy the book and learn a few things about producing live sports events and the talented commentators, celebrities, and others I've encountered.

I look forward to the coming years as I watch my kids continue their thriving careers and raise their growing families. And now I take on perhaps my most important role, being a wonderful grandfather to two girls, Ellory Nora Steinfeld (born October 10, 2022) and Remi Lola Makara (born December 24, 2022). It will be special to behold the first cousins growing up together in Dallas.

# FOREWORD

*3 . . . 2 . . . 1 . . . We're on the Air!* is a fantastic look back at all the consequential moments that my friend Bob Steinfeld experienced during his many decades behind the scenes in sports.

I have been blessed to be a Naismith Memorial Basketball Hall of Famer, a two-time Olympian, and the second woman to be hired as an assistant coach in the NBA with the Sacramento Kings. After that, I became the first female head coach in a man's professional league, the Big3. We won the 2018 championship, and I was named Coach of the Year. You have to think life has been great!

As a broadcaster, I've been working for Fox Sports and other networks since 1980, when I first met Bob Steinfeld. He was bold, hardworking, and always demanded excellence. I knew we would be friends. I have covered NCAA men's and women's hoops and NBA and WNBA games and have served as a studio analyst and sideline reporter. I've also covered four Olympic games for NBC. Many of these events were working with Bob—whom we affectionately call "Dr. Bob" or "Steiny"—one of the best producers in the business.

I can't calculate the number of games we've worked together. They were always epic and a learning experience. Bob wanted our games to be the best and held us to those high standards. You learn a lot about people when you sit around talking to them about life, family, and sports. Both of us loved basketball, baseball, and football. Our conversations were based on trying to see who knew the most about what sport and players.

But I always knew Bob was different. He cared about growing the game, especially for women. I'm sure Bob didn't know he was an activist back in the day, but he was molding women to believe they could be more, and that they deserved opportunities.

After many years of working together we realized we were more than colleagues: we were friends and family. One of the most fun things ever with Steiny was hosting the Dallas Mavericks 2011 championship parade with John Rhadigan for Fox Sports SW. It was a huge moment for me, John, and our producer, Bob. He was an amazing leader with content and a vision for the show. Thanks to his direction, we crushed it.

One of the many things Bob does well is that he pushes you to be better. He can be tough, and you have to have thick skin and not get your feelings hurt. He will explain what you can do better, what you did wrong, and how you can improve it.

Following your producer and working in tandem is a genuine art in sports television. A telecast is never going to be perfect, but if you strive for excellence together, it's rewarding. When we weren't doing a game, we'd get out on the court and play games with the crew. It was gratifying for Bob and the crew to have fun and appreciate our time together.

My foreword for this book is in appreciation for all Bob has done for so many in the industry. He has been a champion for women in sports, whether it's behind the scenes, in the studio, or for the athletes who are performing. He's always been a pillar of fairness for women, and he wants us to get our fair share of the limelight.

When I think of Bob, my thoughts harken to championing the 1996 gold medal–winning Olympic women's softball team in Atlanta and covering the inaugural season of the WNBA and now his work as the executive producer for the WNBA's Dallas Wings and the Commissioner's Cup championships. He's worked with the Dallas Mavericks, San Antonio Spurs, and New Orleans Pelicans and is a ten-time Emmy Award–winning producer. His experiences with Naismith Basketball Hall of Famers like me, Tim Duncan, David Robinson, Dawn Staley, and more, are endless.

So much happens when the cameras are not rolling. Relationships are built in the inner sanctum of an arena. You will find Bob's stories to be real, fun, and educational. He has always been ahead of his time, opening doors for many people to work within the companies that he has frequented. Bob's memoir is a game-changer for anybody who craves tales about the athletes and sports he's covered. Those experiences will keep you riveted to his book.

Bob's commitment to storytelling and excellence will give you a glimpse into why he has those ten Emmys sitting at home. The man never stops, and he's a great husband, father, and friend. He's tough as nails and soft as Charmin. Our decades-old friendship is based on love, kindness, and caring. When Bob had a heart attack, he worked hard to get back, demonstrating the same tenacity he showed each in every broadcast. If you love sports, you will love *3 . . . 2 . . . 1 . . . We're on the Air!*

It's not often that somebody can give you all-access behind the scenes to events, games, and people. Bob's memoir will help you understand what has happened during his many decades in sports television. It will also provide a sneak peek at the athletes, the preparation, and the teamwork that create viewing pleasure for the fans watching sports on their TV. You won't put the book down!

**—Nancy Lieberman,**
Naismith Basketball Hall of Famer, two-time Olympic silver medalist, and Big3 Champion and Coach of the Year

# INTRODUCTION

*Author's Note: Naismith Memorial Basketball Hall of Famer Bill Walton and I worked NBA telecasts together; he was my NBC Sports sideline reporter at the 1996 Summer Olympics in Atlanta and most of all, a friend. He once invited us to his home in San Diego for an interview about his former college basketball head coach at UCLA, the legendary John Wooden. On June 1, 2023, Bill was kind enough to write the following introduction for this book. I learned of his unfortunate passing on May 27, 2024. He had a larger-than-life personality, was opinionated, loved the Grateful Dead, and was one of the best collegiate and pro centers ever. There really was no one like him. He will be missed. I appreciated his kind words here, which echoed his colorful personality. As I read it, I could almost hear his passionate, colorful voice.*

---

*Dr. Bob Steinfeld's latest masterpiece,* 3 . . . 2 . . . 1 . . . We're on the Air!, perfectly captures the essence of our lives: storytelling, which is the basis of knowledge, education, and entertainment.

Leadership (a requisite for success) and production (actually making it all happen) are two elements that define Bob Steinfeld. He has spent his life in the cockpit of high stakes, intense pressure of media content, creation, and delivery. He's forever behind the camera, in the production truck, calling the shots, steering the show, keeping it real, and ensuring his team stays on the tracks.

I know, I was there. He's as good as it gets, as is his tale. Bob is at the top of the mountain. Come with us here on our wild ride through life, on our way to the promised land. The countdown has begun. The pressure's on. This space is getting hot. "3 . . . 2 . . . 1 . . . We're on the Air!"

**—Bill Walton**
Three-time Collegiate Basketball Player of the Year (UCLA) and member NBA 50th and 75th Anniversary Teams; 2001 Sports Emmy Broadcasting Award

# CHAPTER 1

## *Dominate Where You Can*

*Imagine what it would be like to grow up* attending sports events, idolizing college and professional athletes, watching their games on TV, and then one day making a career out of doing just that. I've had the good fortune to realize my dream. If I wasn't working a game, I'd most likely watch it on television, so how exciting would it be to get paid to join the inner circle of those teams and leagues? I am very lucky to earn a living producing and directing sports television, which is a small industry of talented people who get to hang around all levels of athletes, coaches, and professional associates. One of those was National Basketball Association (NBA) hall of famer Tim Duncan of the San Antonio Spurs, who once said to me, "You got to dominate where you can, man."

Another star I learned from was Duke basketball head coach Mike Krzyzewski, who said (during an interview for a special I coproduced) that his advice to a junior high school coach wanting to become a college coach was to focus right now on winning a championship at your level, then move up from there.

This journey over the past five decades has led me to many stellar moments and lessons. My book's objective is to pass along that wisdom—as well as the insights of famed athletes and television broadcasters—as I take you inside the world of sports television.

By entering my world, you'll hear how Alex Rodriguez's admiration for Cal Ripken led to one of the greatest moments in Major League Baseball (MLB) All-Star Game history, due to my association with the two. You'll learn how to implement a big idea and turn it into reality, like getting the NBA's New Orleans Pelicans players an audition on *American Idol*. Under the you-never-know category, you'll see how a show on a regional sports network can compete for a national Cable Ace Award against the big dogs at ESPN and HBO. You'll discover why some superstar athletes and announcers achieve greatness on and off the field, exceeding your expectations. When you get your big break to work the Olympics for NBC, you'll understand why you were compelled to stand up for a favored potential US Olympic gold medal-winning team. And when you work with icons such as Nolan Ryan and Randy Johnson, why not team up with them to produce an instructional video on pitching? Makes sense, right? You just have to do it. You don't win all the time, but when you do, all the effort you made to get there was worth it. And when you don't, well, you certainly learned something useful for the next idea. We'll discuss both sides.

I've produced thousands of events through the years. Each is different. Once the first second of video and audio begins, nothing is the same. Although you begin every game with a plan, you must adjust as storylines develop or change. You come to the show like a doctor approaches each patient, with many instruments but prepared to use the right one. A producer has video tools such as historic flashbacks and graphics to implement. You never use everything, just the ones necessary. It's essentially your call, which is one reason it's fun.

As we approach the top of the hour, my associate director and I are usually on headset with a master control operator (in the studio or network headquarters) to coordinate and make sure we are in sync with the time. Two minutes to air, ninety seconds, one minute, thirty, simultaneously counting down through their headsets or earpieces. "15, 10, 9, 8, 7, 6, 5, 4, 3, 2, 1 . . . We're on the air!"

The countdowns are the same, but the stories and shows can be dramatically different. That's the beauty of live television. It could be the last game of the regular MLB season for the Texas Rangers, and who knows, you might be producing or directing a historic "perfect game."

Enjoy the ride!

# CHAPTER 2

## Carving My Career in Journalism and Sports Television

*I'm often asked* how I started in the television industry. It's simple. I knew what I wanted to do as far back as fourth grade at Arthur Kramer Elementary School in Dallas. My first influence was my father, Fred, who was very artsy. When he wasn't earning a living selling signs or insurance, he was in fact an actor, public speaker, accomplished piano player, and an artist who painted watercolor and oil paintings. He, his father, and two brothers owned Triangle Sign Company in Jersey City, New Jersey, until the early 1960s. He also acted in the Rutherford Players group, which staged children's plays for the kids and their parents in town. I remember going to numerous plays starring my father. It was kind of special attending the theater with my classmates and seeing my dad in the lead.

We lived in Rutherford—about ten miles from New York City—just three miles from where Giants Stadium first opened in 1976. To this day, I'm not sure what happened, but when I was nine years old in 1965, we suddenly moved to Dallas so that my father could have a fresh start in Texas.

He began acting in commercials and posing for print media campaigns. I attended one shoot in a studio near the Southern Methodist University (SMU) campus in North Dallas. It was a 7-Eleven commercial for an Icee (which 7-Eleven now calls a

Slurpee), where everyone had to recite the "Icee Pledge." Perhaps that exposure rubbed off on my future career, and I subconsciously combined show business with my love of sports.

My father's new career in Texas did not take off very fast. He traveled the region trying to acquire and support new sales clients. I recall times when my parents' credit cards were canceled and their checkbooks had negative balances. But my older brother Jay and I were never at a loss for love or emotional support from my parents.

My mother, Elaine, worked as an administrative assistant in the Dallas office of Julius Schepps Community Center (now known as the Aaron Family Jewish Community Center or JCC). It did not pay much, so she diligently toiled in other ways to earn money for our family. She sold jewelry, created decoupage art, sold dining room table mats, and worked at the Carriage House, a retail clothing store in Preston Royal Shopping Center. During our long car trips to visit relatives in Lubbock, El Paso, and Albuquerque, New Mexico, we'd take side trips to Santa Fe, where she'd buy turquoise jewelry to resell back home. She tried hard to balance our family's finances, but it was difficult.

I lived in an apartment my entire life until college. In fact, the first house I ever lived in was the AEPi fraternity house at the University of Texas in Austin. There were times I wanted to participate in classes at the JCC or go to Dick Chaplin's dance classes during my late elementary and middle school years, but we did not have enough money for extracurricular activities. I especially felt left out when I missed those Friday night dance classes which were held at an exclusive country club yet open to our school. While I stayed home, all my friends attended and learned to dance with our female classmates. I'm not sure if it hindered my social development, except to say that I still can't dance very well.

In the early 1970s, we were saddened to learn my mom was diagnosed with ovarian cancer. I was in high school. She fought hard, endured chemotherapy, and for a while went into remission. In 1973, her cancer returned. My father, while not so skilled with finances, was a model of love, caring for and supporting my mom through her final years. He was constantly at her side, making sure she was comfortable. Each time I called home from college—at University of Texas in Austin in August 1974—I could sense my mom was growing weaker. Her voice was becoming faint. I was struggling with losing my beloved mother while busy attending classes and working on the school newspaper. Sometimes I could not hold in the emotion and would begin crying in front of my friends and fraternity brothers. On November 21, 1974, around 8:00 a.m., the phone rang in my dorm room. My roommate, Ted Tobolowsky, answered and handed it to me with a concerned face. It was our family's close friend, Marvin Meadow. He called to tell me my mom had passed away. She was only forty-six. Her spirit, entrepreneurship, love for her family, and lessons about always being honest and punctual remain ingrained in my personality.

My father was an identical twin who was extremely close with his brother, Francis. One time, when I was about seven years old, I actually confused my uncle for my dad. To this day, I remember how embarrassed I was. Around the same time we left for Dallas, my uncle's family moved to Florida. The twins were separated. Each time they spoke long distance, they would remain on the phone for at least an hour. Unfortunately, my father's family had a history of heart disease. On November 6, 1973, my uncle had a heart attack while playing tennis in Miami. It was a sport both he and my father loved to play. Francis was forty-six years old and did not survive. The phone rang in Dallas to inform my dad about the terrible news concerning his identical twin brother. I felt so sorry for my dad as I saw him cry for the first time. To lose his brother and wife, both at the young age of forty-six, must have been emotionally devastating, but he moved on with his life.

My daughter Elaine Frances was named in my uncle's memory.

My father lived until he was seventy-two years old, after battling heart disease and diabetes. He was kept alive in his later years with a defibrillator implanted in his chest to shock his heart when it detected irregular beats. In his later years, he needed support from Meals on Wheels, whose volunteers delivered hot food to his door numerous times a week. I truly appreciated that, and so to this day, I volunteer to deliver meals for the Visiting Nurses Association's Meals on Wheels program in Dallas.

I miss my parents, but know they live on in my heart and have been a big influence and inspiration in paving my way to success. I was determined to work hard to live a life free from the constant financial challenges our family faced growing up—one reason I felt compelled and driven to find my niche early on.

I was always an avid sports fan, especially of baseball, basketball, and football. In Rutherford, my brother and I played pickup baseball, stickball, and wiffleball at George Washington Elementary School. It was a few blocks away from our apartment building on Union Avenue, so we could virtually hear our mom shouting for us to come home. I was pretty good at baseball, so when we moved to Dallas, after a few practices at the JCC, athletic director Hank Bodner put me in a league above my age group. I did not like it, because I was forced to play right field instead second base, which was my best position. After a year went by, my friends graduated up to my league and everything returned to normal.

Besides playing baseball and basketball, my friends and I enjoyed attending sporting events, especially American Basketball Association (ABA) games of the Dallas Chaparrals at Memorial Auditorium and then SMU's Moody Coliseum. The ABA was a rival league of the NBA that instituted the three-point line (which the NBA ultimately adopted), used a red, white, and blue basketball, and hosted the first-ever slam dunk competition at its all-star game. Will Ferrell's movie *Semi-Pro*—about a fictitious ABA club named the Flint Tropics—was about his team's mission to become one of the four ABA teams to merge with the NBA.

Beginning in 1972, we grabbed seats at plenty of Texas Rangers games at Arlington Stadium, where we were fortunate enough to see the exploits of Frank Howard, Fergie Jenkins, Jeff Burroughs, and Jim Fregosi, and opposing legends such as Rod Carew, Carl Yastrzemski, Harmon Killebrew, and Hank Aaron.

Even then, I was thinking of my future career—not as an athlete, but as a media professional.

I once contacted WFAA Channel 8—the local Dallas station and ABC affiliate—to invite reporters to speak to our class. Many did. I was always the first person to meet and greet them and convey my interest in joining their profession. I also had a fascination with weather and often watched Dale Milford, the station's meteorologist, on TV. My parents' friends always called me for the latest weather forecast.

Through my elementary and junior high years, I often went on remotes with the WFAA talent as they shot and edited their pieces. I was thrilled to sit in the studio and watch future network announcer Verne Lundquist write and broadcast sports. I would take the bus from our apartment in North Dallas to downtown and back. Verne went on to an illustrious career with ABC and CBS Sports. In the early 1980s, I hired Verne to work our Southwest Conference college basketball package while he was still at Channel 8.

In high school, I made sure to get journalism training with the award-winning *Hillcrest Hurricane* student newspaper, led by Judy Jeffress, the best teacher I've ever had at any level. She taught me how to write for print, lay out a page, write headlines, and find an interesting angle. I'll never forget one of the first things she taught our class. After you write a lede, read it back. If your reaction is, "So what?" then make it better. Each line and paragraph should entice you to keep reading. Write concisely, succinctly, and clearly. She also taught us to keep a "string book"—journalism slang for your personal portfolio—of every article we wrote for the paper. That lesson came in handy when I arrived at the University of Texas and later when I graduated.

One lesson we learned in Ms. Jeffress's class was the five W's and H: Who, what, when, where, why, and how. Answer all those in your story. Write it in inverted pyramid with the most important facts at the top, because editors trim stories from the bottom, and you want to be sure the five W's and H make print or air. I later discovered, however, that writing for broadcast is a bit different—actually much different—from writing for print. Broadcast scripts need to sound colloquial, as opposed to writing for print, where you're reading to comprehend. Time constraints also limit how many words a writer can use for on-air content.

## Landing My First Professional Journalism Gig (*Dallas Times Herald*)

A career as a journalist was unequivocally my goal. I set my sights on attending the University of Texas, Missouri, or Vanderbilt. I applied to all three of these exceptional journalism schools, but Austin was my preference. If I was accepted there, I'd be following my brother, Jay, who enrolled in the business school two years ahead of me.

Months later, bingo, I received a letter from the dean of the School of Journalism at the University of Texas, congratulating me for acceptance. One of the past editors of the *Hillcrest Hurricane* also wrote for *The Daily Texan*—the UT student newspaper—so I was following his legacy. Buck Harvey was the sports editor when I arrived in Austin for orientation that summer, so I immediately applied to get on the staff and offered my *Hillcrest Hurricane* string book as my resume. It worked. I was writing for *The Daily Texan* before I even started my freshman classes. My first assignment was to cover the UT football team scrimmage, during which a fellow freshman, a running back from Tyler, Texas, made quite an impression. I reported that Earl Campbell "scored three touchdowns and aided on three more" for coach Darrell Royal's Longhorns. Yes, the "Tyler Rose" and I were freshmen the same year! This was an omen that I was destined for a career in sports journalism.

## Campbell Shines in Workouts

Freshman fullback Earl Campbell scored three touchdowns Friday and aided in three more Monday as the Texas Longhorns held their second and third scrimmages of the fall.

Campbell ran for touchdowns of 65, 1 and 2 yards in Friday's scrimmage and assisted first team quarterback Mike Presley in Monday's scrimmage.

With the season opener only 12 days away the starting quarterback position is still open. On Friday quarterback Marty Akins led the first team to three scores in eight possessions and the second team to seven scores in 14 possessions on Monday.

Presley, who was scheduled to lead the second team Friday, sat out with a pulled groin muscle but came back Monday to lead the first team to three scores in seven attempts.

With senior fullback Roosevelt Leaks expected back in two weeks another question will arise with the now first team fullback Campbell.

Though Royal was not optimistic with Friday's scrimmage, on Monday he thought the Horns "have a ways to go but we showed a lot more aggressiveness."

My first assignment for the *Daily Texan* in 1974. *Courtesy of Texas Student Media / The Daily Texan.*

Campbell went on to an illustrious career at Texas, winning the 1977 Heisman Trophy. He became the first overall pick in the 1978 NFL draft by the Houston Oilers, the league's most valuable player in 1979, three-time Offensive Player of the Year, a member of the NFL 100th Anniversary Team, and a 1991 Pro Football Hall of Fame inductee. I was so eager to get my professional career started that I graduated with honors from UT in three years and missed his final season.

I covered many sports for *The Daily Texan*, including the women's basketball team, who played in the Association for Intercollegiate Athletics for Women (AIAW); the men's and women's tennis teams; baseball; and intramural sports and features.

During my time at UT, I became an assistant sports editor, columnist, and page editor and began taking broadcast journalism classes. I knew that having a hard journalism background would be beneficial in many ways, now and down the road. I also interned at a local radio station where I did sports and features, and then for the NBC television station located on MLK (19th Street) in Austin, where I worked in production. On my first day as an intern, the production manager assigned me to run camera on Carolyn Jackson's live lunchtime talk show. I was nervous because I had never run a large studio camera, just one at UT's small TV studio. They were relying on me to keep the picture in focus and understand the director's cues. I could barely move the giant, heavy camera. I'm not sure how well I did, but they didn't kick me out. After I graduated, I was offered a full-time gig, serving both in the studio and newsroom.

This brings me to my advice for aspiring production personnel or announcers: get your foot in the door and pursue as much experience in as many areas as you can. It will help you understand and appreciate the entire process of television production and reporting, and you'll discover what you love to do and where you'll excel. Actually, that applies for most endeavors.

Being a sports columnist at *The Daily Texan* enabled me to pick and choose virtually anything I wanted to cover. Of course, it had to be approved by the sports editor and editorial group from the university. Since I was interested in sports television, I wanted to know why college baseball was not televised by the three networks in existence at the time: ABC, CBS and NBC. College basketball and football earned national broadcasts, but why not baseball? So I phoned all three networks (no internet then) and landed interviews. Each network rep wanted a copy of my story to see how the other networks responded. I subsequently received a call from ABC Sports public relations director Donn Bernstein. He liked my story and asked about my ambitions, so I told him I wanted to get into network sports, possibly as talent or in production. He asked if I'd be interested in going to Waco, about ninety miles north of Austin, to work as a gofer/runner on an upcoming Houston vs. Baylor football game in 1975.

# TV neglects NCAA baseball

By BOB STEINFELD
Texan Staff Writer

College football and basketball coverage on network television has been a big success over the last few years. But what about coverage of the "great American pastime," baseball?

College baseball hasn't been a big success on television. The primary reason is it has not had any substantial television coverage. Most network officials will tell you the only interest in baseball consists of the major league baseball broadcasts by the National Broadcasting Company (NBC) and the American Broadcasting Company (ABC).

Network executives also will tell you college baseball does not draw an audience. What college baseball needs is televison exposure to become a profitable sport for the medium, though the networks don't want to be guinea pigs — a Catch 22 situation.

"There's no time for it," Eddie Einhorn, president of Television Sports (TVS), said. "Statistics show people would rather watch the majors than college."

Statistics also reveal people would rather watch professional football and basketball than college football and basketball, but you still see five or six regionally televised college basketball and football games on each weekend during their seasons.

No plans are being made to introduce college baseball as a regular television sport, but one network representative feels it shouldn't be ruled out altogether.

"I don't feel there's enough interest on a national level to make it work, but I think on a regional basis it could," an NBC spokesman said. "There would be a lot of involved things to be worked out before

## Interpretive

anything could be done, but it's possible."

That brings us down to the local level. Little doubt exists about Longhorn viewer interest. It would seem every attempt would be made to broadcast Texas games.

"It would cost us at least $4,000 to rent equipment for one game," KTVV promotion manager Chuck Smith said, "and that's not including short wave hook-ups or other production costs. If the station owned a remote unit it would not cost so much, but on a local basis you can't find many sponsors to put up that kind of money."

Last year KVUE covered the College World Series from Omaha, but split costs with a South Carolina station to make advertising attrac-

tive and to make money.

"It would be real hard to cover the series on a national basis," ABC-NCAA Public Relations Director Donn Bernstein said. "You see, we can only broadcast five NCAA championship events, and we did track last weekend."

Adding another championship series would mean pre-emption of numerous shows — something the networks are not fond of, especially because college baseball is unproved.

"A minute spot to cover a college baseball game would be about $50,000," Bernstein said, "and when you talk about enormous amounts like that, there's no room for experimentation on network television."

CBS experimented with soccer and track on a weekly basis, but after horrendous Nielsen ratings the programs were canceled. Networks don't want that to happen again, so they won't gamble or feel sympathetic toward a sport.

"College baseball just doesn't have the drawing power, appeal or impact football and basketball have," Bernstein stressed. "From that standpoint there's no way ABC could cover NCAA baseball on a series basis. If we did, in my opinion, it would not survive."

The *Daily Texan* article I wrote in 1976. *Courtesy of Texas Student Media / The Daily Texan.*

Legendary head coaches Bill Yeoman from Houston and Grant Teaff from Baylor ran the sidelines that day. The next weekend, I excitedly made the ninety-minute drive to Waco, where I worked with broadcast associate Bob Dekas, whose distinguished career as a CBS Sports producer included many NCAA basketball championships. I was put to work taping aluminum foil inside the windows of a mobile home that was parked next to the ABC Sports production truck below the press box at Floyd Casey Stadium. The foil blacked out the windows to prevent natural light from interfering with the camera shooting the manual graphics housed in the trailer. Back then, everything was done manually, without computer character generators. Each player's name was printed in white on large, flexible black magnetic sheets that we had to cut up to fit on metal boards and a steel drum. A camera in the mobile unit would shoot the names and stats, and then the director would "key" or "matte" them on the air. The switcher could colorize the text white, yellow, or any color the director requested. When we did scores of other games and credits, we'd put them on the rolling drum. When the director said, "roll scores or closing credits," we'd literally "roll" the drum.

I made a fairly strong impression with ABC Sports. Every Monday, I'd watch *NFL Monday Night Football* to see which regional college football games ABC would televise that weekend. If one was within driving distance, I'd call New York, find out who the production assistant was, then ask if I could work the game. After a while they started calling me on the AEPi fraternity house phone where I lived, because I was rarely in my room and didn't have an answering machine. No cell phones back then, so it was

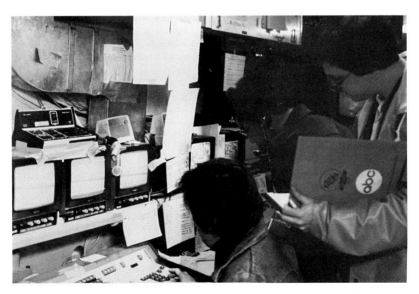

Inside an ABC Sports college football truck, 1977. I was a production assistant on the ABC Sports college football national telecast coordinating the second graphics unit with stats and scores of other games.

13

easier to reach me on the frat house's main line. My frat brothers enjoyed answering phone calls from the likes of Curt Gowdy Jr., the son of legendary hall of fame announcer Curt Gowdy. The younger Gowdy, who made a name for himself in network sports production, retired as executive producer of SportsNet New York in March 2022.

ABC later hired me to work national college football games as a "super gofer" overseeing the second of two chyrons on the show. Chyron was the first generation of computer character generators. I loved it, because I no longer had blisters from cutting those magnetic manual name strips.

In my senior year at UT, ABC was producing a national game in Austin, so I called ABC's Donn Bernstein to invite Keith Jackson, legendary voice of college football, to speak to our journalism school. Not just my journalism class, but the entire journalism school in a large auditorium in the communication building on campus. The school asked me to introduce Jackson, which was a huge honor. Bernstein flew in from New York to watch the speech. Later that night, he took me and my legal-aged frat brothers out to dinner and drinks at the Draught House a few miles north of campus. He said it was on Roone (as in Arledge, the executive producer of ABC Sports). We had a blast.

I continued to work for ABC during football season and earned valuable experience while pursuing my degree.

When I graduated, I tried to land a full-time job with ABC Sports, but it was so competitive. Many of their hirings were children or friends of associates or were from the East Coast schools. All three networks were based in New York City. There were only a few job openings each year, so you had to be persistent, good, and make yourself stand out—especially when there was no one in New York rooting for you. I knew it would take time to land that plum job.

To make an impression and to show my value, I prepped for a game and provided that background information to ABC production associates Curt Gowdy Jr., Bob Dekas, John Faratzis, Jeff

ABC Sports Director of Media Relations for NCAA Football Donn Bernstein and I outside UT School of Communications before the Keith Jackson speech in 1976.

While I was attending the University of Texas at Austin, I worked as a field stage manager for reporter Jim Lampley when ABC Sports came to town, as it did in 1976. That blue ABC Sports jacket was compliments of then ABC Sports Associate Director Jo Umans. I still have it today.

Ruhe, and producer Chuck Howard.

Here's an excerpt from the prep work I distributed for the ABC Sports telecast of Notre Dame vs. Pittsburgh, September 10, 1977:

### Majors Departs Pitt

Jackie Sherrill takes over. Sherrill had been Majors' top assistant for eight seasons, however, last season he was at Washington State (3-8-0). Majors to Tennessee. When Tony Dorsett finished his collegiate career last season and was then picked by Dallas in the NFL Draft, it left Sherrill with a big chore. Who will replace Dorsett? Though Dorsett and 29 others are gone, quarterback Matt Cavanaugh will return for his last season.

### Notre Dame Preview

This year, the Irish return 20 of 22 starters including its entire defense. With most positions filled, coach Dan Devine can concentrate on picking a QB. Though Rusty Lisch did a good job filling in for injured Rick Slager, Devine may also choose from Joe Montana (6-4, 200 pounds) a junior injured in preseason last year, or three freshmen. Whoever becomes starter will get the ball from possible All-America center David Huffman.

I needed a full-time job while pursuing ABC, so following my internship with the NBC affiliate in Austin, I accepted their offer to work full-time in production and in the newsroom. I lived in the frat house during the summer, basically by myself. The TV station was a few blocks away, so I road my bike. After four months with NBC, I returned to Dallas and then New Jersey to live with my aunt Carol, uncle Arthur, and my cousins Nancy, Seth, Marc, Larry, and Sue. Their home was in Princeton, one hour via train to the Manhattan headquarters of ABC Sports, whose lead production associate for college football was the aforementioned Curt Gowdy Jr. I worked national college football games with him at Pittsburgh, Nebraska, and Houston, and then with others at the Gator Bowl game when Ohio State head coach Woody Hayes infamously slugged a Clemson player on the field.

My money ran out, however, so I could no longer fly or drive to the games, especially those on the West Coast. I didn't have the capital that other gofers did. Eventually I made deals to work on *ABC Monday Night Baseball* (including games in Los Angeles and Detroit) plus Major League Soccer and ABC's pro bowler's tour, but it was inconsistent and seasonal. Cable sports games weren't televised every night—ESPN was not born yet—leaving most games on the three networks on weekends. This meant I needed a full-time gig. I wasn't comfortable with my career at that point, so I moved back to Dallas. I was not giving up, but I was back home, living with my dad for a few months in 1977. I started looking for journalism opportunities, knowing my *Daily Texan* string book would help me land a job somewhere in the Lone Star State, if not in Dallas.

I applied for a sports reporting job with the *Abilene Reporter-News*. Its managing editor was excited about having a former Longhorn on staff and complimented my writing and editing. Although my interview with him went extremely well, I drove back to Dallas the same day and thought, what am I getting myself into? But I needed a job, so I accepted his offer to work in West Texas. During the two weeks prior to the day I was scheduled to begin, I frantically searched for opportunities in Dallas. Nothing against Abilene, but I really didn't want to go there. It wasn't my home, and I didn't know a soul.

Would I be able to land another job in just a handful of days? I needed a Hail Mary to avoid heading west. As my moment of truth approached, I started packing my maroon 1972 Impala for the drive to West Texas. In that pre-internet era, a good source for job openings was the classified pages of the *Dallas Morning News* and *Dallas Times Herald*. The day before I was set to leave, I noticed that the *Herald* was seeking a writer and editor for its real estate and homes section. Not sports, I thought, but get your foot in the door and you never know where it might lead. Problem was, I needed to get an interview within twenty-four hours since I was literally leaving for Abilene in the morning. I phoned the *Dallas Times Herald* and arranged for a morning meeting with manager Dwaine Johnson. It was a longshot, but at least I had an interview. My good friend Glenn Bruck took me to dinner the night before to say goodbye and good luck. It was nice, but bittersweet. He knew I really didn't want to go, but I was career driven and ready to gamble on a new adventure. Or was I?

I barely slept that night, nervous about the trip and my pending interview. The next morning, I hugged and said goodbye to my dad and headed downtown with a loaded car bulging with all my stuff. I didn't have any furniture, which allowed me to fit my entire life into that Impala. I found a parking spot in front of the newspaper in downtown Dallas, grabbed my trusty *Daily Texan* string book, then went upstairs to meet Mr. Johnson and five other executives in his office. I placed my string book on Mr. Johnson's desk and pleaded with them to hire me on the spot, because I had a job in Abilene and was literally leaving after I left that office. He either had to hire me on the spot or lose me to West Texas. Did they respect my extensive writing, editing, and page design experience—along with my solid string book? Or did they just feel sorry for me? Or both? I'm not sure. But my sales pitch worked. They hired me! Plop, plop, fizz, fizz, oh what a relief it was.

I was elated. I landed a job at one of the most respected newspapers in the country, and I was staying home. I went to the lobby and called my dad, who was very happy for me. My next call was to my buddy Glenn. "I got the job at the *Times Herald*," I enthusiastically said. There was silence as I was expecting a big congratulations. "That's great," he responded sarcastically, "But you owe me twenty dollars for dinner last night."

I had to notify the managing editor in Abilene that I wasn't coming, after all. Initially I imagined that he might be upset, but then I figured he would be happy for me because I landed a job at the much bigger *Herald*, an opportunity his own staff would covet. Unfortunately, he was upset. He now needed to interview new candidates. If he was honest, however, he would agree that the opportunity in Dallas was better.

The *Dallas Times Herald* job proved to be perfect. It led to a better paying gig a few years later and allowed me to freelance with ABC Sports on the weekends (covering college football and the Professional Bowlers Association (PBA) tour when it came to Grand Prairie for the Quaker State Open. On that bowling show, what a pleasure it was to serve as stage manager for legendary ABC announcer Chris Schenkel.

Schenkel's sidekick/analyst was Nelson "Bo" Burton, a PBA hall of famer. Burton, who compiled eighteen PBA titles, would vacate

I was stage manager for ABC Sports' Chris Schenkel at Pro Bowlers Tour Event in Grand Prairie, Texas, in 1978.

PRO BOWLERS TOUR

One of my responsibilities was making sure the ABC Sports TV pin sweeps were applied correctly.

his analyst gig if he reached the finals. I arrived Friday after the qualifying competition was completed and the TV finalists were set. We took over the bowling alley, dressed up the TV lanes, and put the ABC logo on the ball returns and pin sweeps. Technicians rolled in the cameras and added the lights. We also got fabric to cover the beams and the audience bleachers to make them pretty for television. It was quite an exercise to get the lanes ready for air overnight.

At the newspaper, I wrote weekly stories about the new home communities and more. This helped promote the companies that bought ads in our paper. But I had bigger ambitions for our little section. If there was a new skyscraper or other big transactions happening in "Big D," I wanted to break that news on the front page of our real estate and homes section. And I did. Thanks to my photography classes at Texas, I shot pictures for many of my stories and had the illustrious *Dallas Times Herald* photo department develop and print those for me. One of those photographers was Mark Perlstein, with whom I remain in contact.

My boss at the paper was Alex Acheson, a veteran newspaper man who let me handle everything, including laying out the section, creating headlines, and eventually writing my own column—"Consumer Corner"—where readers (and friends) posed consumer-related questions for me to research and offer advice. Acheson wrote his own weekly column about real estate doings in and around the metroplex.

My duties exposed me to local public relations firms who clamored for publicity for their clients, mostly home builders such as Raldon and Pierce Builders. One firm, the Williams Group, offered me a job for more money. The fact that their North Dallas office was located a few minutes from my apartment convinced me to accept their offer. So, I left the *Times Herald* for the Williams Group, whose clientele was mostly home builders, but expanded to other areas. When I went to central Texas to pitch our services to the founder of Schlotzsky's restaurant chain, our entire office made the trip. I had eaten at their first stores in Austin while I attended UT. I loved it. We didn't land the account, but it was a learning experience. While working at the Williams Group, I continued to freelance in television. And I was about to get my big break in the NBA.

# CHAPTER 3

## *The Role of Producer and What I've Learned*

*"What is the role of a producer?"* I'm frequently asked. In movies, the executive producer is the person (or group) responsible for the film, who buys the rights, sells it to a studio or independent production company, keeps it on budget, hires the director, and holds the money behind the scenes. In sports television, the producer is the show's captain or head coach, who is responsible for executing its format. They decide when to go to break, what to do after those commercials (such as flashbacks, promos, or sponsored elements), and how to: formulate and creatively present storylines; arrange the production schedule; oversee the crew's schedules and issues with operations producers; coordinate with technical managers on employing cameras and other equipment; guide the director on coverage and replay sources; and recommend which crew members to utilize. During the game, producers sit next to the director in the production truck and call out replays. (Although on bigger shows, replay producers assist with that.) Producers keep an eye on the big picture and ensure whatever hits the air is accurate. Their role is to react to the live event and circumstances and interact with the talent or announcers.

An associate director (AD) helps the producer (and the show) with the announce copy, which are the cards the talent reads with promos, sponsor elements, vignettes, and breaks. The AD knows where the production elements exist on the replay machines and helps package the elements—such as graphics and music—to make them ready for air. You don't want your executive producer to have to worry about your show.

For each game, I compile a "Steiny Pack," which includes:

1. *Production Schedule*: The timing of when events will happen, such as the production meeting, rehearsals, breaks, and airtime.

2. *Advancer Rundown*: A line-by-line outline of a piece we'll record and feed to the studio before the game to help promote the show. This includes video and/or graphic elements and our on-camera talent. Routinely, this is shot in the booth ninety minutes before air.

3. *Open Rundown*: What we will talk about at the top of the show. Again, outlined for talent and crew.

4. *Halftime Rundown*: Details of what we at the event (a.k.a. remote) and studio show will produce in each segment.

5. *Run of Show*: What we tentatively plan to run during the game and out of commercial breaks, such as sponsored elements and creative pieces.

6. *Commercial Format*: The number of commercial breaks and lengths. When we go to break, the producer or associate director will count the studio to "roll" or run the breaks.

7. *Checklist*: This contains a list of numbers for the individual announcer cards that the announcers will read, detailing on which machines the video promos exist and their numeric location; production elements such as flashbacks; and pictures and many other elements the producer has ready to go. A single or double page to refer to during the show.

8. *Pregame Timing Sheet*: Minute-by-minute of what the stadium or arena has scheduled prior to the beginning of

the game. The media relations director or arena producer emails it to me beforehand, so we can confirm when the anthem will be played, when and if lights will go out for introductions, and the game's confirmed starting time. For college football and basketball, I will alert the schools a few weeks before with kickoff/tip times, which vary between networks and conferences. For the NBA, Women's National Basketball Association (WNBA), National Football League, and National Lacrosse League (NLL) games I work, those times are predetermined and set league wide.

9. *Transmission Information*: This sheet shows which company will take our signal from the truck and transmit it for air via satellite, fiber, internet, or other methods. It includes key phone numbers in the event you need to reach someone if there is a problem. On most shows, we do a transmission check with our master controls in Atlanta or New York, where we check the video and audio for proper levels and sync. That check-in process can take as little as ten minutes but sometimes takes forty-five when there are multiple studios and networks carrying the game, or if there are problems that need to be addressed.

10. *Talent Copy*: Cards for the talent to read on the air like promos or flashbacks.

11. *Storylines*: In researching the event we are producing, storytelling helps viewers relate to the players and games. The more you know about the athletes, the teams, and the big picture, the more the viewer will be vested in the show. It's not just a game of X's and O's.

12. *Graphic sheet*: This includes the graphic notes you read on the screen about players, teams, and leagues or conferences. These are called "lower thirds" because they're placed on the lower third of the screen. "Full pages" take up most of the screen, "side slabs" occupy the left or right side, and

"chunks" are situated in the lower right or left. I put the information I'd like to see on a "graphics sheet" for our associate producer or graphics coordinator in the truck and email it a few days before the show.

It was coined "Steiny Pack" by my longtime Fox Sports Net director partner Kenny Miller, who kept leaving his production packet in the press box on the day before our Big 12 football telecasts. After the production meetings we'd get back to the truck and he'd say, "Hey Steiny, I left my 'Steiny Pack' up in the press box, do you have another?"

I would just look at him, shake my head, then give him another. From that day forward, I always carried a second "Steiny Pack" for him.

That's a glance at my preparation. It can be a lot of work when you have a tight schedule flying back and forth from different parts of the country and producing many sports for different networks.

Here's an example of my travel/work schedule from Saturday, February 25 through Sunday, March 5, 2023:

*Saturday*: Flew from Dallas to Cedar Rapids, Iowa, then drove to Cedar Falls.

*Sunday*: 5:30 a.m., crew call to produce 11:30 a.m. Belmont vs. Northern Iowa basketball game on CBSSN, then drove back to Cedar Rapids. 7:30 p.m., flew back to Dallas.

*Monday*: 11:20 a.m., flew to San Jose, California.

*Tuesday*: 8:00 p.m., directed Colorado State vs. San Jose State on CBSSN.

*Wednesday*: 6:10 a.m., flew home to Dallas.

*Thursday*: 2:00 p.m., flew to Indianapolis and then drove to Muncie.

*Friday*: 6:00 p.m. Eastern time, produced Toledo vs. Ball State on CBSSN, then drove back to Indianapolis after the game to stay at airport hotel.

*Saturday*: 6:00 a.m., flew home to Dallas. 7:00 p.m., oversaw the NLL Panther City Lacrosse game vs. Saskatchewan Rush telecast on Bally Sports SW as executive producer.

*Sunday*: 7:30 a.m., NBA conference call to discuss afternoon telecast on ABC. Noon, worked Phoenix Suns vs. Dallas Mavericks national telecast on ABC Sports as NBA court administrator/time-out coordinator. 6:00 p.m., saw my new grandkids for the first time in two weeks at family dinner. 10:00 p.m., bedtime.

---

When I speak to organizations and schools, there are a few questions I commonly receive.

"What is your favorite sport to produce and/or direct?" they often ask.

I like producing all events, though some take longer to prepare. The rosters for college football teams change considerably year after year, which creates extra work. Plus, there are many more players, coaches, storylines, and personalities to consider and research. That's why each school's media relations director is critical to a show's success. Also important is the information we receive from our network statistics researchers.

My favorite sport to play growing up was baseball, so I certainly knew the most about its fundamentals and strategy. It can be tough to produce or direct because there is no set time limit or game clock, so games can sometimes drag on. You never know when you are going to get home after a game. (Fortunately, Major League Baseball's pitch clocks and batter clocks have reduced the elapsed time.)

I also played basketball and followed both the ABA and NBA, so I enjoy that sport, too. With basketball, you are usually done in two and a half hours or less, even if it goes to overtime.

College football telecasts can last four hours, especially the high-scoring games and the ones with numerous replay reviews. There are many aspects of each sport I enjoy producing. Football is my favorite, because it's a comprehensive setup with coaches' meetings and the opportunity to capture the color of the collegiate game. The atmosphere at the big conference games is always fantastic. It is humbling when I get to produce college football games at my alma mater, the University of Texas at Austin, where I got my start in professional journalism and sports television. All that college experience has been crucial in setting a path to success in this business.

"What is your all-time favorite event?" is another question I always hear.

I'm quick to say that producing three Summer Olympic Games for NBC—Barcelona in 1992, Atlanta in 1996, and Athens in 2004—was thrilling and fulfilling.

Even on the regional and local level, I experienced special moments, especially when producing and directing the 1987 Major Indoor Soccer League championship game seven, when the Dallas Sidekicks upset the Tacoma Stars. Working with that stellar Pacific Northwest crew was fantastic. I still cross paths with those talented technicians when I am in Seattle and Portland to produce events such as the Nike Hoop Summit or college basketball.

While I mostly produce telecasts, I also direct them. The director—who sits next to the producer in the production truck or control room—guides the camera operators and calls out the camera numbers for the technical director to put on the air. The producer is like the head coach and the director is the quarterback. The producer keeps an eye on the big picture while the director executes the game plan and visually tells the story by documenting the action with compelling, timely pictures. A good director chooses the best camera angle and horizon—whether the shot should be wide, medium, or tight, depending upon the situation. During pregame meetings, a director must address storylines and assignments for camera operators. I have extensive experience directing MLB, college baseball, NBA, college basketball, and college football. It really helps when a producer understands what a director needs to hear from a producer, like where we're going next in the show, before we actually get there. Since I produce and direct, I understand what each position expects communication-wise from the other.

"What is the most challenging sport to produce or direct?" is probably the most relevant question that aspiring journalists pose to me.

Let's go to the directing side of the question. Baseball is the most challenging sport to direct, because it's one of the few sports where points (in other words, runs) are mostly scored away from the ball. Once the ball is hit, the director better know where crucial plays are likely to arise and where the most important perspectives are likely to occur. Growing up playing baseball, we were taught that based on which defensive position you're playing, you should know what you are going to do with the ball before it's hit. Similarly, when you direct a game, you need to put yourself in the minds of all nine defensive position players, the base coaches, the baserunners, and the batter. You must be constantly cognizant of the "situation"—count, outs, runners, score, weather conditions, and more—because when the ball is hit, what are you going to do? If the ball is flying into the right-field corner, when do you cut to the runner rounding third? Will the fielder hit the cutoff man?

Your camera operators must know the sport, too. The crew is crucial in that regard. When I directed games in Arlington, there were none better than those technicians. Working alongside producer David Handler on those historic Rangers games was memorable, and we're still friends and communicate on a personal level. David left the business many years ago and became a successful certified executive coach who works with leaders on achieving their business goals.

## It's in the Box Score

When you're on the NBA beat, as I was for four decades with the Dallas Mavericks, San Antonio Spurs, and New Orleans Pelicans, you establish routines to help you prepare for each game and to make your shows the best. Of course, as you travel, there's a lot of time on airplanes and team buses, which limits your ability to get online. For more than half of my NBA career, there was no internet to help me review games and box scores.

Many times after finishing a game, I'd jump on the team bus to the airport to fly to the next city. I used much of that time prepping for the next assignment. As I prepped, I looked back at previous matchups from the year (if they occurred). Frequently there had been two or three already in the books. It's hard to remember each game of the long season.

That's why I decided to clip the box score, and a paragraph or two of the game story and headline, and glue-stick them into a small notebook I carried in my backpack. I referred to it often, even occasionally during a telecast. When on the road, I would buy the local paper the next morning to clip the story and box score—and to read the local writer's take on the game.

When the season concluded, I would drop my clipbook in a large cardboard box along with the previous seasons. I now have twenty-three seasons of San Antonio Spurs, New Orleans Pelicans, and Dallas Wings notebooks filled with box scores, news clips, and pictures, including historic moments like the NBA championships.

It took extra diligence and dedication to clip and paste after each game, but it certainly helped me as a producer. And now I have an invaluable archive of memorable moments in NBA history.

## Seizing the Moment with the Record-Setting Rourke Brothers

An underrated but paramount skill that every successful producer should possess is adaptability. Your willingness to identify and seize the moment by deviating from your preconceived game plan can pay rich dividends. It's no different than when quarterback Patrick Mahomes walks up to the line of scrimmage, sees something askew, then calls an audible.

My eyes similarly caught something noteworthy when I was assigned to produce the Akron-Ohio football game on Friday, November 24, 2023. (It also marked the third Thanksgiving that I would be on the road and away from home.)

To establish a hook that's meaningful to our viewers, it's the producer's job to identify compelling storylines by reading news clips, reviewing game notes provided by the schools' media relations directors, and having in-person or zoom meetings with coaches and players. At a nationally televised Mid-American Conference game between the Ohio Bobcats and Akron Zips on CBS Sports Network, we felt the most compelling storyline was Ohio graduate quarterback Kurtis Rourke needing only 15 passing yards to tie his brother, Nathan, for second all-time in school history. Nathan starred there from 2017 to 2019, leading them to three consecutive bowl victories. On this day, he was on the Jacksonville Jaguars active roster as a third-string quarterback in the National Football League.

Although this game had no effect on the conference championship, since Toledo would meet Miami (Ohio) in Detroit the next weekend, its outcome was still important to the players, coaches, and fans.

We opened our show with the story of the two Canadian-born brothers, showing Kurtis warming up on the field, with their statistics appearing in an on-screen graphic. Our play-by-play commentator

Carter Blackburn spelled out the scenario to pump up our viewers, reminding them it would be something to watch.

A few minutes into the first quarter, before we even reached our first commercial break, Kurtis tied his brother with those 15 yards for 7,457 career yards. In planning the "run of show" (or my plans for production elements, where I'd place promos and storyline graphics), I correctly anticipated that the record would be broken soon into the game. So earlier in the week, I decided to produce a video of pictures to run under our sponsored opening billboards of Kurtis and Nathan—them growing up in Canada, playing organized football, hanging out together, and then becoming Bobcat teammates in 2019.

I obtained the photographs from Ohio's director of football communications, Sarah Newgarde, edited them together on iMovie, then sent the video to CBS Sports in New York, where it was combined with the sponsored billboards and announcer voice-over. That was step one. Step two was placing that pod out of the first break, when the record would likely be broken. This planned out perfectly, and we ran the billboards out of that break.

"They are even; the brothers are exactly even with 7,457 yards," Blackburn announced to the viewers. "Nathan [is] now on the active roster of the Jacksonville Jaguars and Tyler Tettleton [shown on-screen as the all-time leader] is now coaching him on the Jacksonville staff."

On the Bobcats' next possession, Kurtis passed his brother and became the second all-time leading passer in Ohio University history.

On the Wednesday prior to the game, during our zoom call with Ohio head coach Tim Albin, his offensive and defensive coordinators, and Newgarde, I had an idea. I asked Newgarde to contact Nathan in Jacksonville to see if he would shoot a ten-second congratulatory message for his brother on his iPhone. She said she would try. Wednesday and Thursday passed with no word. Then, two hours before the game on Friday morning, she emailed me Nathan's video. It was a twenty-second, bro-to-bro heartfelt message that he shot himself, from inside the Jaguars' practice facility. We downloaded it in the truck, but had to convert the video file to make it compatible with our replay machine.

Shortly after the milestone was achieved, and out of the next break, our announcer teed up the video on the air.

"Kurtis Rourke has passed his brother Nathan, the terrific quarterback before him, for second all-time in passing yards," Blackburn explained. "And we got a nice message from older brother Nathan."

Next came the iPhone video.

"Hey bud, congratulations on passing me in all-time passing yards," Nathan delightedly told his sibling. "I am super proud. Honestly, I knew it was inevitable, so I can't be all that mad. It couldn't happen to a better person and I am just so happy for you and just so excited to see what the future brings. Go Bobbies!"

Blackburn continued, "Nathan had a good run in the CFL [Canadian Football League], now with the Jacksonville Jaguars, but Kurtis has the bragging rights."

The emotional bond between the brothers was a textbook case of good television. It demonstrated how a touch of creativity—abetted by a school's cooperation—can generate a dramatic moment for a telecast's viewers. The siblings were equally moved.

During our postgame, Blackburn and analyst Adam Breneman (a former Penn State and University of Massachusetts all-American tight end in 2016 and 2017) interviewed Kurtis. We were ready to again run the video message from his brother, so he could hear it live.

"Joining us now is Kurtis Rourke," said Blackburn. "You passed your brother Nathan for all-time passing yards in Bobcats' history. What does it mean to you to move past your brother in the record books?"

"It's great," Rourke replied. "It's nice to be able to pass him, because he's always been great in so many areas. It means a lot for sure. Hats off to the guy [Tyler Tettleton] who's number one at the top. So I'm just glad we came out on top today."

"Well Kurtis, we got a message from your brother Nathan," said Blackburn. "We listened to it earlier, but we want you to hear it as well."

Rourke shook his head and reacted with a wide smile. He was touched.

"Your coach, Tim Albin, spoke about the friendly rivalry between the two of you," Blackburn added. "What has it meant having your brother pushing you to be a better player in just about every way?"

"It means a ton," Rourke responded. "Ever since we were growing up, we instilled that competitive spirit in everything we did. We just compete, because that's what brothers do, and, we weren't short on that for sure. He continues to push me in everything he's done. Like I said, he's accomplished so much on all levels and he'll continue to do so. It pushes me to beat the older brother. He's doing so many great things, and I just want to follow that."

The lesson here? Be prepared. And when you have an intriguing idea, do everything you can to make it happen. As you'll read later, I did exactly that at the 2001 Major League Baseball All-Star Game.

# CHAPTER 4

## *My Entry into the NBA with the Dallas Mavericks*

**My bosses at the Williams Group** public relations firm recognized that sports television was my passion. They knew it would only be a matter of time before I followed my heart and pursued that path. In 1979, the vice president of marketing for Pierce Builders was aware of my love for sports and invited me to attend a luncheon at Brookhaven Country Club in Farmers Branch, Texas. The keynote speaker was Norm Sonju, the president and general manager of the expansion NBA Dallas Mavericks, who were scheduled to begin play at Reunion Arena in 1980. He was invited by home builder Jerry Stiles to speak to fellow home builders and Brookhaven members. This proved too good of an opportunity to turn down. My plan was to get a good meal (single guys love a free banquet lunch), listen to Norm speak, then introduce myself and tell him about my network background in sports television, knowledge of NBA basketball, and to offer my services to the team.

Norm was very nice. He told me to contact producer Dave Burchett and Kevin "Sully" Sullivan in public relations. Sully later worked as vice president of sports communications for NBC Sports in New York and as White House communications director for President George W. Bush.

Once I reached out to Dave and Sully, the three of us began working together, although I was on a freelance basis. Dave and I ran the scoreboard show, including its music, arena announcements, and other elements. That was before the advent of jumbotron scoreboards that were capable of displaying the game. My fee was four season tickets per game, but since I was working all the home games, I always donated them to family and friends. At least I was being paid with experience. During the preseason, the Milwaukee Bucks, headlined by Kareem Abdul-Jabbar, faced the expansion Mavericks in one of the first games ever played at Reunion Arena. I wasn't working that night, so I took a date, my future wife, Sarah Esquenazi. I was really into the game and even brought binoculars. A *Sports Illustrated* photographer decided we were good subjects to demonstrate how excited Dallas fans were for the NBA's arrival. We had no idea. A week later, I had just fallen asleep when my apartment mate Jimmy Weiss screamed, "Bobby, Bobby, you're not going to believe it. You're in *Sports Illustrated!*" Sure enough, a photograph of Sarah and me was forever immortalized in the pages of the most famous sports magazine ever.

The Mavericks began to produce their own telecasts. Dave initially just produced, but eventually directed too, and I was the graphics associate producer. We did home and road games, although when we first started, I went to the Channel 5 studios in Fort Worth to help with the halftime show. It was a bit hard to not handle those duties from the production truck on the road, but fortunately, that didn't last long. Soon I was traveling with Dave, Allen Stone (director of broadcasting and play-by-play), and whoever our analyst was each year.

It was a fun group. Our young play-by-play radio announcer, Dave Barnett, was fresh out of what was then called North Texas State University. Many of the players were friendly, especially Brad Davis, Rolando Blackman, Scott Lloyd, and Bill Wennington. Funny how each of them became radio and/or television analysts. Even NBA hall of famer Bill Walton was hired to work a few games.

Eventually, I produced the games while Dave concentrated on directing. We were a good team for many years. I stayed with the Mavericks from 1980 to 1989 while still working my full-time gigs elsewhere. Dave went on to an illustrious Emmy-winning career directing college football, basketball, and Texas Rangers baseball, and he wrote several successful books. On top of that, Dave's endeared to me for providing a solid opportunity, being a mentor, and most importantly, being a friend.

The NBA was a great start while I was doing freelance events for CBS Sports as a production assistant with dreams of landing a full-time role in New York City.

# CHAPTER 5

# My Entrepreneurial Video Project with Nolan Ryan and Randy Johnson

**While freelancing for the Dallas Mavericks,** I took a full-time job with an upstart subscription television station in Arlington called ON TV. It was a hybrid pay service like HBO in that it had the latest movies, rock concerts, and sports, including pay-per-view boxing. You had to subscribe to it and have an ON TV antenna installed on your roof or in your attic. That was cutting edge then. It was a new breed of television broadcast over an encrypted signal on an ultra high frequency (UHF) television station (in this case KTXA-21) which loaned decoders to subscribers.

I worked for Ed Frazier and Glenn Gurgiolo, doing programming, production, monthly programming logs, making sure the movies were in the control room each day, and returning them to the file room after they aired. ON TV offices were in Arlington on Randol Mill Road, a half mile south of the original Arlington Stadium, which you could see from our offices. We also had a neat view of Six Flags across the street. Eventually, the Rangers' third stadium, Globe Life Field, would be built on the exact site of our ON TV offices. Today, every time I drive down Randol Mill Road to watch the Rangers or Cowboys at AT&T Stadium next door, I flashback to those ON TV days and shake my head with what has emerged there forty years later. It's quite astonishing and impressive.

ON TV faced competition from Video Entertainment Unlimited (VEU) and Preview (yet another subscription service in the area which eventually merged with VEU). This prompted Ed Frazier to team up with the Houston Sports Association and begin an all-sports regional cable network called Home Sports Entertainment (HSE). Actually, there were two HSEs: one in Houston, which was already established, and one in Dallas, where Ed ran the company and Glenn was executive producer and program director. We were one of the first small, fledgling regional sports networks in the country. We obtained rights to Southwest Conference basketball and football, and more importantly, Texas Rangers baseball home games (which previously aired on VEU subscription TV). That was great news! The stadium was right across the street, and I would produce the games while future TNT director Lonnie Dale, from Kansas City, flew in and directed.

I produced or directed Rangers home games from 1983 to 1995. That era featured future hall of famer Ivan "Pudge" Rodriguez's first game as a Ranger, the historic Rangers years of Nolan Ryan, plus two perfect games (pitched by California Angel Mike Witt in 1984 and the Rangers' Kenny Rogers in 1994). At that time, I was lucky to be the only director to have worked two perfect games. Lucky not so much as an accomplishment, but for being at the right spot at the right time.

My Rangers tenure was packed with wonderful memories, including working with the team's great staff. Our telecast crew was also terrific, such as our announcers Merle Harmon, the former NBC Sports commentator; all-star pitcher Steve Busby (who threw two no-hitters for the Kansas City Royals); analyst Norm Hitzges; play-by-play announcers Mark Holtz, Dave Barnett, Bob Carpenter, Josh Lewin, and Greg Lucas; plus commentators and former Rangers Tom Grieve and Jim Sundberg.

I was welcomed in the clubhouse before games, especially during the Bobby Valentine managerial era. Bobby allowed me to suit up in Rangers practice gear during early batting practice to shag balls in the outfield for hitters such as Pete Incaviglia, Larry Parrish, and Buddy Bell. I remember playing home run derby with my brother Jay while growing up in Dallas at the Jewish Community Center, imagining what it would be like to catch a major league fly ball or hit the gap to steal an extra-base hit.

Now, I was realizing my dream at Arlington Stadium, running on the warning track and jumping (barely two inches off the ground) to catch the balls against the outfield wall. I loved it. The ball zigged side to side when it hugged the dense grass at Arlington Stadium and would roll around your glove if you were not concentrating. After I made the grab, I threw the ball back to the infield where coach Wayne "Twig" Terwilliger would catch it. Twig played nine seasons between 1949 and 1960 as a second baseman for the Chicago Cubs, Brooklyn Dodgers, Washington Senators, New York baseball Giants, and Kansas City Athletics. He joined the Rangers in 1981 for Don Zimmer and then went on to coach for Darrell Johnson, Doug Rader, and Valentine. Interestingly, Twig was on the Rangers' original 1972 coaching staff as third-base coach under manager Ted Williams for one season. Yes, Ted Williams, the Red Sox legend.

On the evening of September 14, 1990, during HSE Day at Arlington Stadium, I was asked to throw out the first pitch right before the game began. Even though I was directing that night's telecast, I managed to make my way from the production truck—just behind the Rangers clubhouse—to the pitcher's mound, where I was met by Rangers staffers in charge of the first pitch. They asked if I wanted to throw the ball from the front of the mound, like most people did. Not me. I wanted to go sixty feet, six inches from the rubber to home plate. They warned me that most folks fail to reach home plate. My baseball background, combined with the fact that I was playing softball at the time, convinced me that my arm had the right stuff. But with over twenty thousand fans watching, could I handle the pressure? Texas Rangers catcher Bill Haselman took his place behind home plate. The HSE crew was recording it, not for my benefit, but to hopefully have something funny to play in case I short-hopped it to the plate, threw it wildly, or slipped off the rubber.

I took the mound, got comfortable, channeled my inner Nolan Ryan, and unleashed a 53 mile-per-hour "fastball" (as clocked by radar) right into Haselman's mitt. Cool. Haselman stepped in front of home plate to present me with the souvenir American League ball. The Rangers staff were impressed, because I had thrown the fastest ball of any first pitch participant that season, which was nearing completion. So there.

During my Rangers tenure, I got to know and work with their pitching coach, Tom House, who played for the Atlanta Braves, Boston Red Sox, and Seattle Mariners from 1971 to 1978. Tom is most famous for catching Hank Aaron's historic, record-setting 715th home run in the fourth inning of a game against the Los Angeles Dodgers on April 8, 1974. The ball reached the Braves' bullpen in left center, where House caught it on the fly. The game stopped to mark the milestone. House could have kept the souvenir, but he sprinted to the infield where cameras captured him presenting the ball to Aaron near home plate. After his playing career, House established himself as an out-of-the-box pitching coach . . . at least at that time. His techniques (like throwing a football for arm efficiency) were well ahead of the curve and caught the eye of Nolan Ryan. During his Cooperstown speech, Ryan credited House for extending his career into his mid forties.

"While I was with the Rangers, I was very fortunate to have a pitching coach by the name of Tom House," Ryan said. "Tom and I are of the same age, and Tom is a coach that is always on the cutting edge. I really enjoyed our association together. He would always come up with new training techniques that we would try and see how they would work into my routine. Because of our friendship and Tom pushing me, I think I got in the best shape of my life during the years that I was with the Rangers."

I was honored to the throw the first pitch at the Texas Rangers game September 14, 1990, on HSE (Home Sports Entertainment) Day at Arlington Stadium.

While House helped Ryan on the field, I established a business relationship with both. Tom and I produced five instructional videos:

The cherished ball I threw for the first pitch was clocked at a season high, 53 mph, according to Rangers official on the field.

- "Pitching Absolutes"
- "Pitching Mechanics," which sold more than ten thousand videos before the internet existed.
- "Pitching Strategies and Tactics"
- "Pitchers Fielding Practice"
- "Nolan Ryan's Fastball Pitching Instruction Video with Randy Johnson," which also did well.

I sold those videos on HSE, thanks to commercials that ran day and night, including during Rangers games. I hired a company to answer the calls to an 800 number, after which the orders were shipped by my video fulfillment house in Irving, Texas. The masters could be dubbed into two hundred VHS tapes or DVDs at a time. I advertised in national baseball publications and attended the annual American Baseball Coaches Association Conventions each year, including the one in Texas. I paid for booth space, brought a video monitor to show the footage, sold the videos, and provided order forms for coaches to bring back to their schools for purchases. Another marketing strategy I employed was to buy mailing lists of high school and college baseball coaches, then send them pamphlets and order forms. I was doing it all, but it was worth it. I learned a lot about publishing your own videos, including cover design, how to license with Major League Baseball, and more.

We used celebrity extras to demonstrate the pitching tips in those videos, such as Texas Rangers Bobby Witt, Mitch "The Wild Thing" Williams, and Jamie Moyer. Tom recruited Nolan's sons, Reid and Reese Ryan, plus Tom Grieve's kids, Tim and Ben (Ben was the future American League Rookie of the Year).

We shot each video in one afternoon, on the Rangers' off days, at the old Arlington Stadium. We needed to stop every few minutes, whenever the noisy flights from DFW Airport took off overhead.

"Nolan Ryan's Fastball" was shot in the offseason in Alvin, Texas, on the high school field where he played ball and lived nearby. I flew Randy Johnson down from Seattle, where he lived while playing for the Mariners. This was early in Johnson's career. He looked up to Nolan as a mentor and was eager to fly to Alvin to learn from his idol. Nolan and Randy were similar. Both threw hard and sometimes lacked control, especially in their early days. Nicknamed "The Big Unit" because he was 6 foot 10, Randy eventually earned five Cy Young Awards, was named the 2001 World Series MVP, won the 2002 Triple Crown, pitched a perfect game in 2004, and was a ten-time all-star. He amassed 4,875 strikeouts, second only to Nolan Ryan. After becoming a first-ballot hall of famer in 2015, Randy attributed his development to working with Nolan.

In the April 1996 issue of *Mariners Magazine*, Randy spoke about how Nolan and Tom helped fix his mechanics in 1992:

I don't think it's any secret that I struggled early on in the Major Leagues and throughout parts of my minor-league career. I don't think I had any breakthrough to where I am now until I met with you [Nolan] and [Texas Rangers pitching coach] Tom House. A great deal of my success started after that meeting. I had some success in the minor leagues and early on in my major league career, but not even close to the extent that I have now. Lots of people tried working with me and they were all helpful, but it was the one thing that the two of you taught me about landing on the ball of my foot as opposed to landing on the heel of my foot that has helped me the most. I was always throwing the ball hard, but I was never consistent with my mechanics. The ability has always been there and I've always worked hard, but that seemed to be the one little element that wasn't there—being consistent with my arm angle and mechanics.

I have been very fortunate to run across some very giving players, the most generous being you, Nolan. It's unheard of, unfortunately, to have other people on another team take the time to help another professional athlete. Sure, hitters will talk about their swings here and there. But you and Tom House didn't have to help me. You two guys are good people and you've taught me more than proper mechanics. You've taught me to go up to a young player when he's struggling and maybe try and help them. So, you've helped me not only physically and mentally, but as a person to go and try and help other people.

I drove to the then Intercontinental Airport near the Woodlands, fifty miles north of Alvin, to pick up Randy. Since I funded the entire production and paid Randy, Nolan, and Tom House, I wanted to be sure Randy arrived at the shoot on time. You could say I was nice, smart, or both. I hired a local crew to shoot it, led by Steve Henry, whom I knew from working ESPN college baseball. We shot the

Shoot day with Tom House, Nolan Ryan, Randy Johnson and our production crew at Alvin High School in Texas.

sixty-minute video in one day. Then I brought the videotapes to Dallas to edit at Video Post & Transfer. I knew during shooting that we were making something special and historic: two future hall of famers collaborating under the coaching of Tom House. It was great hearing Nolan offer his tips to Randy and how the average pitcher could utilize those same words of wisdom.

Eventually I made a deal with Word Publishing to publish, distribute, and sell the tape. The arrangement wasn't exclusive, so I could sell it, too. The video proved to be an excellent documentation of two pitching legends talking baseball and providing insightful coaching tips for amateurs and professionals. Even MLB players bought copies.

During this Nolan Ryan era, I directed his five-thousandth-strikeout game on HSE on August 29, 1989, and produced his three-hundredth win for ESPN at Milwaukee County Stadium on

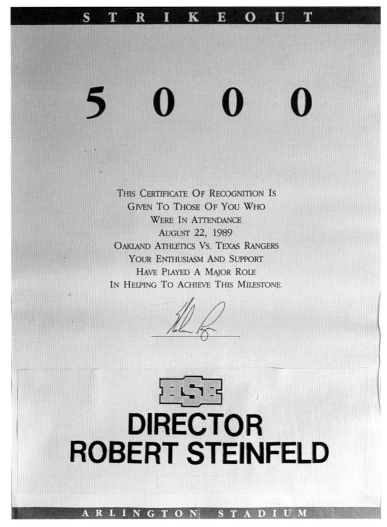

This historic souvenir certificate was distributed to everyone leaving the ballpark that night. I added the HSE logo and name.

July 31, 1990.

My background in producing and directing MLB caught ESPN's eye in the late 1980s, just as they secured the rights to air Major League Baseball beginning in 1990. I couldn't ask for better timing for Nolan's three hundredth victory.

# CHAPTER 6

## CBS Sports: My Decision on a Dream Opportunity

*In 1980, CBS Sports ramped up* its sports division to emulate ABC and NBC. Terry O'Neil, whom I met when I was a runner for ABC Sports in the late 1970s, was named executive producer for CBS. Although I kept pursuing my dream to work for a major network, three years had passed since I graduated from the University of Texas. I was persistent in my efforts to land an interview for a CBS broadcast associate (BA) job in New York City, something I had chased since 1976. Finally, CBS Sports administrator Kay Wight called to ask if I'd be interested in interviewing for the next class of entry-level broadcast associates. Of course I was. Yet my personal life was changing. In 1981, I married Sarah, who was extremely close to her family. And I was already producing games. Although she had family in New York, it would be very difficult to leave her parents and brothers in Dallas. Nonetheless, Sarah and I flew to the Big Apple for the interview. We had to.

On our way from Penn Station to CBS headquarters, a.k.a. Black Rock, on West 52nd Street, we experienced some memorable, disturbing NYC moments which seemed like omens. As we approached Times Square, we saw a high-speed police car in pursuit of a passenger car. The getaway car veered onto the sidewalk—

nearly hitting us—then returned to the street where it struck a lady and launched her through the air. It was like an episode of "Law and Order," except that it was real. Fortunately, the lady was alive and immediately attended to. Minutes later, as we approached CBS, the street was blocked off. We were told to detour to the other side, because granite and steel debris had fallen from a sky-scraper. A crane atop a skyscraper under construction collapsed, hit the side of the building, and wreaked havoc on the street below.

Later, on our return to the train to Princeton, I saw the after-noon edition of the *New York Post*, whose banner headline read, "Tower of Terror Rains Doom on City." I will never forget that dramatic headline, as only the *Post* would publish.

Amid our "peaceful" mental state, Sarah and I arrived at CBS, where I faced the first of three or four interviews with the CBS Sports executive team. (Weeks before, I had spoken to the current broadcast associates to learn what to expect during the interview process.) I met with executive producer Terry O'Neil, longtime NFL senior producer Charles H. Milton III, and a few others. I prepared a report on the NFL with my predictions for the upcom-ing season and handed a copy to each interviewer. They inquired about my ambitions, work ethic, and knowledge of sports to see how I would fit in with their culture. Securing that interview was an accomplishment unto itself, because Kay Wight told me hun-dreds had applied. From my research, I expected Chuck Milton would give me a sports quiz. That was exactly the case. He asked about current NFL head coaches and past champions. I believe what separated me from other candidates was that I was already in television, had worked with Terry O'Neil, had been persistent with my communication over the years, and I knew sports. More-over, I answered every sports question correctly.

I left CBS feeling good about the interview and then flew home to Dallas.

Days later, Wight called to congratulate me for being chosen as one of the new broadcast associates. She asked me to respond to their offer soon, but she seemed convinced it was a formality that I would be moving to New York. As much as I wanted that job, I would be separating my new wife from her family, and I would often be gone. I'd be working late nights in the broadcast center, preparing for games or events, and traveling on the road for weeks, perhaps in Europe or other distant destinations. I wrestled with one of the hardest decisions of my life.

While I pondered my dilemma, CBS flew me to a championship boxing match in Albuquerque, New Mexico, to shadow broadcast associates Bill Brown (who later became an executive with Fox Sports) and Richie Zyontz (who now produces Fox's top NFL game). Chuck Milton, who was producing, introduced me to the crew as their new BA. Unfortunately, I had not accepted the job yet.

I discussed it with Bill Brown and others. No one could believe I was contemplating rejecting an opportunity that I worked so diligently to get. I couldn't believe it, either. Yet something inside of me was saying that it came too late . . . just by a year or two. I was now married and had a good life in Dallas. Who knows what might have happened with my career at CBS Sports, but I decided to turn it down.

Nobody else had ever rejected such a coveted BA gig, I was later told. Granted, the entry-level salary was low, but with hard work, it would lead to much bigger opportunities. Although I was aware of that, I decided my life was fine. I have no regrets. As you'll read later, I eventually was hired by CBSSN to produce college basketball and football, as well as WNBA national telecasts for CBS in 2021 and 2023.

I learned many incredible lessons and experienced many exhilarating events during those early years working for all the national networks, the NBA, and for NBC at three Summer Olympic games.

# CHAPTER 7

# The Amazing—and Surreal—Celebrity Guest List for *Tailgate Party*

**While I was producing live shows** for HSE, Prime, ESPN, ABC, NBC, Fox Sports Net, the Cotton Bowl, and more, I also created original shows that aired locally, regionally, nationally, or not at all.

In 1988, I developed a variety show, along with producer Greg Mauiro, for Home Sports Entertainment regional cable and Six Flags Over Texas in Arlington. Growing up in Dallas, I attended Six Flags amusement park, which presented live shows several times a day, but not all day. The park's captive audience loved going inside air-conditioned rides and buildings, especially during the steamy Texas summers. My idea was to see if Six Flags would allow us to use their Southern Palace auditorium to host a sports variety show hosted by HSE's Norm Hitzges, who also had a daily radio show on KLIF/570 AM radio.

Six Flags execs loved the idea: an attraction that didn't cost them anything. We'd roll in our production truck during the week and invite celebrity guests each day. Six Flags would post signs at the park entry and make announcements each morning to promote our guests. We called the show *Tailgate Party* and created a festive, colorful logo that we animated for our opening sequence.

Bill Land, just getting his feet wet in sports television, served as Norm's sidekick. Our director was Kenny Miller from Denver, who spent the summer in Arlington just to direct this show. Years later, Kenny and I teamed up again to direct and produce college football on Fox Sports Net. Bill later became the longtime TV voice of the San Antonio Spurs. Kenny was an executive producer and general manager of a regional sports channel in Denver, and he more recently joined Amazon Prime as director of live production and technical operations.

Norm opened the show with a monologue, which was funny most of the time, and at other times moving. He was a master storyteller. Then we'd have a few guests on stage. Many were current or former major leaguers, since we were in the middle of baseball season and next door to Arlington Stadium. Back then, the teams stayed across Interstate 30 at the Hilton Inn or the Sheraton. Norm's radio station producer, Greg Mauiro, booked our guests.

Then managing partner of the Texas Rangers, George W. Bush was a guest on *Tailgate Party* at Six Flags Over Texas with host Norm Hitzges, 1989.

The only time a guest got upset was when three-time Indianapolis 500 winner Johnny Rutherford showed up, as Greg had accidentally double-booked another guest. Former Brooklyn Dodger Bobby Bragan, who later managed the Atlanta Braves, played piano and sang on one episode.

When George W. Bush was a managing partner and minority owner of the Texas Rangers, he bowled frozen turkeys with Norm and turkey bowler Derrick Johnson.

Norm handed Bush a frozen, still-wrapped turkey, and just before Bush took aim, he said "Turkeys Vote." Norm and the audience laughed as Bush reared back and slid the turkey on the stage—down the imaginary lane—toward ten plastic Coke bottles. While he didn't strike, he did knock down nine bottles, to everyone's delight.

"You know when you run for president, Mr. Bush," Norm said, "the Democrats are going to use this against you." Years later, when George W. Bush became president, we did get requests for that video. I'm not convinced the Democrats took advantage of the footage, though.

As executive producer, I sent reports to my bosses Ed Frazier, Joe King, Jack Stanfield, and John McIntyre. Here's a snippet from my first one:

> After two weeks of refining the audio and lighting aspects of our show, we have finally reached the point of acceptability. We realize the Six Flags Southern Palace is a stage for live theater show performances. It is not television-ready, so we dramatically enhanced the lighting.
>
> The new directional microphones have reduced the echoing effect caused by the large theater. Earlier in the week, we added transformers to the wireless microphone transmitters to eliminate humming. Don Covington was here this weekend to work on the cameras which have been presenting us with problems. He discovered some bad tubes, which will have to be ordered.

The concept of the show has never been a question. Now, the technical aspects have reached the same point. We are now shooting two shows per day. Our shooting schedule has been designed around the availability of guests, usually Friday, Saturday, and Sundays, but sometimes during the week. The dual shoot days allowed us to re-channel production budget capital into the lighting. Everyone on the crew has given more than 100% of their time and energy to make sure this show is a success. We are very serious about it. Almost every day we are adding something to improve production quality.

The studio audience increased this week. Saturday and Sunday we had our biggest crowds yet, with more than 300 people. We attribute that to the increased awareness of the show and a new sign we placed outside the Southern Palace.

*Tailgate Party* was a fun project where everyone enjoyed the unique setting, live nature of the show, and the format. It was an easy set and strike—many times, just leaving the camera and audio cables inside for the next show.

Our show's guest list was as astoundingly impressive as it was quirky, ranging from future President George W. Bush, to singer Charley Pride, to Mark McGwire, to the guy who invented pom-poms. (To get a glimpse of all the notable stars we hosted, go to Appendix 1.)

## The Skip Bayless Show

In 1993, I became executive producer of another original pilot. We shot the show in downtown Dallas, in a makeshift studio on the event level of the old Reunion Arena. Yes, the home of the Dallas Mavericks and soon the National Hockey League's Dallas Stars, who were leaving their home in Minnesota.

I had been following a young, opinionated columnist named Skip Bayless, who wrote for the *Dallas Times Herald*. He liked to stir

On set with host Skip Bayless during the shooting of the pilot episode of the *Skip Bayless Show,* 1993.

up controversy, so his point of view often challenged the consensus of Dallas–Fort Worth sports fans. I thought that would work well on TV. But at that time, newspaper columnists were, well, newspaper columnists, and they rarely, if ever, appeared on TV. It was even rarer that they starred in their own program. I conceived a thirty-min-ute show that focused on current sports events. I also devised the incredibly catchy title, *The Skip Bayless Show.* We taped the pilot and shopped it around, but word kept coming back that Skip was a "newspaper guy" and would not be accepted as a "TV guy," too. I could not believe it. Why pigeonhole someone? This was espe-cially dumb logic because viewers outside of Dallas would have no clue whether his media roots were in print or broadcast. To me, his newspaper columnist expertise gave him credibility, and his Vander-bilt-trained journalism background didn't hurt, either. I paid for the crew and editing, but we didn't make air. Fortunately for Skip, it was good training, which helped him down the road when he launched his national television career on ESPN and on FS1's "Undisputed."

## Lone Stars

A few years later, announcer Dave Barnett and I reteamed for an hour-long series we developed, called *Lone Stars*. There wasn't anything else like it at that time: a long-format interview show starring great athletes in Texas. We shopped it as a regional show and shot the studio segments at KTVT-11 in Fort Worth. Raycom Sports helped syndicate it. One of our best episodes featured San Antonio Spurs All-Star David Robinson, who is one of the most impressive athletes I've encountered. We had some success with that show in syndication.

## Icons Of Coaching

In 2013 and 2014, Dave and I collaborated once more on a sports interview show called *Icons of Coaching*, which won two regional Emmy Awards. I was able to clear this series nationally on Fox Sports Net regionals due to my relationship with FSN in Los Angeles and with our Fox Sports SW executive producer Mike Anastassiou. Mike afforded us a budget which allowed us to travel the country seeking the top "icons of coaching." Dave and I established criteria for guests to qualify as an iconic coach, but the main one was championship pedigree. Our lineup was incredible. True icons. Here's the list, with some quotes pulled from specific episodes:

**Mike Krzyzewski**—Head coach of the Duke and US Olympic basketball teams (shot in Las Vegas during Olympic practice). He discussed guiding Team USA's superstars:

> Every team needs coaching. If it doesn't get coaching, it has a
> chance to splinter. So, the Dream Team of '92 was not coached

I knew Coach K when I produced *ACC Sunday Night Hoops*, so it was especially gratifying to include him as a guest on Icons of Coaching, shot in Las Vegas in 2014 while he was head coach for Team USA.

as much by X's and O's as much as it was coached as trying to develop a collective ego representing our country. Chuck Daly did that in a magnificent manner.

Let's see how all of your egos—a collective ego—play for the United States and that's the beauty of it. You have to be careful if you ask guys to take away from something they do instinctively or that killer instinct they normally have just to fit in, [then] we're not going to be as good.

A couple of our standards . . . We are always going to tell the truth. You could have a rule, "don't lie." I'd rather have a standard to always tell the truth. We're always *on time*, because we have respect for one another.

**Jimmy Johnson**—Head coach of Oklahoma State, Miami Hurricanes, and Dallas Cowboys (recorded at his home in Key West, Florida). He addressed Jerry Jones adding him to the team's Ring of Honor at AT&T Stadium:

> Actually, Jerry told me three years ago that he was going to put me in the Ring of Honor. I think it's great for players and it's a really great honor for those players, but for coaches we've done our work. You can see the records, so that accomplishment is fine enough for me.

Jimmy was inducted in the Cowboys Ring of Honor December 30, 2023

We traveled to the Florida Keys the summer of 2013 to interview former Dallas Cowboys Head Coach and Fox Sports commentator Jimmy Johnson for *Icons of Coaching*.

**Barry Switzer**—Head coach of Oklahoma and Dallas Cowboys (shot in Norman, Oklahoma). He described phoning Oklahoma Sooners recruit Billy Sims during halftime of the 1974 Oklahoma–Colorado game when they were leading 28-0:

> I get in the locker room and [see] a pay phone. And I said to one of my coaches give me a nickel. That was back when there were pay phones. I walk over, put a nickel in the pay phone, and I called Billy at the gas station where he was working in Hooks, Texas. The phone rang and I asked to speak to Billy. The guy said Billy couldn't talk "cause he was pumping gas." I said, "I don't give a damn. Go out and pump it for him, get him on the phone!"
>
> He dropped the phone and went out to get him. The man said, "Hey Billy, Coach Switzer is calling you from the locker room of the game today."
>
> A disbelieving Sims came to the phone to hear Switzer say:
>
> "Billy, this shows you how we feel about you and how much we want you. I came here and used this telephone to call you personally to talk to you about coming to Oklahoma."
>
> The game officials came to the locker room, because the Sooners were late returning to the field.
>
> "You hear that Billy? I got to finish this ass-kicking. I'll call you later tonight."

Sims went on to win the 1978 Heisman as an Oklahoma Sooner.

**Larry Brown**—Head coach of SMU and championship coach in both the NCAA and NBA (shot in Dallas). He stressed the value of "playing the right way":

> I should have coined that, 'cause now I hear everybody saying it in every sport. And I really believe I was the first one to say that, even though I always thought that way. . . . Dean Smith

Host Dave Barnett with then Texas Longhorns Head Coach Mack Brown and me in Austin.

was a big influence on my life. . . . And every day I write on the board, "play hard, play smart, play together, have fun." . . . And it would be nice if we could defend and rebound.

**Mack Brown**—University of Texas football coach (shot in Austin, Texas)

**Béla Károlyi**—US Women's Olympic gymnastics coach (shot at Karolyi Ranch, his gymnastic complex in Huntsville, Texas, north of Houston). This was filmed before his complex was closed due to USA Gymnastics terminating their agreement with Károlyi. USA Gymnastics doctor Larry Nassar, an employee of Karolyi Ranch, was convicted in 2017 of sexually assaulting hundreds of young women and girl gymnasts. The Károlyis were exonerated and never charged with a crime.

**Mary Lou Retton**—Olympic gold medalist gymnast. I set up the interview with Mary Lou Retton when I was in Houston to produce Texas Rangers telecasts for Fox Sports SW. We met at the Four Seasons Hotel in downtown Houston, where the team and media stayed while playing the Astros. My crew set up cameras, lights, and background in a meeting room. I had been emailing with her for several weeks and felt like we were acquaintances, so when she arrived punctually in the lobby, I greeted her with a smile and was about to give her a hug. To my surprise—or should I say my naivete?—she looked at me like I was a stranger. Which, of course, I was. Although I had never seen or met her before, I felt like I knew her well. How could I not? After her gold-medal performance at the 1984 Summer Olympics in Los Angeles, she was America's darling, the glorified face on a box of "The Breakfast of Champions" Wheaties cereal and a popular guest throughout television. Once I introduced myself, she apologized. "This happens to me all the time," Retton explained. "People just come up to me as if we were lifelong friends."

The interview went well, and I thanked her for her time and thoughtful words. Remembering her kindness, I was deeply concerned when I heard about her serious health scare due to pneumonia in October 2023, but thankfully she recovered.

**Nadia Comaneci**—Romanian gymnast who scored the first perfect 10 in Olympics history at the 1976 Montreal Olympics (shot in Norman, Oklahoma). She discussed Károlyi, her former coach:

Gymnast Mary Lou Retton also provided her thoughts about her former coach Bela Karolyi for our Icons episode shot in Houston in 2013.

With 1976 Olympic Gold Medalist and former Romanian gymnast Nadia Comaneci before we interviewed her for our Icons episode about her former coach Bela Karolyi. She scored the first perfect "10" in Olympic history in 1976.

> He used to take us to ski. He never told us [laughing] that we had to climb the entire mountain for an hour and a half and then ski down in a minute and a half. I remember that because that was his tactic. He wanted us to walk the entire mountain with big boots and skis. Man, we were so strong after we came back home after the two weeks of the mountain experience.

**Bart Conner**—Two-time gold medalist Olympic gymnast

**Kim Mulkey**—Baylor women's basketball head coach (shot in Waco, Texas). She assessed her coaching style: "I am up on my feet, I am pumping my fist. I am trying to give my team everything I can."

**Wayne Graham**—Baseball coach at Rice (shot in Houston). He shared his experience playing for hall of fame manager Casey Stengel for the 1964 New York Mets:

> Casey described me one time to writers within my hearing as a mediocre baseball player. You know, when Casey says that, you've got to kind of take it to the bank, because I think Casey Stengel knew as much about baseball than anyone who ever lived. And on the bench, he gave a running commentary, which I listened to carefully. If you listened, you learned a lot.

**Roger Clemens**—Famed Boston Red Sox pitcher

**Tommy Lasorda**—The hall of fame manager of the Los Angeles Dodgers (shot at Dodger Stadium). He elaborated on his managerial style:

> My major philosophy was to get a group of guys—a team— and number one, make them believe in themselves. Number two, to play and be like a family; a family attitude on the team. I knew everyone's wife. I knew everyone's children's names. It wasn't just a manager and a player, it was a manager and a family. And I felt if I could be like a family, I could get them to play better. I wanted them to believe in themselves very, very much. . . . Self-confidence is the first step to success.

**John Wooden**—We interviewed disciples of the late UCLA head coach, including Bill Walton and Marques Johnson, as well as coaches such as Duke's Mike Krzyzewski, UCLA's Steve Alford, and Wooden's daughter, Nan. (Shot on the UCLA campus and at Walton's home in San Diego). Walton, the Naismith hall of famer and former UCLA Bruin all-American, commented on his mentor's "Pyramid of Success":

What a treat it was to meet Hall of Fame Manager Tommy Lasorda at Dodger Stadium for another episode of *Icons of Coaching*.

He had so many great maxims. Be quick, but don't hurry. Failing to prepare is preparing to fail. Happiness begins where selfishness ends. Never mistake activity for achievement. If everyone thinks alike, nobody thinks. It's not how big you are, but how big you play. It's not a game of size and strength, it's a game of skill, timing, and position. It's not how high you jump, it's where you are and when you jump. And on and on and on, but the thing is that he lived. . . . He lived all of that stuff. . . . He constantly would tell us, "When you are through learning, you're truly through." And he never stopped learning.

Walton's heartfelt soundbite, recorded in his guest home adjacent to his house in San Diego, was also where he went to play drums and listen to Grateful Dead music. Its living room doubles as a music studio outfitted with sound and percussion instruments from Grateful Dead drummer Mickey Hart. Walton, a self-described "Deadhead," had seen the band perform countless times and had hosted podcasts and radio programs featuring their music. His property also features an additional, eclectic place for visitors to stay: an actual teepee with sleeping arrangements. Unfortunately, we lost Bill Walton to cancer in May 2024. His friendship, personality, and love for his family and basketball will be missed.

Weeks after the episode aired, I received a letter in the mail, postmarked July 9, 2014, from Santa Clarita, California. Its return address read, "Ms. Nan Wooden." That was exciting. I opened the envelope and found a beautiful greeting card inside. On the cover was this quote: "The main ingredient of stardom is the rest of the team. — Coach John Wooden."

On the backside of the card was a picture of Coach Wooden with another quote: "I wish you good luck on your own journey to achieve success. Make each day a masterpiece."

I opened the card. On the right side was an additional message from him:

Barnett and I met Hall of Famer and former UCLA Bruin Bill Walton at his guest house in San Diego to record an interview for the John Wooden tribute episode in 2014.

I'm asked, "Coach Wooden, how did you win those champion-ships?" My response was factual. "I didn't win all those cham-pionships. Our team did." In my 27 years at UCLA, I didn't score a single basket. My job was to help others do it. The star of the team is your team.

On the left inside panel was a handwritten, heartfelt note from Wooden's daughter, Nan:

Dear Bob,

Thank you so much for the DVDs 'Icons of Coaching' John Wooden. . . .Watching the DVD was awesome and emotional. Your tribute to my Dad was perfect and I really appreciated your effort, Bob. . . .

I wish you continued success on you next projects as well as your health and happiness to you and those you love.

—Nan Wooden

What a charming note, but not unexpected coming from the Wooden family. I proudly keep the framed card hanging in my office.

**Lenny Wilkens**—NBA hall of famer and coach for Atlanta and Seattle (shot at his home in suburban Seattle). Bill Walton praised Wilkens as such:

Lenny Wilkens was fantastic . . . the perfect coach. Would have been, except I couldn't play (in Seattle) when the string of stress fractures started for me. Lenny Wilkens was so much like John Wooden. [He] had that spirited force of character of quiet leadership—that aura that surrounds him.

The Károlyi and Jimmy Johnson episodes each won 2014 Lone Star Emmy Awards for Outstanding Achievement in Sports Inter-view/Discussion.

2014 Emmy Award for *Icons of Coaching*, "Jimmy Johnson." We also won for the Bela Karolyi episode simultaneously.

# CHAPTER 8

## Making All-Star History with Cal Ripken Jr. and A-Rod

*I've been fortunate* to work and cross paths with some of the finest athletes and personalities in sports history, including David Robinson of the San Antonio Spurs and strikeout king Nolan Ryan of the Texas Rangers. Both played for teams whose telecasts I produced for years. Another athlete on that pedestal is Cal Ripken Jr., who played his entire career with the Baltimore Orioles and is considered one of baseball's greatest shortstops, along with Honus Wagner.

I produced or directed many of Cal's games nationally on ESPN, ABC, the Baseball Network, plus regional sports networks HSE and Fox Sports Net. But it gets more personal. Cal and I are linked to one of the most memorable moments in MLB All-Star Game history.

Cal Ripken—a.k.a. the "Iron Man"—played in a record 2,632 consecutive games; was voted into nineteen all-star games; was a two-time American League MVP; was twice named all-star game MVP; captured the Silver Slugger Award eight times; won a 1983 World Series ring; and was inducted into the Baseball Hall of Fame in 2007. He ranks even beyond the legends glorified in Kevin Costner's movie *Field of Dreams*.

For four years, I produced Fox Sports Net's national telecasts of the Cal Ripken World Series, which is the Babe Ruth League's youth equivalent of the Little League World Series.

The 2000 game took place in Mattoon, Illinois; 2001 in Vincennes, Indiana; 2002 in Mattoon again; and 2003 at Cal Ripken Stadium in Aberdeen, Maryland, where one of the Orioles' minor-league teams, the Aberdeen IronBirds, called home.

For those first two telecasts, Cal was playing for the Orioles and could not attend the championship games that we were televising. We arranged for a live satellite hookup from Camden Yards baseball stadium in Baltimore so he could virtually join our telecast in Mattoon. I was nervous about the technical integration, but both times, it worked out fine.

I was impressed with Cal's involvement on conference calls leading up to the event at his hometown stadium. His brother, fellow MLB player Billy Ripken, was our analyst on a few telecasts.

Cal's love of baseball was so ingrained in his psyche that he felt obligated to try to grow the game by enhancing its grassroots, hence the Cal Ripken World Series.

For the 2001 Cal Ripken World Series—during Cal's final playing season—I decided it would be fitting to interview Cal's admirers and roll those bites into our telecast. We'd be congratulating the Iron Man for his contribution to baseball and his work with kids.

Since I lived in Dallas and produced Texas Rangers games, I thought an ideal interview would be with Rangers' star Alex Rodriguez, who was making his first start at shortstop in the 2001 MLB All-Star Game at Safeco Field in Seattle. The significance was that it was Cal's last all-star game and the first time he would not join the starting lineup as a shortstop; he was instead slated to start at third base. A-Rod always looked up to Cal. Both were tall short-stops and hit with power, so A-Rod would be realizing a dream, playing next to his idol.

I phoned Texas Rangers media relations director John Blake, who arranged the interview with A-Rod before a game at the Rangers' ballpark in Arlington. This was on Thursday, July 5, 2001, five days before the all-star game in Seattle.

I was honored to work directly with baseball Hall of Famer Cal Ripken for four years, including the 2002 Cal Ripken World Series in Matoon, Illinois.

Fox Sports Net camera op David Mammeli and I set up our camera and two chairs in the Texas Rangers press conference room located near the Rangers locker room. I would interview A-Rod, which was fulfilling in itself. He was very pleasant and looked forward to speaking about Cal. Here's what A-Rod told me about taking over Cal's position at shortstop:

> That's very special to me, because '97 was the first season I
> started off, and it was the first year he moved over to third
> base. And I felt that was kind of neat, someone who played
> so long and now you were going to replace him [at shortstop]
> after sixteen or seventeen years and then to play in his very last
> game . . . and to have the opportunity to play with him at third
> base. I definitely want a picture of that game. Both [of us] in it,
> one of those side shots to show my kids one day.

As he was answering, a light bulb went off in my head. I waited for A-Rod to finish his thought. Then I suggested:

"Have you ever thought at all about—not that this would ever happen—but do you ever think to yourself, because it's his last game, that maybe for one batter you switch positions and let him play shortstop?"

A-Rod chuckled and smiled. "That's an idea," he responded.

He didn't shoot down my creative scheme, so I pressed on. "It would be an unbelievably classy thing, not that it would be your call…"

"That would be cool. I would be willing to do anything. Whatever he wants to do, I'm down, he said."

"I don't think [Cal] would want to do it," I added. "Maybe if you talk to the manager [Joe Torre]. That would be unbelievable if he came out there for one play. It would be kind of neat."

"I'm going to have a great time playing with him," A-Rod vowed.

Although A-Rod didn't seem overly excited about it, I planted something tangible in his mind. Unbeknownst to me, that same afternoon he phoned Joe Torre in New York with the idea. I later discovered that Torre consulted with the offices of Major League Baseball.

It was a longshot that something would happen at Tuesday's all-star game on Fox, yet I alerted three people: my wife, Sarah; Fox Sports Net media relations director Ramon Alvarez; and my longtime friend Mark Bodzin, a childhood baseball teammate who had attended many sporting events with me. "Something might happen before the first pitch tonight," I told them. "Keep your eyes on A-Rod and Cal."

The game on Fox Sports was about to begin as my wife and I were eating dinner at our home. Suddenly, a shot of Alex Rodriguez at shortstop popped up on the screen. Here's how it sounded on the air:

"Alex Rodriguez thought of this," said play-by-play man Joe

Buck. "He grew up in Miami idolizing Cal Ripken Jr., and he thought this year should be the year…"

The director cut to a tight shot of Ripken.

"…that Cal Ripken Jr. should finish as an all-star and start this game as a shortstop, where he—as Kevin Kennedy said in the pregame—revolutionized the position of shortstop."

Next came a wider shot of A-Rod walking from shortstop to Ripken at third.

"Cal has no idea. And Alex Rodriguez said, 'You know what? I want Ripken to play short.'"

A-Rod pointed to Ripken, who remained oblivious to what was transpiring.

"We'll see if Ripken is accepting."

As A-Rod asked him to switch, Cal looked hesitant. Then A-Rod pointed to American League manager Joe Torre.

The other Fox commentator, St. Louis Cardinals hall-of-fame catcher Tim McCarver—a two-time World Series champion in 1964 and 1967—chuckled at Ripken's reaction.

"You knew he wouldn't want to go," Buck observed.

Torre motioned Ripken to move to shortstop. While Ripken decided what to do, A-Rod gestured towards the manager.

"Joe Torre [is] back up for Alex Rodriguez," said Buck. "And in this seventy-second all-star game, the nineteen-time all-star deserves to go out and play this first inning as a shortstop."

McCarver gleefully added, "And he's gotta [do] what your manager tells you, right?"

"Hey, he's only following instructions," Buck replied coyly.

Ripken wandered into shortstop territory as McCarver laughed some more.

Fox then offered close ups of both A-Rod and Ripken, after which the latter said something to American League starting pitcher Roger Clemens.

Buck astutely guessed, "I think he just said to Roger Clemens, 'Strike him out. Don't have him hit it up the middle.'" Ripken was referring to the National League's leadoff hitter, so he wouldn't need to field a ball at short.

Ripken acknowledged the applause of the roaring Seattle crowd witnessing this historic moment in baseball history.

"So a classy gesture, from a classy, classy man," Buck continued. "Alex Rodriguez, his idea, and Cal Ripken fought it. But Junior finally gave in when Joe Torre said, 'Get over there.' So, there's the surprise for Cal already."

Within seconds, my friend Mark Bodzin phoned me and screamed, "You just changed the course of all-star history!" Perhaps a mild exaggeration, but at minimum, a notable chapter in baseball lore.

Fox media relations director Ramon Alvarez soon called to add, "It was like an out-of-body experience. I knew what was going to happen. It was like I was dreaming it."

Later in the telecast, Fox Sports reporter Jeanne Zelasko interviewed Torre in the dugout and asked how that switch came about. Torre said that last Thursday afternoon—the same day I interviewed Rodriguez in Arlington—he received a phone call in his office at the stadium. It was A-Rod, explaining that he had this great idea.

Few people might believe I played a fundamental role in Major League Baseball all-star history, but I have it on tape and DVD. Even better, I have written proof from A-Rod himself.

When the Rangers returned to Arlington a week later, I caught up with A-Rod to ask about the switch. He said he received so much positive response from that gesture, including one lady who was in tears. He thanked me for the idea and signed a photograph of that historic moment.

I also gave him a picture to keep for himself. He appreciated it and wanted to give it to his kids someday. It meant a lot to him. And to me.

It was exhilarating that an all-star would take my off-the-cuff idea and literally execute it. I came up with a good premise on the fly, but it was Alex Rodriguez who took it to market. Ripken told the *Daily News*:

Alex Rodriguez acknowledged my idea for the switch with Cal Ripken at the 2001 All Star Game with this autographed picture.

It seemed like I was the only one in the stadium who didn't know what was happening. Alex came over to me and told me that we were going to switch positions and I wanted to tell him what I thought about that in a direct sort of way, but then I remembered that I was wearing a microphone from MLB. I then looked into the dugout and Joe Torre was waving me over. When it happened, I really was a little uncomfortable, because I don't like surprises, but looking back, it was such a wonderful tribute by Alex and something that I will always remember.

MLB.com ranks it as one of the greatest moments in all-star game history. In Ripken's first at-bat, the crowd gave him a standing ovation. Then on the very first pitch by the Dodgers' Chan Ho Park, he hit a rocket home run to leftfield. He went on to earn MVP honors.

On a personal note, Rawlings sent me an official 2001 all-star game ball that Ripken later signed for me at the 2002 Cal Ripken World Series. It's a cherished memento. When I handed him the ball and a black Magic Marker, he said, "No, let me get a ballpoint pen. Collectors say that's the best way to sign it."

Those four years working with the Ripkens and Ripken Baseball rank near the top of my career memories.

What's the lesson for aspiring journalists (or anyone) meeting an important, influential, and famous leader or athlete? Don't be intimidated. Observe and seize the moment. When you come up with an idea, pipe up. Make the suggestion. Don't keep it inside then later wish you mentioned it. Who knows, your idea might make headlines and become a historic memory for two of the greatest baseball players ever.

# CHAPTER 9

## *Verne Lundquist and "Six Others" Withstand a Nail-Biting Flight*

*In the early '80s* while working for ON TV—a subscription TV network in Dallas–Fort Worth—I became the staff producer for live sports events as we acquired games and packages. We carried a special series of games that was brokered by Keith Samples at Sports Production Inc. (Samples became a successful Hollywood producer/director, whose film and TV credits include *Felicity*, *Walking Tall*, and *Oz*.)

The package of Southwest Conference basketball games aired simultaneously on our network and USA Network. This was when the Houston Cougars, "Phi Slama Jama," were wreaking havoc on the conference with future hall of famers Clyde Drexler and Hakeem Olajuwon. I devised a unique plan to rank each dunk graphically with something I affectionately coined the "Dunk-O-Meter." We had plenty of opportunities to implement it whenever the Cougars hit the court. Each time Clyde "The Glide" Drexler or Benny Anders stuffed the rim, our "Dunk-O-Meter" ratings— solely determined by me—were proudly announced on the air by Verne Lundquist. Following his tenure as our play-by-play voice, Lundquist became one of CBS Sports' top talents, calling March Madness, PGA golf, and SEC football. The Cougars were not televised every week, but often.

I also devised the idea of using a different expert analyst every week, usually a coach who had the night off. I hired Robert "Snake" LeGrand, head coach of the University of Texas in Arlington, who was a genuine character and an excellent coach. He knew the players and had fun on the air. We used Abe Lemons, who had just finished his stint as Texas head coach and was returning to coach at Oklahoma City, where his career began in 1955. I gave Baylor head coach Jim Haller his first analyst job. We employed Dallas Cowboys wide receiver Drew Pearson, who retired in 1983 and was also an excellent basketball player. His obvious star power made him a natural for TV. He led the Dallas Cowboys Hoopsters in nationwide exhibitions, with Tony Hill, Ed "Too Tall" Jones, Roger Staubach, Danny White, Robert Newhouse, Charlie Waters, Butch Johnson, Billy Joe DuPree, Tony Dorsett, Ron Fellows, Mike Hegman, Ron Springs, and more.

Our boss at ON TV, Ed Frazier, had connections with a private airplane pilot whose twin-engine turboprop plane we could charter. The plane, which was catered and comfortable, flew us to the games each morning, then returned us afterwards. Clarence, the pilot, picked us up at the general aviation gate at Love Field, which was convenient to all living in the area. That was a key reason that Verne agreed to do the games. It enabled him to get home the same evening to honor his commitments to local Dallas television station WFAA Channel 8 and to the Dallas Cowboys, since he served as the team's radio voice.

One such game took place in Fayetteville, Arkansas, home of the Razorbacks. The flight there was notably bumpy while soaring over the rolling hills as we approached Fayetteville. After the game, we returned to the airport at 9:30 p.m. Clarence alerted us that there was heavy weather between Fayetteville and Dallas. He recommended staying the night and returning in the morning when flying conditions would be safer. Sounded like good idea, but Verne said he needed to return that night, per our agreement. So, it was wheels up. Oh my!

As soon as we lifted off, the plane went side to side, up and down, rocking and bumping. I'm not even sure if Clarence had control. I looked at the cockpit and he seemed okay, though most of us were feeling queasy. Especially yours truly. Director Dave Burchett, sitting across from me, said I was turning green. I was holding onto my seat so tightly my fingernails must have pierced the armrests and left marks. I managed to muster enough courage to open my eyes and ask Clarence what he saw on the radar. He pointed to the scope and it was entirely green, meaning storms. Oh, no. It got so bad that most of us thought that it was doomsday. Mayday. We were unsure whether the small craft could withstand the bouncing and constant shifting from the heavy rain, hail, wind, and lightning bombarding us. Clarence said that the trip (if we made it) would take at least twice as long, because the wind was driving us off course, and he had to steer against it to keep us headed in the right direction. Oh no, again!

At that point, Burchett, whose sharp-witted, perfectly timed humor could always calm the storm in our production truck, quipped, "You know, the unfortunate thing for most of is that in the newspaper tomorrow, the headline will read, 'Verne Lundquist and Six Others Die in Plane Crash.'"

Verne would, of course, earn the headline while the rest of us were incidental. It was just a joke, but the timing was perfect. It even elicited a terrified giggle from Mr. Greenface.

What seemed like the longest flight ever—even longer than my nonstop flight to Germany—settled down when we broke through the clouds a few miles north of Dallas Love Field. Seeing that runway was the best sight in the world. We made it through the rain, hail, wind, and storms thanks to our excellent pilot and G-d's will.

Verne thanked us all for returning that evening. You're welcome.

# CHAPTER 10

## *Producing the Summer Olympics for NBC in Barcelona, Atlanta, and Athens*

*I tried quite hard* to land a producing role with NBC Sports, not only for the challenge and prestige, but also for what I might learn from being around the best production personnel, artists, talent, and technicians in the world. The Olympics were the place where state-of-the-art, next-generation media technology was often introduced. Every four years, those games provided an outstanding introduction to new equipment and production techniques.

In my attempt to land a producing gig for the XXV Olympiad at Barcelona in 1992, I introduced myself to NBC Sports coordinating producer David Neal via letter and phone calls in the early '90s. It was a long shot for a producer from Texas who had never worked for NBC Sports. Nor had I even met him. But I kept in touch and visited him in New York when I was in town with the San Antonio Spurs. My association with the NBA provided some credibility, since NBC had carried the league from 1991 to 2002.

Because I was producing and/or directing MLB for Home Sports Entertainment—a regional sports network in North Texas—it was natural that I lobbied to produce baseball and basketball for the Olympics. I wrote a report on the top international baseball teams and their star players. It was well received. I told David about my best-selling instructional videos that I made with Rangers pitching coach Tom House. I handed him a copy of "Pitching Mechanics: Problem Recognitions & Solutions" and left the meeting feeling pretty good. The 1992 games were still months away from crewing, so I gave it my best shot.

Months later, David offered me a gig producing weightlifting and possibly wrestling for NBC Sports. I was familiar with those sports, but did not know the international stars or weight classes. Luckily, I had time to prepare. I was very excited. With persistence and hard work, I reached my goal to produce at the summer games and work for NBC.

So, cram I did. For the next few months, I followed international competitions and watched whatever events aired on television. Remember, there were no internet files then. One month before I was set to leave for Barcelona, David assigned me to another project, a bigger one for the network. He wanted to know if I'd produce the official highlight video of the games for NBC Sports in association with Blockbuster Video. It would be called "NBC Sports Presents Barcelona '92 Olympic Games: The Greatest Performances and Stories behind the XXV Olympiad," hosted by Bob Costas.

Besides my credit as "producer of Olympic videocassettes," the team behind the highlight video included Dick Ebersol, president of NBC Sports; Terry O'Neil, executive producer of NBC Sports; David Neal, coordinating producer; Molly Solomon, writer of Olympic videocassettes; Randel A. Falco, senior vice president of Olympic coverage; and Martin J. Yudkowitz, vice president of business affairs. The music was composed by John Tesh. I was thoroughly humbled to see my name included amongst the greats in the business.

As cool as my title was, David had yet another big assignment for me. This was the first year that NBA players would participate in the Olympics, so NBC and Blockbuster wanted to document and sell an official highlight video of Dream Team I. It was titled, "NBC Sports Presents Barcelona '92 Olympic Games: Featuring the Greatest Moments of the U.S. Olympic Team," hosted by Marv

With NBC Sports Olympics basketball director Kevin Shank outside Pavello Olimpic de Badalona in 1992.

Albert. The credits were the same, yet with the addition of Tommy Roy, basketball venue producer, and Kevin Shank, director. The back cover boasted this pitch:

> Watch America capture the gold with the greatest U.S. basketball team assembled in nearly 100 years of Olympic tradition. From the hardwood of Barcelona, Spain, relive the legendary U.S. Olympic basketball events on this exclusive videocassette.
>
> Witness the pursuit of the gold through the awesome talent and power of the greatest basketball team in history. With a legendary lineup including Michael Jordan, Larry Bird and Magic Johnson, surely there will never again be such a formidable Olympic basketball team. They had a mission; a quest to regain the gold.

Here are the American basketball triumphs of the XXV Olympiad captured exclusively on videocassette. You'll want to watch these spectacular moments over and over again.

I asked for a challenge and this was going to be it. Not only would I produce one historic highlight video, but the second one had to be completed *before* I left Barcelona. That required me to focus on it during and after the games. David promised I would have a crew of editors working around the clock, which meant *I* would be working around the clock organizing and producing highlight reels for both videos simultaneously. Blockbuster wanted these videos mass-produced and distributed nationwide just weeks after the game to capitalize on the momentum and excitement. Such videos normally take months to complete. We were still using videotape in the early '90s, so moving things around, shortening, lengthening, adding, or removing effects took much longer. Sometimes we needed to completely restart a segment. Reediting segments took hours. Today, it would be far easier to do digitally, in mere seconds or minutes.

I accepted the challenge and flew to Barcelona that summer. Little did I know it would take six months to physically recuperate after completing the projects. There wasn't any specific physical ailment, just the substantial drain on my body and mind. In the end it was worth it.

My family and I arrived in Spain in the summer of 1992, one week before the games began. My daughter Elaine was seven, and my son Leon was five. The NBC hotel was on the historic La Rambla, a tree-lined pedestrian street stretching about a mile with cafes, kiosks, and infamous pickpockets. It connected the Placa de Catalunya in its center with the Christopher Columbus Monument at the port. Behind the hotel was a small street and another boutique hotel where the Dream Team stayed. Everywhere they went, cheering fans and helicopters followed their entourage. My kids spotted a young actor named Will Smith hanging out at that hotel—a fan just like us. As the weeks went by, many NBA players visited our hotel lobby, which was bigger and gave them an escape from the commotion anytime they were spotted at their hotel. Our NBC hotel was secure from fans.

One week after we arrived, my family returned to Dallas so I could concentrate on my tasks. I had to keep my eyes on every venue to see which records would be broken and the best stories to document.

Evelyn Ashford won her fourth Olympic gold medal in the 4x100 meter relay. Derek Redmond of Great Britain tore a hamstring during a 400-meter semifinal heat. As he struggled to finish the race, his dad entered the track without credentials, put his arm around his son, and helped him complete the race as the crowd gave him a standing ovation. Sixteen-year-old Jennifer Capriati won the gold in singles tennis. But the big story overshadowing everything was the Dream Team's ascent to Olympic gold.

I had access to any video that NBC had in its file or aired during the Olympics. One challenge was that archived footage was recorded on tapes that you had to check out of NBC's tape library in the Barcelona broadcast center. There was not a virtual video file that anyone could access, as producers do today. That single tape had to be dubbed or passed around as needed by the numerous producers and editors in the center and on remotes. The good news was that I was able to start on the general highlight video soon after the opening ceremony. I was able to complete the opening ceremony and teases right away. It was a little different for the Dream Team video, since we had to wait for games to be played and features to be produced.

I went to specific venues to let talent introduce their sports. Tom Hammond did track and field; John Tesh did gymnastics; Charlie Jones did swimming and diving; and of course, Marv Albert and Mike Fratello introduced basketball.

Traveling around Barcelona proved challenging, especially since I had to take a forty-five-minute subway ride to get to the Pavello Olimpic de Badalona arena.

Once the Olympics ended, I had eight edit stations going simultaneously. My editors were already tired from working long hours and were ready to go home. Unfortunately, I was just beginning and under extreme pressure to finish both highlight tapes in one week. One by one, each editor said they had nothing left. Too worn out. There was no way I could complete the videos. Moreover, the International Broadcast Center (IBC) was being dismantled around my edit bays. We barely had one week until technicians would cut the cords. By the time the final day arrived, all I had left were two edit bays. We had made progress, yet needed more time. I alerted David Neal, who let Blockbuster know about the delay. He allowed me to fly to Dallas with the tapes and complete them at a facility of my choosing . . . but quickly. I was already dragging, having endured many late nights. Welcome to the Olympics.

After completing the editing in Dallas, I needed the host, Bob Costas, to revoice and lay down new tracks. David arranged for me to fly to St. Louis where Costas resided and set up a session at a professional audio house to record his voiceover. We only had one day.

The audio session took longer than planned, so Bob could not finish. He had promised to take his son to the Cardinals game that night. I understood and asked if he would just lay down a few lines that I thought we'd need. He kindly agreed. I thought that would be it, so I thanked him for his time. My plan was to fly back to Dallas that night, but the editing (syncing his voice with the video and mixing) took more hours than I expected. My editing crew and I were still there when I received an 8 p.m. phone call from Bob Costas. Wow, was there a problem? No, Bob called to see if I was happy with his work. I said he did fine, but there were spots I thought could be improved with different wording. "We'll make it work," I assured him.

Instead, Bob promised to return to the audio house immediately following the Cardinals game to finish the job properly. He wanted me to be satisfied that things were perfect. About ninety minutes later, he was back in the studio, revoicing his segments. I was beyond impressed with his professionalism and dedication to his craft. He understood the significance of this project to NBC Sports.

That's what makes Costas one of the elite broadcasters—his drive for perfection. On top of that, he knew I planned to fly to Dallas that night and correctly assumed that I missed my plane. He then invited me to stay at his house, which I really appreciated. I had a few more hours of editing to do, however, so I would contact NBC, get a hotel, then fly back the next morning. He insisted, but I simply could not intrude like that. Again, what a class act. We could have had some great conversations about the old American Basketball Association, as he was the voice of the Spirits of St. Louis while I was a teenager attending Dallas Chaparral games.

The two videos were successfully completed and were well received.

NBC Olympics host Bob Costas and I at a St. Louis recording studio to complete voiceover work for the official 1992 NBC Summer Olympics highlight video from Barcelona.

Four years later, the games were held in Atlanta. My family again joined me for the first week—this time attending the opening ceremonies—highlighted by the lighting of the Olympic flame by Muhammad Ali. What an iconic sports moment we shared.

I was hired to produce beach volleyball, which was making its Olympic debut. I was excited to be assigned to one of the best venues. Each match was played at Clayton County International Park in Jonesboro, Georgia, about seventeen miles or twenty-five minutes south of downtown Atlanta. It was constructed exclusively for the beach volleyball competition.

My broadcast team featured commentator Randy Rosenbloom; analyst Kirk Kilgour, a three-time all-American volleyball player who led the UCLA Bruins to a national championship in 1971; plus NBA hall of famer and former beach volleyball player Bill Walton as our reporter.

There were no lights or night matches, so I worked from early morning to dinner hour. I was editing packages on beach volleyball, for both men and women, to help promote my venue and the very first beach volleyball Olympians. Occasionally, my offers were granted, and we got extra exposure. David Neal asked me to produce other venues/sports in Atlanta once beach volleyball ended, so I handled volleyball games downtown. One match was scheduled for July 27 at the Omni, about a half mile from Centennial Olympic Park.

During the early morning hours of July 27, 1996, I was sleeping at our NBC hotel, one mile from Centennial Olympic Park and very close to a major hospital. At Centennial Park, a melting pot for tourists attending the games and a major sponsor hub, the band Jack Mack and the Heart Attack was performing. At 1:20 a.m. a pipe bomb exploded under a bench near the base of a sound tower. It contained masonry nails. One person died and 111 were injured. Another person died later of a heart attack. I didn't hear the bomb, but I remember hearing myriad ambulances delivering patients to the hospital emergency room. I had no idea what had transpired until I woke up that morning to go for a jog and heard people in the lobby talking about it. NBC informed me that we'd have to take a special route to get into the Omni for a mid-morning volleyball game to produce, since the area was considered a crime scene.

Once I completed the volleyball match, I was not done in Atlanta. David asked me to stay to produce the potential gold-medal game of the US women's softball team . . . presuming they lived up to predictions and reached that far. I was pumped to get the assignment. The games were held at Golden Park in Columbus, Georgia, less than two hours away. I attended the sold-out semi-final on July 29, when the United States edged China 1–0 in ten innings. Lisa Fernandez, a two-time national champion and four-time first-team all-American at UCLA, pitched a three-hit shutout.

The venue was electric, with excited fans cheering "U-S-A!" It was everything that Dick Ebersol, the NBC Sports president and executive producer of the Olympics, wanted from an Olympic event: emotional stories, dramatic moments, electric atmosphere, and a memorable accomplishment by our female Olympians. It was about athletes daring to dream big.

I drove back to my Atlanta hotel to get some sleep, anticipating at least a portion of our gold-medal game airing on NBC prime time the next evening. In 1996, however, women's sports were struggling for coverage and exposure.

When I woke up, the NBC day and evening show rundowns and formats were delivered under my door. (Again, the worldwide web was in its infancy, so no email communication.) I scanned the schedule as fashioned by Ebersol. A Team USA Softball gold-medal game segment, except for brief highlights, was nowhere to be found. I was astonished. How could there be no extended live coverage of the possible gold-medal crowning moment? Or at least a package that was virtually live, that presented the last half-inning? NBC would not air the entire game live in prime time. Yes, an alternate outlet was carrying it for the world feed, but if NBC network could show the potential climactic moment—and the atmosphere and emotions leading up to it—it would be spectacular. As the game's producer, I expressed my concerns to David.

"NBC might miss a tremendous opportunity in prime time," I cautioned him.

David's boss, Dick Ebersol, was the greatest programmer in Olympic television history. The ratings proved it. There was no disputing his genius in knowing what scored in prime time. In his 2022 book, "From Saturday Night to Sunday Night: My Forty Years of Laughter, Tears and Touchdowns in TV," he wrote how important the female viewing audience was to ratings. That's why he fundamentally decided not to program certain sports in prime time, like boxing.

I was convinced that this women's softball championship would satisfy his criteria. Having attended the semifinal, I knew how to present it to viewers. The championship, however, was merely one chapter in the saga. The stories leading up to that moment, as well as the struggles and drive of the women—many of whom delayed their nonsports professional careers while representing their country—was where the real drama lay.

Captain Dot Richardson, for example, took a year off from her five-year residency as an orthopedic surgeon at the University of Southern California Medical Center to pursue her softball dream.

This was the inaugural Olympics for Team USA Softball. Many of these women had never had this opportunity, and like Richardson, were nearing the ends of their playing careers. That made this moment highly emotional. I was certain the crowd would be spirited, vocal, and patriotic. And if they won the gold, it would happen on home turf. What a story! David invited me to attend the morning table read of the programming schedule/format to state my case and fight for Team USA Women's Softball. In attendance were top NBC executives including Ebersol, producer Tommy Roy, and David, who sensed my excitement. He felt I could make a compelling argument to carry it live or virtually live. It clearly merited more extensive coverage than just a brief highlight.

Carrying it live would have been difficult. In a live sports event, you never know when you will reach the final inning, the final out, or game-winning hit. And what if the US team was trailing badly? That would hardly be compelling prime-time viewing. An occasional live check-in would have been nice. Then we could bring our viewers to softball during the scheduled gymnastics gala, which Ebersol counted on for high ratings and familiar stars. I attended the morning meeting, quite confident in the event's credibility and the possibility of gold for a women's team sport. I was ready to campaign for that, but was nervous as I entered the room with about twenty people. Everyone knew I was an outsider. As Tommy Roy and Ebersol reviewed the prime-time schedule, we all remained silent. Sport after sport was mentioned, until it came time for Bob Costas to present brief Olympic notes from the evening and a highlight from softball.

After Ebersol concluded, I raised my hand. Everyone in the room stared in my direction. Ebersol acknowledged me, though I was unsure he even recognized me. I introduced myself.

"Dick, you mentioned at our meeting before the Olympics began how important it was to tell stories, and that women made up a large part of our viewing audience," I told the room. "David asked me to stay and produce the potential Team USA women's gold-medal game, and now we have it. The atmosphere was so electric in Columbus last night, with a win in 10 innings. If they capture the championship tonight, it will be an unbelievable moment for those women and our country."

He wasn't sold on changing his plans. That part of the coverage "will be highlights of women's softball," he responded, before moving on to the next event on the prime-time schedule.

I felt terrible, as if my comments were unimportant or perhaps categorically dismissed. Yet I was nonetheless proud to stand up for Team USA and the women who represented our nation that summer. I did not leave the room, however. The meeting wasn't over.

Minutes later, Ebersol mentioned a segment in the schedule which called for brief highlights of women's softball if they won the gold. I persistently raised my hand once more. I didn't want NBC to pass on this historic moment with only marginal coverage, so I again pleaded my case. I reiterated that my announcers would be there in case he changed his mind. This time, he replied, "I believe Bob Costas can do a nice job with that." I felt like an embarrassed Fred Flintstone, shrinking in size in a cartoon. No one came to my defense . . . until the meeting ended. I felt disappointed as I left the meeting, but one female programming executive quickly approached me to say, "Hey, I know you feel bad about what happened in there. Most everyone in that room agreed with you and admired the fact that you fought for what you believe, but at NBC, whatever Dick says is what we do."

I now felt slightly better, even in defeat. I fought for the women's softball team.

David Neal gave me an opportunity to voice my opinion, and I chose not to waste it. Because I didn't work full-time for NBC—I was only contracted for the Olympics—I had nothing to lose. I *did* want to work again for NBC, so I hoped that Ebersol was not upset that I presented my case. While I wasn't disagreeing with his programming brilliance, the reality is that employees whose boots are on the ground (or in my case, sneakers on the field in Columbus, Georgia) are often better positioned to recognize something special and pass along that knowledge. Ebersol knew what generates ratings, but sometimes it's crucial to think outside the box. I hoped he'd like my input, which he values from his employees. I was proud of what the softball players were accomplishing and felt enthusiastic about sharing my view. That's all. I was not trying to be disrespectful.

I stood outside the building afterwards. I was done. No more events to produce. Then I thought about it a bit more. Why should I be upset? If I hadn't stood up for America's softball players, I would have felt like a coward. I may have been turned down, but at least I tried.

I drove to Columbus to attend the game, anyway. The venue was again sold out, and the crowd roared at every moment as the game reached its climax. Dot Richardson's third home run in the Olympics, a two-run shot, proved to be the game winner as Team USA again toppled China, 3–1. As she rounded the bases, she trotted past many former softball superstars and felt she won the gold "on behalf of everyone who played the sport."

"This is awesome!" Dot exclaimed. "It doesn't get any better than this."

The Chinese disputed Dot's home run, arguing with umpires for nearly fifteen minutes that it was foul. In 1996, replay was unavailable to the umpires like it is today. The world feed replay clearly showed the ball passed just fair inside the rightfield foul pole, but it could not be used to challenge the call or satisfy the Chinese players or coaches.

After pitcher Lisa Fernandez dramatically ended the game by striking out the final batter, pandemonium ensued. The players were extremely emotional. It embodied the essence of the intro to ABC's pioneering show *Wide World of Sports*, as voiced by Jim McKay: "Spanning the globe to bring you the constant variety of sports. The thrill of victory . . . and the agony of defeat. The human drama of athletic competition. This is ABC's *Wide World of Sports*."

For the 1996 Summer Olympics, it was all there: the thrill of the USA victory; the agony/disappointment of the Chinese athletes; and the drama of capturing the first gold medal for the USA Softball team during the sport's first official foray into the Olympiad.

"As we all were standing on the gold-medal podium with Olympic gold medals put around [our] necks for the first time, representing [our] sport in the history of the games, knowing that [we were] in the biggest athletic moment of our lives . . . I felt so small," Richardson said. "The only way I can explain it is I felt this overwhelming sense of humility that we were chosen. We were the chosen fifteen to represent all who'd ever dreamt of it all, all who were deserving before us, but never given the opportunity."

"This was the best dream, hitting it out in the gold-medal game," she declared. "The power of the mind and the power of dreams, they do come true. They do!"

*USA Today* TV columnist Rudy Martzke wrote a review of NBC's Olympics coverage that evening. He acknowledged that for all the impeccable decisions that Dick Ebersol has made throughout his career, not carrying Team USA's gold-medal game live was a mistake.

I was in Atlanta when that story was published. Some were convinced that I was vindicated. All I knew was that it was a lost opportunity.

"I do regret the women's softball," Ebersol told the *Atlanta Journal-Constitution* in August 1996. "It's the only regret I have of the entire Olympics that we didn't put at least 20 minutes of the women's softball on."

On July 31, 1996, *Tampa Bay Times* guest columnist Ernest Hooper concurred. He wrote:

> With coverage limited to one network, there was no way NBC could please everyone, but solving the riddle of the sphinx would be easier than determining who the target audience was Tuesday night. At the heart of the mystery is the United States's gold medal softball victory over China. The teams considered the best in the world. Fast-pitch softball, springing up with new collegiate programs around the nation, continues to rise in popularity. And the U.S. team has a wealth of colorful personalities. NBC has aimed for more women viewers, and here it had an up-and coming women's sport dressed in red, white, and blue and gold. But the network passed on softball for a potpourri that included weightlifting, diving, and a gymnastic "gala." This was the day's only significant gold-medal victory involving a team or athlete from the United States, but it was reduced to two brief highlights packages and a post-game interview. Unbelievable. You saw the team's joy, you saw Dot

Richardson's tears on the medal stand, but you never saw the game. Style did not triumph over substance this time.
*From* Tampa Bay Times. *(c) 1996 Tampa Bay Times. All rights reserved. Used under license.*

On September 1, 2023, I was in Lynchburg, Virginia, helping my CBS Sports production crew prepare for Liberty University's football game against Bowling Green the next day. Dot Richardson was Liberty's softball coach, so I arranged to meet her for breakfast to relive those moments. She recalled that one of those NBC highlights was when Bob Costas (who was in the studio) remotely interviewed her and her teammates on the field. She was the only one who could hear Bob through her earpiece, so she instinctively interviewed her fellow athletes herself. Dot took charge like she's done her entire career and unselfishly shared the limelight with her teammates.

The next morning she was on the set of the *Today* show. Afterwards she took a car to Atlanta's Hartsfield Airport to head back home to California. At the airport in Atlanta, mobs of people cheered and congratulated her. On her flight to Dallas, the pilot made an announcement that they were proud to be flying an Olympic gold medalist home, and everyone applauded and asked for autographs. Dot was honored to oblige. At her stopover in the Dallas-Fort Worth Airport, she was greeted with more cheers and accolades in the terminal. Upon arriving at her destination in Los Angeles, more adoring fans, and a plethora of electronic and print media, were craving autographs and photos. The spoils of a champion.

Dot further demonstrated her selflessness when she lauded my efforts to give her teammates the respect they deserved. "I appreciate that Bob fought for increasing national television exposure and reach for elite women's athletics," she stated. "His stance for adding coverage for the 1996 USA Softball team in their quest for the Olympic gold medal was honorable."

In 2004, I was back working the Olympics for NBC in Athens, Greece. What a treat and honor to work this event, the site

I relived 1996 Olympics memories with Team USA Softball gold medalist Dot Richardson when I was at Liberty University on September 2, 2023, where she is head softball coach.

of the first-ever international Olympic games in modern history, held in 1896.

As cool as that was, the mid-August start was uncomfortably hot for competitors and fans. Many athletes were affected. Attendance suffered. Numerous venues were sparsely attended. Some locals didn't want to host the games due to the anticipated increased traffic, cost overruns, and unfavorable press. International terrorist threats also deterred tourists from traveling there. Although many Athenians left town for the month to get away from it, there still was traffic. NBC Olympics president Dick Ebersol told us that anyone who used "traffic" as an excuse for not being at their venues or stations on time would be immediately flown back home. My venue was about twenty minutes from our hotel by Olympic buses, so to be cautious, we always left ninety minutes early.

Athens was iconic. From many vantage points, you could see the Parthenon on the summit of the Acropolis. Like the previous Olympics, my family joined me for the first week. My kids were older now and could appreciate the gravity of the event and its historical location. By chance, we ran into a celebrity in the lobby of our NBC hotel, who proved to be approachable and cordial. Befitting the locale, it was actress Nia Vardalos, an emerging star fresh off her runaway hit 2002 movie *My Big Fat Greek Wedding*. She was there to meet friends and was waiting like a normal person, with no entourage. We struck up a conversation, and she seemed happy that we did. It proved to be a good start of the trip for my family. After a week, they flew back to the states while I got ready to brave the long hours.

NBC assigned me to produce the high-definition coverage of track and field, but primarily the preliminary heats outside the main finals at Olympic Stadium. Back in 2004, NBC's feed was standard definition, which meant I was on the pioneering side of the network's Olympic broadcasting. Few people even had HD sets then. Now, all sets are HD, 4K or 8K.

As far as storylines, American Justin Gatlin won gold in the men's 100-meter; American Allyson Felix won silver in the women's

200-meter; and American Jeremy Wariner won gold in the 400-meter. Those wins came in the Olympic Stadium and were covered by NBC staffers.

Another noteworthy moment was Michael Phelps winning his sixth gold medal of the games in the 4x100-meter swimming medley relay.

I was allowed to bring an associate director with me from the states, so I invited my San Antonio Spurs producer/director friend Daniel Ashcraft. The days before and after the events, we attended other venues, including table tennis, gymnastics, and swimming/diving. We were excited to watch light heavyweight boxer Andre Ward win the gold medal. Soon afterwards, I had the pleasure to produce many of Ward's professional fights on Fox Sports Net.

Matt Devlin, an NBA play-by-play announcer, was our host commentator, along with analysts Frank Zarnowski (a highly regarded track and field coach, historian, author, announcer, and inductee to the 2016 National Track and Field Hall of Fame), and 1996 Olympic gold medalist in the decathlon Dan O'Brien.

The Barcelona and Atlanta games provided me with indelible memories and fulfilling career achievements, yet my role producing and directing the high-definition track and field events was extremely challenging and left me disappointed. I had to make split-second decisions on when to cut from live event to live event and turn it into a comprehensible telecast with no editing. Amid the crowning moment of the high jump, a heat for the 400-meter was taking place, forcing me to quickly weigh which one to cover. NBC instructed me to carry specific events they promoted that day, making it essential to bounce back and forth to events happening simultaneously. This change of disciplines also made it difficult for the talent. Ultimately, we pulled it off, working fifteen-to-twenty-hour shifts, with both day and night sessions.

I only had a handful of free afternoons during my three weeks. That's when I went to the neighborhood park and played pickup basketball with the locals. The second time I played, an organized

My track and field HD announce team for NBC Sports at the 2004 Athens games. *Left to right:* me, host Matt Devlin, analyst Frank Zarnowski, and 1996 decathlon gold medalist Dan O'Brien

team of men assembled, then briefly watched me shoot and run the court. Instead of kicking me off, one player asked me to scrimmage with them. It turned out to be a Greek League semipro team. Their gesture was quite gracious. I was the shortest, slowest, and oldest guy on the court at forty-five years old. Fortunately, I was in good shape from running every day. Once play began, they deliberately passed the ball to me, which I found amazing. They played a more physical style of basketball, only calling a few fouls they deemed egregious. The result was plenty of arguing and cursing. The funny thing was that they argued in Greek, but cursed in English. Don't know why, but I didn't care. I laughed except when they cursed at me—which never happened—or did it? I survived the games and thanked my new Greek basketball friends for letting me hoop with them.

Memories like these, whether from Barcelona, Atlanta, or Athens, made me grateful to NBC Sports for utilizing me in the rings.

# CHAPTER 11

## *The White House and Producing Golf with President George H. W. Bush*

*In the summer of 2008,* my family and I had the privilege of visiting the West Wing of the White House for a private tour. President George W. Bush was in office toward the end of his second term. His communications director was Kevin "Sully" Sullivan, who previously served as the Dallas Mavericks media relations director and senior vice president of communications for NBC Universal. He arranged our private tour of the Oval Office, rose garden, and cabinet room. He and the president were off visiting a nuclear power plant, so we didn't get to thank him in person. Regardless, it was something my wife Sarah, eighteen-year-old daughter Elaine, and sixteen-year-old son Leon will never forget. Thanks, Sully.

Bush's father, George H. W. Bush, the 41st president of the United States, was a lifelong sports fan. He played baseball at Yale University and frequently attended Texas Rangers games when his son, George, was the managing general partner.

More frequently, "41" attended Houston Astros games in his hometown and still loved to watch and play golf at his Houston-area course, Shadow Hawk Golf Club.

At that course in Richmond, Texas, Fox Sports Southwest was taping a tournament called the Direct Energy Texas Grand Slam. The 2006 telecast featured a four-man stroke play format between touring professional golfers from the state of Texas who had won at least one major championship.

The guests were Tom Kite (1982 US Open), Mark Brooks (1996 PGA Championship), Ben Crenshaw (1984 and 1995 Masters), and Justin Leonard (1997 British Open).

As producer, I was responsible for the look, storytelling, and editing of the event, which was owned by Terry Jastrow Productions in Los Angeles. Terry and I worked together at ABC Sports in the late '70s. He was a director and producer while I was getting my feet wet as a production assistant, a.k.a. gofer (not golfer).

To open the show, I thought it would be crucial to share the history and evolution of golf in Texas. I also wanted to tease the viewers about Shadow Hawk's participants. Who better to do that than 41 himself? A lofty goal, but why not aim high?

I wrote an opening tease, plus a feature on the history of golf in Texas. (To read my "Evolution of Golf in Texas" story in its entirety, go to Appendix 2.)

I sent the scripts to Shadow Hawk general manager and head golf professional Paul Marchand, a friend of the president. He said that 41 was vacationing in Maine, then gave me the name of his assistant. I forwarded the copy to her and waited. A month passed by without any reply, so I called to see if she received it. She said the president read my script and would be glad to tape the on-camera lead-in and voiceovers when he returned home to Houston in two days.

The president was flying in from Maine that afternoon and would stop by his office to do some work before heading home. He would grant me twenty minutes, which meant we should be set up and ready to go. I wasted nary a second to arrange a Houston camera crew to meet us at his Memorial area office. We were required to send our personal information to Bush's assistant for Secret Service clearance.

Everything with the president was scheduled to the second. His whereabouts were always known to his aides and the Secret Service, who had an office in the same building.

When I arrived an hour early for the 3 p.m. taping, it didn't seem like the Secret Service was around, but they knew I was there with my crew. Within seconds, my identity was confirmed and our crew's camera and bags checked before we were permitted to set up in a room adjacent to the president's office.

At 2:40 p.m., the president's office manager and personal assistant said she just heard from the Secret Service. Bush would be here right on time.

"How do you know exactly when he will arrive?" I inquired.

"It's my job to know," she proclaimed.

Sure enough, at 3:00 p.m. I could hear the staff greeting the president. Moments later, I heard his recognizable voice. Strangely, I thought it sounded like the Bush impersonation by "Saturday Night Live" comedian Dana Carvey. Could it possibly be the former leader of the free world? To paraphrase another Carvey character from *Wayne's World*, "I'm not worthy!" But indeed, it was President George H. W. Bush.

He entered the office, quickly said hello, and accepted my gift: a Fox Sports golf shirt to wear for the shoot. A few minutes later, 41 emerged wearing the maroon shirt, strategically picked because it's the color of the Texas A&M Aggies. The George H. W. Bush Presidential Library is located on that campus in College Station, Texas, an hour north of Houston.

I remember how friendly he was and how receptive he was of my input and comments. Fortunately, he had previewed the copy and made revisions of his own. As his assistants recommended, we used a teleprompter. We only had twenty minutes of his time, and that's how long it took to record his on-camera pieces and voicing of the scripts. Here is what he read:

**Texas Grand Slam**

"Why I Love Golf," as read by President George Herbert Walker Bush:

It was an incredible moment to be granted 20 minutes with President
George H.W. Bush "41" at his office in Houston to record an opening segment and features for a national golf event on Fox Sports Net in 2006.

Golf is a game with a seemingly simple goal. Deliver the ball from tee to green and into the hole in the fewest shots possible. And hopefully less than your opponents'.

To accomplish that, it takes years of practice, athletic ability and, of course, an occasional break along the way. But golf is so much more. Golf, like life, is a virtue. It's a sport which displays moral excellence and competitive fortitude. And just like our lives, the game provides its share of ups and downs. One minute you're on top of the world; the next you're gasping for optimism. And in both instances, you look toward your partner and say, "Well, that's golf."

Last year, in the inaugural "Direct Energy Texas Grand Slam" at Dallas National Golf Club, 1992 U.S. Open champion and golf hall of fame inductee Tom Kite sank this brilliant putt early in the round.

1996 PGA champion Mark Brooks stayed in contention with shots like this.

1997 British Open champ Justin Leonard led the tournament late in the round, but it was two-time Masters champion and Texas legend Ben Crenshaw who captured the tournament title.

While I was guiding this country, and throughout my life, I've enjoyed the opportunities to tee it up with the pros and friends alike, because golf is a game I enjoy playing and watching. So join me now as Tom, Mark, Justin and Ben meet again, but this time on my home course in Richmond, Texas for the "Direct Energy Texas Grand Slam at Shadow Hawk."

Golf is a wonderful sport. I'm glad you'll be here to share it with me today.

The president finished his contribution, thanked everyone, then went into his personal office. As we were cleaning up the equipment, and before I was about to leave, I noticed his office door was open. I admired how generous he was to grant us his time, but more importantly, the years of public service he dedicated to our nation.

On September 2, 1944, while flying on a bombing run for his Torpedo Squadron 51 in the North Pacific during World War II, his plane was shot down. He managed to swim to a life raft and remained afloat until he was rescued by the submarine USS *Finback*. The historic footage of his rescue was famously recorded on newsreels, allowing modern-day Americans to witness his heroism.

In 1967 he was elected to the House of Representatives; became United Nations Ambassador to the UN under Richard Nixon in 1971; was director of the CIA from 1976 to 1977; was vice president under Ronald Reagan from 1981 to 1989; and then became president of the United States from 1989 to 1993.

As I passed by his office, he looked busy going over mail and messages, since he had been out of town for months. That didn't stop me from knocking on the door and asking if I could come inside for a second. The president granted my wish.

He stopped what he was doing and had a smile on his face, putting me at ease.

"Mr. President, first of all thank you for taking time to tape the intros and features for the show."

"My pleasure," he assured me, "no problem at all."

"But I really wanted to say thank you for the many years of public service for this country."

Again, he smiled, paused, looked me in the eye, and said, "Thank you very much. You know, that really means a lot to me."

And it did. He could have just shook his head and took it as a common compliment, but his sincere reply to me was truly satisfying. I was happy I took the time to convey my gratitude. I knew for sure that he was a pleasant and great person.

Later that night, after flying home to Dallas from Houston, I turned on Fox Sports Southwest and saw Roger Clemens pitching for the Astros. At that instant, the camera panned to President

George H. W. Bush watching the game . . . wearing the maroon Fox Sports Southwest shirt I had handed him hours earlier.

The Fox Sports Southwest Astros announcers wondered where the president had obtained that shirt.

Now you know.

# CHAPTER 12

## *Producing the San Antonio Spurs during Their NBA Dynasty*

*In 1988,* the San Antonio Spurs director of broadcasting Lawrence Payne and play-by-play announcer Dave Barnett were looking for advice on improving their telecasts, so I accepted their offer to consult and then ultimately produce and direct the telecasts on HSE (a regional cable sports network) and over-the-air stations such as KSAT 12.

My wonderful twenty-three-year journey with the Spurs began in 1989 when I lived in Dallas. I'd commute to San Antonio for home games, then jump on the team charter when they left for a road trip. Other times I flew from Dallas to meet them at the first stop of the road trip. My first full season was Naismith Memorial Basketball Hall of Famer David Robinson's rookie year, which was akin to hitting the jackpot. Eventually I focused on just producing the games, sitting next to directors Mike Kickirillo or Daniel Ashcraft. During my tenure, the Spurs won four championships (1999, 2003, 2005, and 2007). The team's fifth title came in 2014, one year after I left for the New Orleans Pelicans.

I was blessed to witness and get to know many of the top players and coaches in the NBA annals, including Robinson and four other Spurs whose numbers were also retired: Sean Elliott, Manu Ginobili, Tony Parker, and Tim Duncan.

The coaches I worked with were equally impressive: Larry Brown, Bob Bass, Jerry Tarkanian, John Lucas II, Bob Hill, and Gregg Popovich.

Our announcers included play-by-play men Dave Barnett, Ron Thulin, Dick Stockton, Greg Papa, Joel Meyers, and Bill Land; analysts Coby Dietrick, Sean Elliott, P. J. Carlesimo, Bernie Bickerstaff, Rolando Blackman, Greg Simmons, Lance Blanks, and Steve Kerr; and sideline reporters Brian Anderson, Andrew Monaco, Jim Knox, Don Harris, and Michelle Beadle.

One amusing incident occurred in 1993 at HemisFair Arena, the Spurs' original home. HSE had a small cable audience in the region. We wanted to have some fun, so we asked head coach John Lucas to sit alongside our crew and announcers in the stands before a game. We set up a shot to resemble a crowd cutaway of fans cheering after an exciting basket. I instructed everyone to look to their left as if they were watching the action, then, at the count of three, react wildly to an imaginary slam dunk. We'd record it and have it ready at the right moment and roll it in as if it was live during the telecast. But would we actually do it?

Of course, we did. We could not stop laughing at our stunt. Even to this day, we laugh. I doubt that anyone watching at home realized it. Unlike today's viral videos that get scrutinized a zillion times, viewers in those days could not record and instantly rewind or freeze action. If anyone caught it, they might have thought it was brilliant. Instead of occupying their usual locations, the announcers, head coach, and the production team were somehow in the stands, cheering. How could that be? TV magic, of course.

Although that was fun, it was the only time we took the liberty to use that cutaway. We took immense pride in the production of our games.

Prior to the 1989–1990 season, I produced and directed a telecast on HSE, when Spurs star Mike Mitchell returned for the playoffs. He had not played in that game, but the HemisFair Arena crowd wanted head coach Larry Brown to put him in. Our shot of

Mitchell on the bench was shown on the jumbotron. I wasn't aware that the arena director simultaneously took our shot live. The fans chanted for Coach Brown to put Mitchell in the game. In a matter of moments, one of the assistant coaches ran to our production truck, which was parked in the loading dock 100 yards from the court, demanding that we never again put a shot of Mitchell on the screen. Coach Brown did not want the crowd to dictate when or if he would hit the court. That, my friends, is the only time in my five decades of television that an assistant coach left the court to demand we *not* show a player on the bench while the game was in progress. We explained to him that we did not control the jumbotron, but granted his wish by not shooting Mitchell on the bench again. Just in case.

## The Admiral

People have asked me, is David Robinson really like he appeared on television? I say no. When you meet him in person, he exceeds your perception. "The Admiral," so named because of his Naval Academy background, is outgoing, smart, caring, sensitive, well educated, and grounded. These traits were instilled by his parents. He also was talented on the court. The 7-foot-1 center was a ten-time all-star, NBA Defensive Player of the Year, a member of the NBA's 50th and 75th Anniversary Teams, and his number 50 was retired by the Spurs. I don't believe he was exceptionally passionate about the game, yet he was smart enough to know that athletic success would help him achieve his ultimate goal of helping others and improving his community. He and his wife, Valerie, founded the Carver Academy in San Antonio, which is now an IDEA Carver Academy (a public charter school). They also formed the David Robinson Foundation.

My kids still remember when we were on a road trip with the team in the early '90s on Christmas Day in Los Angeles and David invited them to his table to meet him.

My son Leon with Spurs great David Robinson during a holiday game lunch in the '90s.

David became a family man and always maintained a squeaky clean image, which can be hard for an NBA player on the road. David always said, to stay out of trouble, "Don't put yourself in a position to fail." It's a smart lesson anytime. It's no wonder he's enshrined in the hall of fame and loved for his work in the community.

When we traveled with the players on the team bus to and from the airport, David Robinson was often nearby. His outstanding

Spurs point guard Avery Johnson at a holiday luncheon with my daughter Elaine and my son Leon in the '90s.

personality was easy to observe. He was one of those people you hold in high regard before you meet, and then they exceed your respect once you do. I recall him telling a teammate why he grew so tall, despite having parents who weren't as tall as him. He said his mom made him drink milk all the time, and that strengthened his bones. What a ringing endorsement for the dairy industry. If they only knew.

## The Worm and the Material Girl

Dennis Rodman was quite a character. During the 1993–1994 season, he had a highly-publicized relationship with Madonna, although I had yet to see them together. While the team was in Salt Lake City, we were staying at the Marriott a few blocks from the then Delta Center, which the Utah Jazz called home. At 1 p.m., before I was about to walk to the arena, I heard a loud banging on a door. When I looked through the peephole, there was a short woman banging on the door across the hall. I couldn't believe my eyes. It was Madonna, screaming for Dennis to open the door. Eventually, he did.

This confirmed to me that the rumors about their fling were true. What was she doing in Salt Lake City? She did not have a concert, so she flew in to see Dennis. He wasn't overly thrilled at that moment. How did I know that? A few minutes later, I approached the elevator to go to the game. Nobody was around as the open elevator door began to close. I stepped inside, expecting to be the only one heading to the lobby in the middle of the afternoon. I was not alone, however. Two others were in the elevator with me: Dennis and Madonna. And they were arguing. Dennis had a car waiting for him outside and Madonna wanted to go, too, but he didn't want her to accompany him. I stood there like a fly on a wall. They kept bickering as if I wasn't there. I can understand why their relationship barely lasted a couple months.

Rodman's autobiography, "I Should Be Dead," had this to say: "I think back in '93, '94 her career was more at a standstill. I think that's when I came in the picture. I was a bad boy; she loved hanging out with bad boys and guys that were controversial. I think at the particular time I was the interesting one to pick."

## Sean Elliott

Sean Elliott was a tremendous player for the Spurs from 1989 to 1993, and then again from 1994 to 2001. He was a two-time all-star and member of the 1999 championship team. His number 32 is retired by the Spurs. He will be remembered forever in San Antonio for the "Memorial Day Miracle." During game two of the 1999 Western Conference Finals against Portland, the Trail Blazers held a two-point lead with nine seconds remaining in regulation. Elliott received a pass within an inch of the sideline and managed to keep the back of his feet inbounds. On his tippy toes, he hit a twenty-one-foot shot to give the Spurs a one-point lead and eventual win. His shot catapulted the Spurs to meet the Knicks and win their first-ever NBA title. After that season, he announced he had kidney disease and needed a transplant.

On March 13, 2000, I produced the game when he got back on the court against the Atlanta Hawks, becoming the first player to return to the NBA after a kidney transplant. Two years later, he retired as one of the most beloved players ever. He remains with the Spurs as the expert analyst on their telecasts. I savored working with him for many years. Always one of the nicest guys in the league and broadcasting.

Fox Sports Net asked me to produce the annual March of Dimes award show for a few years. The event, honoring major athletes for their accomplishments, took place at the Fox Theatre in Detroit. We had NASCAR drivers, NFL and MLB players, and iconic coaches. One year, I nominated Sean Elliott for the Courage Award for resuming his career after his transplant.

Sean is highly generous. Many times when we went out to dinner or lunch, he picked up the tab. He has also publicly expressed gratitude for our professional partnership. "I began my now twenty-year broadcasting career under Bob's tutelage and owe much of my success to Bob," said Sean. "His meticulous production skills set a high bar for sports television."

Once, during an off day in Los Angeles, Sean, director Mike Kickirillo, and I played golf in the foothills of the Lost Canyons mountains in Simi Valley, forty-five miles north of Los Angeles. The beautiful courses, named Sky and Shadow, were designed by

Pete Dye with consultation from Fred Couples.

We decided to play a skins game. Although we weren't gambling large sums of money—no more than ten dollars per hole—pride was on the line. Sean is a very good golfer. Loves the game. Can hit it a mile. No surprise for a pro athlete. After the first nine holes, Sean led 8 to 1 to 0. The goose egg was mine. At the turn, Sean asked if anyone was hungry. The cart person was conveniently driving by with sandwiches and beverages. I said I'd take a peanut butter and jelly sandwich and water, and thanked Sean. That proved to be his mistake. Sean's moment of generosity came back to haunt him. After munching that delicious sandwich, I felt energized. There was something magical about that delicious combination of protein and sweetness that supercharged me. I won holes ten through seventeen. Now the score was 8 to 8 to 1. Was I just teasing them on the front nine, or was it that sandwich?

It boiled down to the final hole on the eighteenth. Sean had proven he could handle pressure, as he did on the Memorial Day with millions watching on TV. But could he handle it when skins were on the line in front of a flock of seagulls and hawks flying above?

Indeed, I won the final hole and the money. The real prize, however, was seeing Sean and Mike's disbelieving eyes. Sean laughed. Mike was definitely upset. To this day, if you mention peanut butter and jelly sandwiches to Sean or Mike, they will not be too happy. It was *my* Memorial "Mountain" Miracle.

## Coach Pop

I have a very different perception of Gregg Popovich than the average person who doesn't truly know him. Those who do know how loyal and dedicated he is understand how much he cares about his players, the team, the community, and his country. I had the opportunity to travel on the road with the team for twenty-three years and many times spoke with him one-on-one. I saw how he treated his coaching colleagues, players, team broadcasters, and

I had the privilege to work with two of the nicest guys in sports television for many years in San Antonio, broadcasters Bill Land and Sean Elliott.

even me. After a game against the Golden State Warriors, the team buses drove to Ill Fornio, an Italian restaurant near the wharf in San Francisco. It was late, and the place was closed . . . except to us. There were appetizers on each table, followed by what seemed like everything on their menu. Pop covered the entire tab as a team-building exercise and to thank everyone. Wonderful evening.

After I left the Spurs to produce the New Orleans Pelicans around 2020, the Pelicans were hosting the Spurs in New Orleans. I had not seen Pop since I left the Spurs, so I wanted to stop by the locker room for his 5:15 p.m. pregame presser with the media and extend my condolences for the recent passing of his wife. That is, if I had a chance, since he was busy preparing for the game. I waited with the rest of the media in the hallway as he exited the Spurs' locker room to address the reporters. When he saw me, he said in front of everyone, "Steiny, how are you doing?" which caught everyone by surprise. I smiled, exchanged greetings, and explained, "I now produce the Pelicans games."

"No," he replied. "I mean, how are you, personally?" That's the Pop that most people don't know. He really cared about me as a person, not just professionally. He cared about my family and my life away from the court.

All of the media witnessed this conversation. Pop remarked how nice it was to come across people he worked with, or players he coached, in virtually every NBA town.

I told him that the Pelicans' next stop was Philadelphia, where we planned to interview Sixers assistant Monty Williams, the former Spurs assistant and former Pelicans head coach. Pop said he recently spoke to Monty and that he was doing well. I then offered my condolences on the passing of his wife. He responded with a heartfelt thank you.

Those few minutes were very special to me. I was quite moved that he singled me out in front of the media when he really didn't have to. But that's Pop. He always watches out for those he cares about. When his coaching buddies or former players were out of work or off from the WNBA season, he would find them work on our telecasts. This included Bernie Bickerstaff, John McLeod, Dan Hughes, Lance Blanks, Sean Marks, and more. Some even became full-time staff members working with Pop in the front office. He also gave former San Antonio Stars alum Becky Hammon a chance to work and excel on his coaching staff. She was later named head coach of the Las Vegas Aces, where she won WNBA titles in 2022 and 2023.

## The Big Fundamental

Tim Duncan was involved in all five NBA titles in San Antonio. I did not get to know Timmy as well as David, but I had a few encounters simply from traveling with the team.

During the team's shootaround practice one morning in Toronto, I arrived early at the Air Canada Centre as the team was wrapping things up. I took a seat near where they were shooting free throws and exiting the court to retrieve their warmups. Tim, who had not been feeling well, was putting on his warmup near my seat in the corner of the court.

"How are you feeling today?" I inquired.

"Fine," Tim answered. "Much better. How about you?"

I was stunned. Was he really interested in how I felt? Yeah, he's a nice guy, but most likely it was just conversation. Which was rare, but acceptable. It was Tim Duncan.

"Yes, I feel great," I told him. "I scored 20 points yesterday in the JBA, the Jewish Basketball Association in Dallas."

Tim looked me right in the eye and said with a serious tone: "You got to dominate where you can, man."

That was the end of our brief conversation. I headed off to produce the game that evening. Smiling all day.

I felt very fortunate to be a part of the Spurs family for over two decades. During their run of four NBA titles, the team generously included me in the celebrations. They even presented me with a championship watch for the first title and personalized NBA championship rings for the other three. What an honor and treasure. Franchises don't often bestow rings to production personnel. I also rode on one of the decorated riverboats during a championship parade on San Antonio's Riverwalk, which was a genuine rush.

# CHAPTER 13

# Indoor Soccer's David vs. Goliath Hollywood Ending

**When you're employed in sports television** or participating in sports, it doesn't matter which level you're in. Whether it's youth league, high school, college, or pro, your goal is to do your best job and see your team win the championship. In sports TV, you want the team you cover to win, because it makes the games and season much more fun and stimulating. Who knows, you might even get lucky and receive a championship ring from the team you represent. The San Antonio Spurs made me living proof of that.

In the 1986–1987 season of the Major Indoor Soccer League, the Dallas Sidekicks, run by the legendary soccer guru and coach Gordon Jago, won the MISL championship against long odds. Down three games to two in the best-of-seven series against the heavily favored Tacoma Stars, the Sidekicks won the final two contests 5–4 and 4–3, respectively, both in overtime and both in front of raucous fans at a sold-out arena.

Game six was played at Reunion Arena in Dallas, former home of the Dallas Mavericks and Dallas Stars. The deciding game seven took place in the Tacoma Dome, where Tacoma Stars fans were confident they would close out the series and win the championship at home. So many fans tried to enter the Tacoma Dome, the fire marshal directed the box office to stop selling standing room-only tickets as a safety issue. Hundreds of balloons, held up by nets attached to the ceiling, were ready to shower down on the floor during the certain postgame celebration.

Tacoma led 3–1 with less than three minutes to go when fans began to celebrate, sensing an imminent win. Dallas, however, never gave up. With 2:25 remaining, Sidekicks forward Mark Karpun took a Kevin Smith pass, shot, and scored to bring the Sidekicks within one. Just 27 seconds later, league MVP Tatu (known for throwing his shirt in the stands after each goal) struck a ball into the left side of the net to tie it 3–3. The capacity crowd now stood silent. What just happened? What was going on? Not again? Just two nights before, the Sidekicks stunned the Stars in double overtime.

Less than ten minutes into overtime, Tatu rushed down the right side of the goal and took a shot. Instinctively, Karpun raced to the goal and redirected the shot into the net. That was it. Karpun was again heroic, scoring the game and series winner. The Sidekicks were the 1986–1987 MISL champions, much to the dismay, disbelief, and astonishment of the Stars and their fans.

I produced and directed that telecast for HSE, relying on a stellar regional crew, some of whom I still see when I produce games in Portland and Seattle. Memorable camera shots depicted the final goal by Karpun and Tatu's reaction. Thanks to the audio picked up from our handheld camera on the turf, viewers could hear Tatu exclaiming, "We are the champions!" Our camera operator and audio technician captured that jubilation, as well as the stunning live visuals and sounds on the turf. Great instincts by our crew.

Even our announcers, Norm Hitzges and Mike "The Snarler" Renshaw (who unfortunately passed away in 2021), sitting high up at their broadcast position, could hear the voices of the celebrating Sidekicks. That's mostly because the home crowd had fallen so silent.

The third magical, memorable camera shot revealed the fans in the Tacoma Dome. They remained standing. No one left. They were stunned, unable to believe what they saw. The crowd was convinced they would be celebrating a Stars title. Instead, their eyes and minds were paralyzed by witnessing the Sidekicks savoring "their" championship.

I'll never forget Norm's line as we showed the fans and then the balloons still hanging in the rafters.

"Look at the Tacoma people, I don't think they realize it yet. It hasn't sunk in that these balloons are not going to come down this season."

It was a great comeback victory from the "never say die" Dallas Sidekicks. The next morning, we flew back from Tacoma on an American Airlines commercial flight. As our plane taxied on the DFW Airport tarmac, I peered through the window and saw a big congratulatory banner hanging on one of the terminal buildings. Even more impressive, hundreds of fans were cheering as we pulled up to the gate and opened the door. I was quite moved, but could see it was even more emotional to Gordon Jago, Tatu, Karpun, and the rest of the team. It was a special moment. What a feeling to be part of that "family."

Months later, I submitted the telecast to the ninth annual national ACE Awards (Awards for Cable Excellence). This was before cable entities competed against broadcast networks for sports Emmys. The ceremony was to be broadcast simultaneously on various national cable networks, including HBO, on January 24, 1988, live from the Wiltern Theater in Los Angeles.

My submission was a longshot to be nominated, but I gave it a chance. Sure enough, our telecast earned the nod. It was an underdog to win, since our fledgling regional cable network was going up against ESPN, TNT, HBO, and other national cable channels. Yet I felt the show captured everything the awards were meant to showcase: a dramatic, well-done production. We were entered in the live sports category.

On the entry, I wrote, "I have produced and directed major league sports for 11 years, and judge this game coverage to be the most exciting, entertaining and emotionally charged event I've been associated with. And that includes a baseball perfect game by

Mike Witt, NBA playoffs and football."

When the nominees were announced in the category of Sports Event Coverage Special, I was unbelievably excited to see in the following order:

- HBO Boxing: "Marvelous" Marvin Hagler vs. Sugar Ray Leonard (executive producer Ross Greenburg)
- HSE: 1987 Major Indoor Soccer League Championship game #7 (executive producer Jack Stanfield; producer/director Robert Steinfeld)
- NHL on ESPN: (producers Bruce Connal, Bryan Cooper, and Barry Sacks)
- 1987 Aspen Winternational ESPN: (coordinating producer Terry Lingner; associate producers Neil Goldberg and Kim Whitelaw)
- ESPN: NCAA basketball, Indiana vs. Wisconsin (producer John Wildhack; coordinating producer Steve Anderson)

This was a signification accomplishment for Home Sports Entertainment from Dallas. We were nominated with the big boy cable networks. Many of the above nominated producers and coordinating producers hired me to work for them at ESPN a few years later.

Certainly, we would be able to attend the ceremonies in Hollywood a few months later and be on national television. Right? Right!

HSE general manager Ed Frazier and programming director Glenn Gurgiolo consulted with our executive producer Jack Stanfield, who decided that Jack and I could attend. The invitation allowed each nominee to bring a guest. In my case, of course, it was my wife, Sarah. We were excited to mingle with the day's nominees and prominent celebrities such as Billy Crystal, Helen Hunt, Rod Steiger, Shelley Duvall, Paul Simon, Hal Holbrook, Robin Williams, The Muppets, Max Headroom, Judi Dench, Garry Shandling, and many more.

Weeks before the ceremony, I attended a Cable Ace Awards nominees party and presser at Spago's famed restaurant on Sunset Boulevard in Los Angeles. Ed Frazier granted me the opportunity to fly to the event, which was one of the most entertaining nights of my life. My first cousin, Seth Frank, who lived in Los Angeles, attended the star-studded affair with me. There was a red carpet outside the restaurant for nominees. Entertainment Tonight, plus other networks and paparazzi, hovered outside.

I was a nobody in that setting. Surrounding me were familiar faces such as *Star Wars* actor Mark Hamill, Academy Award-winning actor Rod Steiger, and sports luminaries including programming legend Don Ohlmeyer and ESPN host Roy Firestone. Comedian Elayne Boosler greeted me, took me under her wing, and introduced me to nearly everyone at the party as the guy from Texas and a fellow nominee. There was no reason she would do that, other than to be kind and friendly. She made me feel comfortable and part of the honorees. As I said earlier, it doesn't matter how big or small your network may be. Your work simply needs to be worthy.

On January 24, 1988, Sarah and I, along with Jack and his guest, flew to Los Angeles. The ceremony was at the Wiltern Theater, so we settled in at the Sheraton Universal Hotel and got ready. Like most awards shows, handheld cameras shot the nominees in their seats—including us—as our names were announced. That was fun, especially since many friends and family back home were watching. We didn't have much of a chance against the major networks, so it was no shock that HBO's Hagler–Leonard boxing match captured the award. Yet that never detracted from how gratifying it was to be nominated and attend the celebrity-packed gala.

Afterwards, guests attended a dinner under a tent adjacent to the theater. It was a typical Hollywood over-the-top affair with drinks, lavish food, and decorations. Billy Crystal was seated at the table adjacent to ours. I trust he was delighted to be in the vicinity of such stars as the HSE group.

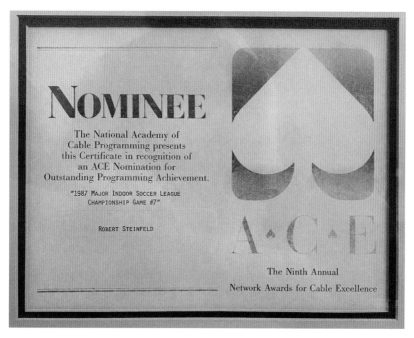

National Award for Cable Excellent (ACE) in 1987. The awards show was January 24, 1988, at the Wiltern Theatre in Los Angeles and was nationally televised across numerous networks including HBO.

That evening felt like our fifteen minutes of fame in Tinseltown. Quite an achievement for the little regional sports network from Texas and the fledgling Major Indoor Soccer League Dallas Sidekicks. It's one of my finest career highlights.

"I didn't expect to win. Just getting nominated was a big honor," I told the *Dallas Morning News* in a story published in 1988. "The sad thing is, I can't even take credit for it. We just happened to be in the right place at the right time."

# CHAPTER 14

## *Heavyweight Boosts from Harry Connick Jr., Wendell Pierce, and Trombone Shorty*

*In 2012, regional sports network Fox Sports* SW acquired the rights to produce telecasts of the New Orleans Hornets, as they were called until 2013. The original producer they hired did not pan out that first season. Fox Sports SW executive producer Mike Anastassiou asked if I'd be interested in leaving the Spurs to cover the newly nicknamed "New Orleans Pelicans" and get their production up to speed. Dallas to New Orleans wasn't much farther than San Antonio, maybe fifteen more minutes in the air, so I accepted the challenge.

I conceived an ambitious idea to open the season with a video tease of the players—including second-year player Anthony Davis—auditioning for Fox's *American Idol*. David Hill, an innovator who led the startup of Fox Sports and the NFL on Fox, was also creatively involved in *American Idol*. On top of that, one of the show's judges was Harry Connick Jr., a New Orleans native. The singer was a big sports fan, especially of the New Orleans Saints. My logic was that this could be excellent publicity and goodwill for *American Idol* itself. I also knew that Connick was friendly with the family of Tom Benson, who owned both the Saints and the Pelicans.

The premise was that the players may not have the talent to win *American Idol*, but Harry Connick Jr. would be convinced that they had the talent to begin a new era of NBA basketball in New Orleans, thanks to Anthony Davis, a renovated arena, a new name, and swagger. Good idea, but first I had to convince seven constituents:

1. My executive producer
2. New Orleans Pelicans media relations director Matt Ryan
3. Other Pelicans team executives
4. Pelicans head coach Monty Williams
5. The players
6. Fox Network, who had to persuade the producers of *American Idol* to endorse my idea and let us use their set, logos, etc.
7. Harry Connick Jr., who could do it as a favor for friend and owner Tom Benson, the network, and the team

First, I wrote a script and an outline. It took many renditions before I felt comfortable presenting it. I sent it to Matt Ryan, who liked the idea and forwarded it to his Pelicans bosses. They agreed it was fine, assuming coach Monty Williams signed off. He did. They pitched it to the players, who embraced the idea and were enthusiastic about showing off their singing (or nonsinging) ability. Anthony Davis, Jrue Holiday, Eric Gordon, Ryan Anderson, Tyreke Evans, and Austin Rivers were all up for the fun competition.

Next, I presented my case to Fox and the *American Idol* production company. To pull that off, I let our Fox Sports executive team in Los Angeles work their magic in the corporate chain of command. Fortunately, David Hill liked my concept. With assistance from Fox Sports talent relations, he contacted the production company and Harry Connick. Days later, Fox emailed me to say that *American Idol* and Connick liked the idea and would shoot it on their set, while taping segments in Detroit for the upcoming season. It didn't matter where they shot it, as long as it was on the *American Idol* set. I presented the formal script and the video of the players' audition, which we shot in New Orleans on media day. We recorded the Pelicans singing over what is called a "green screen," to allow our Fox Sports SW editors to key branded graphics behind them, so it appeared as if they were on the set with Harry. We sent those files to Fox and the production company to show Connick.

As anticipated, the players had a ball. Most of them couldn't carry a tune, which made it extra funny. Connick played along cleverly. The producers, directors, and editors from Fremantle North America and 19 Entertainment production companies color-corrected the clips and provided us with solid video and sweetened audio. (Incidentally, we had to use public domain music so there would be no copyright infringement on the songs the players sang.) It really looked like the players—who were wearing their Pelicans uniforms—were standing a few feet in front of Harry Connick Jr.

Editors Tim Evans and Greg Flick took the clips and edited them into the final product at our Fox Sports SW studios in Irving, Texas.

The lesson here? If you set your sights high, you never know. You need support from the right people and lots of things to go your way. It takes patience and persistence to get everyone on board. The entire process from inception to final product took ten weeks. Here's how it went, with some amusing ad-libbing by Connick:

> "Hey everybody, Harry Connick Jr. here. I want to say hi to all my friends back home in New Orleans. Now, some of you have heard I'm going to be a judge on the upcoming season of *American Idol* right here on Fox. Well, apparently many of the New Orleans Pelicans players are aware of that and they've already sent me some singing tapes to judge. It seems they feel they have the talent to star on the court and now on the stage and in the recording studio. Well, let's take a look."
>
> "She'll be coming around the mountain when she comes . . ." sang Austin Rivers.
>
> "I wouldn't say it's *Idol* material," Harry commented, "but that's not bad."
>
> ". . . and the skies are all sunny all day," Jrue Holiday crooned. "Eeeeeeee!"

Speaking with Pelicans guard Eric Gordon before he auditioned for our *American Idol*.

"Oh, my God!" barked Harry.

Eric Gordon then belted out his tune: "For he's a jolly good fellow, for he's a jolly good fellow for he's a jolly good fellow . . ."

"Uh, uh, uh. I'm not sure autotune is going to help that, man," Harry said. "That's more 'out of tune' than autotune."

"Old McDonald had a farm," Tyreke Evans sang, "ee-i-ee-i-o . . ."

"Somebody is not going to Hollywood unless they are playing the Lakers," joked Harry.

Next it was Anthony Davis's turn at the microphone: "He's got the whole world in his hands . . . "

"Sorry," Harry insisted, "no golden ticket. But you know, the good news. Hey, Anthony Davis, he's the future of the team. He's a great blocker. You got incoming star Jrue Holiday.

I mean, he's going to be a 'hit' on the court. Pelicans newcomer Tyreke Evans, he was the Rookie of the Year. And veteran guard Eric Gordon, he gets my vote to handle all the scoring. While Austin Rivers can carry a tune on stage, I think he's more likely to star on the court in New Orleans. We have a new spirit, a new bolstered roster, we have a newly appointed arena, we have a new name, this is a new season. Hey, it's opening night, New Orleans Pelicans basketball takes flight right now on Fox Sports. And I will be watching!"

## Cooking Up a Good Idea

New Orleans is known for its food, excellent restaurants, and world-renowned chefs, so I came up with an idea for our opening night theme for the next season. With a little research, and after speaking with sideline reporter Jen Hale, "the unofficial mayor of New Orleans," we shot an opening night piece at a seafood restaurant near the arena, owned by a celebrity chef.

The concept was to bring players to a restaurant kitchen and show that you can make something special by mixing together the proper ingredients. We filmed real chefs cooking meals, then cut to head coach Monty Williams, Anthony Davis, Jrue Holiday, Ryan Anderson, Tyreke Evans, and Austin Rivers posing as chefs on opening night. They prepared savory dishes and served them to the team's owners, Tom and Gayle Benson, and their granddaughter, Pelicans executive Rita Benson, who were inside the restaurant waiting to be served. It took plenty of preparation and coordination to get everyone there on the same day and time and to get the script approved, shot, and edited. It was tremendous fun.

## Trombone Shorty

My goal the following year was to incorporate more of the Big Easy's flavor into opening night and during the season. What

I met Trombone Shorty in New Orleans while we shot opening segment for Pelicans.

better way than to utilize one of the team's most dedicated fans, Grammy-winning musician and philanthropist Trombone Shorty? The New Orleans-born horn player attended numerous games and had performed there. I gathered the players and Trombone Shorty at various New Orleans landmarks such as the French Quarter, a historic streetcar, Café du Monde, and the Garden District. The hurdles were many: acquiring permits to shoot in the city; music clearance rights; and coordinating everyone's time.

First, I cranked out a script. After it was approved, we had camera crews and audio personnel flown in from Los Angeles. Fox Network in Los Angeles provided additional support. Thanks to vice president Laura Mickelson for that. We used the footage and music—"You and I (Outta This Place)"—all season. Anthony Davis joined Trombone on a streetcar while players such as Dante Cunningham and Alexis Ajinca visited landmarks around the Crescent City.

The video began with shots of a vintage music store in the Garden district and of an indistinguishable man picking up a trombone, exiting the store, then approaching a streetcar. After the door swings open, it's revealed that Trombone Shorty is boarding the car, and the conductor is Anthony Davis. Trombone begins singing his song as we cut to shots of Pelicans basketball action and the various landmarks: "You and I, you and I, let this be our battle cry."

The piece powerfully conveyed the essence of New Orleans, and it linked the Pelicans to its culture. It was a terrific way to kick off the season. You should have seen the eyes of tourists and New Orleanians as the streetcar passed by with Anthony Davis and Trombone Shorty conducting.

## Actor Wendell Pierce and the Playoffs

In 2016, the Pelicans reached the postseason, and we carried first-round games on Fox Sports SW. I wanted to make a statement by shooting an original tease with alternate pieces that we could use during the playoff series. Through my association with the team, I contacted Tony Award-winning actor Wendell Pierce, star of two hit HBO dramas—*Treme*, which was set in New Orleans, and *The Wire*—as well as USA Network's *Suits*. The New Orleans-born actor has appeared in a slew of major movies and TV series.

I sent my script to Wendell's agent. Weeks later, we agreed on a fee and a time when he would be in New Orleans. I picked him up at his rebuilt home in Pontchartrain Park, which had been submerged by fourteen feet of water during Hurricane Katrina in 2005.

Native New Orleanian actor Wendell Pierce recorded various on-camera and voice-over segments for the Pelicans playoff run, 2016.

We drove to the Pelicans Smoothie King Center to shoot the pieces on the basketball court in front of the spotlit team logo. I directed the handheld Steadicam camera operator to circle Wendell as he dramatically delivered his lines.

Afterwards, I asked Wendell to ad-lib a surprise video that I could use at my son and future daughter-in-law's upcoming wedding rehearsal dinner. He generously agreed.

Wendell and I stood midcourt as I discussed producing the playoff games. When I asked the actor to shoot the tease for my Fox Sports telecast, he interrupted me and said, "Hey, wait a minute, we're not here to talk about work. I want to congratulate Rebecca and Lee for the wedding! I've heard it will be as big as Meghan and Harry's." (Meghan Markle starred with him on *Suits*).

Those teases were challenging to organize, execute, and bring to fruition. But that's what makes producing fun.

Wendell later invited me to brunch at a historic, generationally owned small restaurant in nearby Treme, where everyone knew him. The food was fantastic.

It was thoughtful of Wendell to cooperate, and everyone at my son's rehearsal dinner was thrilled by the actor's unexpected cameo.

# CHAPTER 15

## LeBron Will Have to Wait— Emergency at 30,000 Feet

*On December 19, 2014,* I had a big day planned. I woke up, jogged three miles, worked out with my trainer for an hour, returned home, showered, and then headed to the Fox Sports Southwest offices in Irving, Texas, to gather my materials for that night's Cavaliers vs. Pelicans game in New Orleans. LeBron James was in town, and the game was sold out.

After doing a little research in the office, I headed to DFW Airport for my late morning flight to New Orleans. I arrived at the airport at 10:30 a.m. with plenty of time to spare before my 11 a.m. production call. I boarded the flight and emailed the production rundowns and opening tease script to the talent and production crew in case I was delayed. That was normal procedure.

We departed on time, and the flight was smooth. Sitting beside me in first class (I was bumped up due to my platinum status on American Airlines) was a lady from Austin who was flying on short hauls solely to accumulate enough American Airlines Advantage miles to maintain her elite status before the year ended. As we descended to New Orleans, I started to feel nauseated and began sweating profusely. I assumed it was motion sickness, so I shut my eyes and told myself I'd be fine once we landed.

133

As we touched down, I opened my window shade to look out. For a second, I was disoriented, but never lost consciousness. As we taxied to the terminal, the lady next to me asked if I was okay. "No," I answered.

She immediately signaled for the flight attendant, who alerted the captain to report an emergency.

When we arrived at the gate, paramedics came aboard. Although they determined my vital signs were good—heart rate, blood glucose level, blood pressure—something was not right. I said I did not want to go to the hospital, because I had a game to produce in a few hours and that most likely it was motion sickness. The paramedics wheelchaired me into the terminal, and I still felt ill. I thought I might recover with a Gatorade, but then I started sweating again and felt lightheaded.

I agreed to be taken to a hospital, but requested I go to one closest to the downtown Smoothie King Center, where the Pelicans played. Another emergency crew put me on a gurney and off I went from the gate to the airport terminal where an ambulance awaited. What a terrible, bumpy, uncomfortable ride in that ambulance. Glad I didn't have back issues. A paramedic again took my vitals, which remained good.

About twenty-five minutes later we arrived at the Tulane Medical Center emergency room. I hoped I'd be cleared to go to work. Doctors took my vitals. Still good. I was told that if my blood work came back OK, I would be cleared very soon.

But when the results came back, troponin enzymes were found in my blood, and the 1.79 level indicated some sort of cardiac event. According to the doctor, the only way for troponin enzymes to enter your blood is by leakage from the heart. This red flag is sometimes a false positive, so they retested my blood on another floor that had more reliable equipment. Another hour later, the results indicated my troponin level was higher (1.84), which convinced them I had suffered a heart attack.

They needed to keep me there for evaluation. Since it was a

Friday, I had to wait until Monday to have a heart catheterization, since the cardiac crew was off until then.

My wife, Sarah, flew down from Dallas and arrived at the hospital at 12:15 a.m. I was still in the ER. They could not get a room for me until 1 a.m. that morning.

I was hooked up to EKG and other monitoring systems. The doctors assessed the EKG and felt I had a cardiac event in the lower right part of my heart and that, most likely, plaque got loose, stunned my heart, then dissolved. They also performed a sonogram and gave me blood thinner medication.

I felt much better, but had to remain in the hospital until after Monday's test. By the time Monday arrived, I hoped to be cleared to go home after the test. I was scheduled to produce the University Interscholastic League Texas high school football state championships that weekend, so while in my hospital bed, I was on conference calls with my announcers and high school coaches. Little did I know, I would not be producing any games that weekend.

I waited all morning, but the doctor and attendants did not come for me until midday. I requested they make a DVD of the heart catheterization so I could provide it to my doctors, even though I did not have a cardiologist yet.

The procedure went well. As I lay in recovery, the doctors told me and my wife that I was lucky I had that cardiac event, because the test revealed four arterial blockages. One of them— "the widowmaker"—reflects a 95 percent block in a main artery. We couldn't believe it. I was an avid runner and ate healthy, but family history caught up to me.

Still in denial, I contacted the Pelicans to see if the team's cardiologist would provide a second opinion. Moments later, I received a text with a number for Dr. Stephen R. Ramee at Oschner Medical Center. He was the cardiologist for team owner Tom Benson. I called from the recovery room. His assistant asked my wife to immediately deliver the DVDs to Dr. Ramee, who would review them right away. Sarah flagged a taxi, and off she went.

Dr. Ramee concurred with Tulane doctors that I needed bypass surgery within a few days. I wanted to return to Dallas for that, but the Tulane team wasn't keen to comply. Dr. Ramee felt I could fly home, so he consulted with Tulane. The next evening, my wife and I flew to Dallas with a small vial of nitroglycerin in her purse, in case I had another cardiac event. A big thank you to Dr. Ramee for treating us so well, like part of the family.

On Wednesday, we met Dr. Trent Pettijohn, a cardiologist in Plano, Texas, as well as cardiac surgeon Dr. Kelley Hutcheson. My bypass surgery was set for Friday at Baylor Plano Heart Hospital, five minutes from my house. Much better for all parties.

Funny, but I wasn't nervous. I knew this procedure would improve my health and felt I was in great hands, literally. I kept busy the day before surgery by getting my Cotton Bowl Classic production up to speed for the person who subbed for me during my recovery.

The operation took place Friday morning. I was back in my Plano Baylor Heart Hospital room that afternoon. My intensive care unit room was exceptional, private, and it offered my own nurse.

My heart was now okay, but recovering from the broken chest bone from surgery was my worst problem. Boy, I had no energy. My body was using all of it to mend the broken bone and heart. Getting my stamina back was a long, slow process. Three weeks after surgery, I started to feel comfortable showering and doing normal stuff, thanks to Sarah's constant support.

My aunt Carol arrived from New Jersey for a few days to provide emotional support, while my good friends helped me exercise and regain my stamina by walking me around the block or at shopping malls. Standing up to take a shower took all my energy, and I had to get back to the bed as soon as I could to catch my breath.

Miraculously, six weeks after surgery, I returned to producing New Orleans Pelicans games. Sarah joined me on that first trip to be sure everything went smoothly.

Today, I feel terrific. I'm cleared to do anything, with no limitations, according to my cardiologist Dr. Pettijohn.

I run every day, lift weights, do yoga, play golf, or go for long walks. I eat right, except for dessert after dinner. But even then, I limit my sugar intake. Fortunately, my most recent physical test results remain good.

# CHAPTER 16

## *Launching My National Cable Network Career on a Fledgling Network Called ESPN*

**My early career coincided** with the emergence of cable television and outlets like ESPN. As Will Ferrell's *Anchorman* character Ron Burgundy cluelessly predicted about twenty-four-hour cable networks: "That is without a doubt the dumbest thing I've ever heard. A channel that's never off? No offense, but you are stupid!"

I remember writing a slightly more optimistic report in elementary school about the future of television and "CATV," or Community Antenna Television. Cable systems frequently used a "community antenna" to receive broadcast signals from communications satellites, then retransmit them via cable to homes. It's also another term for cable television service. I followed the industry from its infancy to where it is today.

Storer Communications was being awarded cable franchises in many Texas locations, so when I was old enough, I bought stock at about $24 per share. Eventually, Storer was acquired by Comcast and TCI for about $1.55 billion. I still own the stock (which has since converted to Comcast, and now sells at more than $40 per share plus splits). Even then, I was fascinated with that side of the business. It's no coincidence that I produce games for networks still on cable, DIRECTV, or streaming services such as Amazon Prime.

In the mid '80s when I served full-time at regional sports network Home Sports Entertainment, my boss said I could keep producing events, but it would have to be on a freelance basis. He blamed dwindling budgets. Although it meant no more health benefits and no security, I felt comfortable enough to give it a try.

During that era, I freelanced for other stations and networks. One day I was contacted by ESPN producer Bruce Connal, son of Scotty Connal, one of the network's original founders. Bruce was the top live-event remote producer for the fledgling network, handling its big sports events such as tennis, college baseball, and football. ESPN did not cover major college football games, MLB, NBA, or NFL yet.

As ESPN acquired more events, they needed more people with expertise, albeit on a freelance basis. When Reunion Arena hosted the world championship tennis finals from 1980 to 1989, Bruce was in Dallas to cover them. He asked me to help with the production, and we got along well. Soon he recommended me to coordinating producers Terry Lingner, John Wildhack, Mo Davenport, and Jed Drake, each of whom offered me assignments during the next few years. Bruce knew I was producing Texas Rangers games, so he asked if I would guide their national *Sunday Night College Baseball Game of the Week*. Having written on why college baseball was not on TV (for *The Daily Texan* at the University of Texas), it was ironic that I was now being asked to produce it on ESPN. This even included a few Texas Longhorns games.

The *Sunday Night College Baseball Game of the Week* was a staple on the network. One week it could be Texas vs. Texas A&M, or Stanford vs. LSU, or UCLA vs. USC, or Arizona vs. Arizona State, or Miami vs. Florida State, or Mississippi State vs. Vanderbilt, etc. ESPN brought college baseball to the forefront, spotlighting its coaches and the caliber of play.

Bruce asked if I would observe him producing the first week at Stanford's Sunken Diamond stadium. After that, he and ESPN handed me the reins. I worked with Mike Patrick, Ron Franklin,

Sean McDonough, Sam Rosen, Steve Physioc, Jim Kaat, Joe Morgan, and analyst Ray Knight, who had retired from the Detroit Tigers in 1988 after playing for the Reds, Astros, Mets, and Orioles. Ray was one of the nicest and most competitive guys I've worked with. He was a novice broadcaster yet wanted to be the best.

One of Ray's first games with me was at Wichita State early in the season. It was cold, and the forecast in Wichita called for snow. We were convinced that the game would be postponed, but WSU head coach Gene Stephenson said, "We don't get a chance to play on national TV too often, so we're playing." So we did televise the game.

Ray and I went from college baseball telecasts to working MLB games together at ESPN. One of those was historic. On July 31, 1990, at the old Milwaukee County Stadium in Wisconsin, Nolan Ryan had been sitting on 299 career victories for ten days. That night was his chance to win his three hundredth. Fewer than twenty pitchers had ever reached that milestone.

As usual, we rehearsed our opening on-camera segment. We wanted to record it to be sure we were timed perfectly to reach break and not miss the first pitch. We kept redoing it, because Ray stumbled or didn't like what he said. With only minutes left before airtime, I insisted, "Look, we need to do this live."

I knew Ray could do it, because he deftly handled pressure during his thirteen years on the diamond. (As MVP of the 1986 World Series, Ray scored the winning run in one of the most famous plays in baseball history: Bill Buckner's game-six fielding error that lifted the Mets over the Red Sox in the dramatic tenth inning.) Some players can't handle the pressure of the big leagues, but guys like Ray feed off it.

When airtime arrived, Ray stepped up to the proverbial plate and hit a home run. His opening was perfect. Sure enough, Nolan captured his three-hundredth victory. It was a historic moment for MLB, ESPN, Nolan Ryan, and Ray Knight. And an evening I'll never forget.

Eventually, I produced *Tuesday Night Baseball*, *Wednesday Night Baseball*, *Friday Night Baseball*, holiday games, and of course, opening days and nights.

In ESPN's early years, it did not have a stable of full-time producers with vast experience handling MLB. Although I was only in my mid-thirties, I had already been producing Texas Rangers baseball for a decade.

One idea that I innovated during our Rangers telecasts was a small baseball diamond graphic we placed in the upper right-hand corner of the screen. It offered viewers a quick visual shorthand to indicate who was on base. The diamond was green, and each base changed colors if a man was on base. I formulated various versions of that graphic for the Chyron IV character generator: runner on first only; first and second; second and third; bases loaded; and every possible scenario. Our graphics operator would call up the appropriate one, and it would seamlessly change on the screen.

ESPN loved it. They thought it was so clever, they copied it and soon employed my "men on base" graphic on the network. Incidentally, my diamond graphic was patterned after the cover of a book written by Houston Cougars baseball coach Bragg Stockton. Thanks, coach.

I produced many NCAA baseball College World Series games at the old Rosenblatt Stadium in Omaha, featuring schools such as Texas, Stanford, Florida State, Cal State Fullerton, Miami, Mississippi State, and LSU. This was heaven for me, working with ESPN announcers Mike Patrick and analysts including Boston Red Sox outfielder Fred Lynn (a nine-time all-star and 1975 American League MVP), Knight, and Kaat. The coaches were legends as well: ASU's Jim Brock, Texas's Cliff Gustafson, Stanford's Mark Marquess, Florida State's Mike Martin, LSU's Skip Bertman, Cal State Fullerton's Augie Garrido, Miami's Ron Fraser, and Mississippi State's Ron Polk.

ESPN College World Series director Scott Johnson and I enjoyed working together. We often spent our off days playing basketball or golf, or having a postgame refreshment at ESPN's favorite watering hole, Pauli's on Leavenworth Street. If you were a College World Series fan or had any connection to the event, you probably stopped by Pauli's at least once during your visit to Omaha.

Adjacent to venerable Rosenblatt Stadium was a place for burgers and the best milkshakes in the world: Zesto's Ice Cream and Grill. It wasn't your typical chocolate, vanilla, or strawberry shake. My favorite was the hot fudge/banana shake, made with vanilla ice cream, real bananas, and real fudge. Scott and I downed a shake every day. Oh, to be young again.

In 1995, the *Omaha World-Herald* did a behind-the-scenes story about ESPN producing the College World Series. Its reporter, David Hendee, hung around the compound and sat in the truck for our USC vs. Florida State game. The Trojans' lineup featured outfielders Jacques Jones (a future Minnesota Twin, Chicago Cub, Detroit Tiger, and Florida Marlin) and Geoff Jenkins (a first-round draft pick of the Milwaukee Brewers, who became a 2003 all-star). The Seminoles' lineup boasted star outfielder J. D. Drew, who hit three home runs in the game. Drew, the first player in college baseball history to hit thirty home runs and steal thirty bases in the same season, later played for the St. Louis Cardinals, Atlanta Braves, Los Angeles Dodgers, and 2007 champion Boston Red Sox.

Hendee's article for the *Omaha World Herald* was titled "ESPN Unleashes Its All-Seeing Eye." Here's an excerpt:

> Scott Johnson's biggest error of the day came two hours before the first pitch.
>
> A former Ohio University baseball player and now a director for ESPN, Johnson's mistake was to show up to work the afternoon of the College World Series game with a Zesto's milkshake in hand—and not one for his producer, Robert Steinfeld.
>
> It was a setback for Johnson's bid to win the second and last gag trophy known as the "Steiny"—that Steinfeld gives

ESPN colleagues to recognize exceptional achievement in broadcasting the national college baseball championship at Rosenblatt Stadium.

Hustling and fun describe the atmosphere behind the screens in the 24-hour cable sports network's high-voltage, trailer-city command post, which parked at Rosenblatt during the nine-day tournament.

My ESPN resume expanded to sports beyond college basketball and football, namely World Cup Soccer, NCAA championship events, softball, volleyball, lacrosse, and Little League World Series regional championships.

In 1998, I was assigned to produce the FIBA (International Federation of Amateur Basketball) women's world championship in Germany with many of the top USA players ever, including Lisa Leslie, Dawn Staley, Sheryl Swoopes, and Rebecca Lobo. We also produced many of the exhibition games domestically. To my dismay, a few weeks after I traveled to Germany to do site surveys with NBA operations personnel—and just before we were about to leave for games—the telecasts were canceled. My friend, play-by-play announcer Dave Barnett, was also scheduled for it.

Here's the tease I wrote for those games:

### World Championship of Basketball, Opening Tease

Lisa Leslie has a story to tell. Despite an All-America career at USC, an Olympic gold medal and an all-pro season in the WNBA, that's not enough.

Natalie Williams was an all-American volleyball player at UCLA and Pac-10 basketball player of the year. And now she's the ABL's most valuable player. But that's not enough.

Jennifer Azzi and Nikki McCray, accomplished professional all-stars, have won gold for the USA in Atlanta, and they're coming back for more.

Kara Wolters won it all at Connecticut in 1995, has played

on numerous USA national teams, and just completed her first professional season. But she's not satisfied, either.

Former Ohio State Buckeye Katie Smith had a stellar collegiate career and now two professional championships on her resume, but . . .

Dawn Staley was named 1994 USA basketball female athlete of the year, national collegiate player of the year in 1991 and 1992, and just completed a grueling professional all-star season. Isn't that enough?

As these veterans of foreign battles continue to press on, an incredible insurgence of new talent, Chamique Holdsclaw and Delisha Milton, will add fuel to the U.S. dreams of capturing a world championship this year.

Tara VanDerveer capably guided 1996 Team USA to Olympic glory. Now, the torch has been handed to her former national team assistant Nell Fortner, who has shown the personality and deft of a pedigree coaching background.

But it won't be easy. The 16-team international world championship rosters assembled today in Germany are dotted with players equally motivated and talented. The United States will begin its quest for the gold tonight. An attainable goal, but one, as history suggests, is anything but assured.

I also produced ESPN's first-ever Major League Baseball telecast, which was an exhibition game in Scottsdale, Arizona, the spring training home of the San Francisco Giants. Here's a story that ran in the *San Francisco Examiner* on March 26, 1990:

### ESPN Readying For Exhibition Opener Like It's Game Seven

SCOTTSDALE, AZ – To watch ESPN's 43-man crew scurrying around Scottsdale Stadium this weekend, you'd think they were preparing to telecast the seventh game of the World Series instead of the first game of the Cactus League.

The truth is, Monday's noon (PST) national broadcast of

the game between the Giants and the Cleveland Indians is of major significance to the cable network, and they are treating is as such. It is ESPN's first-ever major-league baseball game.

"To us, it's a historical game, a milestone," said ESPN producer Bob Steinfeld. We're approaching it with all the energy and fervor we have."

ESPN will use six cameras, some of them mounted on the scissor-lifts they've been hurriedly installing. Steve Zabriskie, voice of the New York Mets for the past seven years, and former Texas Ranger announcer Norm Hitzges will call the game. Veteran Ken Fouts, who worked for years on NBC's Game of the Week, will direct.

"People say, 'How can ESPN do a good job?,' but we have people who have done it for years," Steinfeld said. "You'll be really, really impressed with our graphics, which are brand-new, as is our animation. Our theme song was produced at Tallman Studios, where Billy Joel cut his album. We're doing things first-class."

ESPN will broadcast nine exhibition games and 175 regular-season games in 1990.

The coordinating producer was Jed Drake. I owe much of my ESPN career to Jed for hiring me for baseball, the 1994 World Cup, college hoops, football, and NCAA championship events including women's volleyball in Honolulu and men's lacrosse in Syracuse. My work was also initially recognized by coordinating producers Terry Lingner, John Wildhack, Mo Davenport, Dave Miller, and Tim Scanlan.

Scanlan, I should add, has been a tremendous advocate for all my accomplishments. "Bob Steinfeld is one of the most talented people in the sports television industry. Full stop!" said Scanlan, the vice president of sports broadcast and media at Octagon, former ESPN vice president of talent planning and development, and coordinating producer for Major League Baseball. "His ability to lead a production and technical team through a live sports television event is similar to a conductor with an orchestra: on point and brilliant."

Other exciting events I produced were the Heroes of Baseball and Celebrity All-Star games played the day before the MLB All-Star games in Chicago (1990 Wrigley Field), Toronto (1991 SkyDome), Philadelphia (1996 Veterans Stadium), and Cleveland (1997 Jacobs Field).

ESPN allowed us to use commercial music during our telecasts. Using just one or two of these cuts required rights approval by artist and publisher, and a signoff from the higher ups who paid the copyright fees. For the first game at Wrigley Field in Chicago, I found the perfect song to open the show. It was "Take Me Back to Chicago" by the band Chicago. Another song approved for our telecast to use in and out of breaks was "Old Days," by the same band.

For the 1991 Heroes of Baseball game in Toronto, I opened the show with a creative idea that incorporated one of my childhood heroes, Brooks Robinson, who played in the game. The hall of fame third baseman played twenty-three seasons, all for the Baltimore Orioles. He participated in eighteen consecutive all-star games, won sixteen Gold Gloves, and led the American League in fielding percentage eleven times. While he was known more for his glove than his bat, in 1964 he led the league in runs batted in and finished his career with 2,848 hits, 268 home runs, and 1,357 RBI. His uniform number 5 is retired by the Orioles. He is arguably the best third baseman in the history of the game. Brooks passed away in September 2023 at the age of eighty-six.

My idea was to magically transport Brooks from his playing days in Baltimore to the SkyDome in Toronto. To do that, I had to get permission from my bosses at ESPN to fly to Baltimore, arrange for Brooks to meet me at Memorial Stadium (where the Orioles used to play), show him fielding a grounder, then transport him twenty years later to Toronto. Brooks was game for it, as was ESPN.

I flew to Baltimore to meet Brooks along with our camera and audio crew at the old stadium. Once inside, I flashed back to the 1966, 1969, 1970, and 1971 World Series games played there. I remember bringing my transistor radio to school to listen to Jim Palmer pitch and Brooks make spectacular plays in the field. After coming back to reality, we took about an hour to shoot it and then used creative editing to take him from Baltimore to Toronto.

A year or two later, I was privileged to work with many big-name stars when MLB changed the format from Heroes of Baseball to Celebrity All-Stars.

I concocted this premise to open the show: two celebrity captains—actors John Ritter and Drew Carey—would meet at home plate and exchange lineup cards with the umpire. Then suddenly, *Saturday Night Live*'s Jim Breuer would interrupt their conversation as his popular Goat Boy character. This agitated Drew Carey into wanting to trade him to Ritter's team for Lee Ann Rimes. They were skilled at improvisation, which made the bit incredibly funny.

The star-studded humor in the prerecorded opening did not end there. When John Grisham—author of the bestseller *The Runaway Jury*—was involved in a baserunning controversy, a jury then assembled in the stands to judge whether he was safe or out. Singer Lee Ann Rimes sang her hit song "Blue" to persuade the umpire to reverse an out call. ESPN's Charley Steiner got "annoyed" and punched a mascot. When a former Cleveland Browns quarterback stepped to the plate, the pitcher hurled a football instead of a softball.

Another year, we enlisted Rob Schneider, another *SNL* alum, to participate in our open.

———

I was now producing ESPN's *Tuesday Night Baseball*, *Wednesday Night Baseball*, *Friday Night Baseball*, and special holiday and event games. During one year, I produced four opening-night games in one week, in four different cities.

One opener took place at the old Cleveland Municipal Stadium for an ESPN baseball game on a miserable night. It had rained most of the morning. I was at the stadium at lunch time when the game was called off, so I alerted coordinating producer Jed Drake in Bristol.

"How fast can you get to the airport?" he inquired.

"Why?" I replied.

He said the backup game was in Toronto. ESPN planned to use the Blue Jays' feed, but wanted an ESPN representative—namely me—to attend and ensure everything proceeded smoothly. I rushed back to my downtown hotel and got my stuff. ESPN took care of my flight. Fortunately, the airport was only thirty minutes from my hotel, and Cleveland to Toronto was only a seventy-minute flight. The trick was getting through Canadian customs and to SkyDome. Toronto's airport was forty-five minutes away. I made it to Toronto by 5 p.m. and reached the ballpark at 6:15, barely in time for the 7:00 p.m. game. ESPN was relieved that I was on headset to Bristol master control. Wow. I began the day at Municipal Stadium in Cleveland and ended it at SkyDome in Toronto. I am still catching my breath.

During my tenure at ESPN, I worked with someone I considered baseball's finest commentator. Joe Morgan, a National League MVP and World Series champion in 1975 and 1976, is arguably the greatest second basemen ever. The ten-time all-star and five-time Gold Glove winner was inducted to the hall of fame in 1990 and was named to not one, but two teams' hall of fame: the Houston Astros and Cincinnati Reds. The Reds retired his number 8 uniform, as well. "Little Joe" hit for power and had an 80 percent successful stolen-base rate.

This all-time great broadcaster was all about observation and taking you inside the game. The night before our first telecast—an ESPN college baseball game in California—I knocked on his door at the hotel to deliver research and game notes. I was astonished to hear that he didn't prepare by reading notes, bios, or stats. His broadcasting style, he insisted, was about telling viewers what was happening in that game and in that moment. He was hired for his expertise and experience, not stories about the players. Such stories, he said, were the responsibility of his play-by-play partner.

Understood. I was familiar with Joe's work on ABC and NBC Sports, and now I was familiar with how he prepared to take the booth.

Quite simply, he was the best analyst I've met. Here's why. He broadcast each game as if he was playing it. Thinking—what the pitcher might throw, where the batter should hit it, whether the baserunner should steal (and if so, on which pitch), if the manager should hit-and-run, if the fielders are situated in the correct spots for the batter and that situation, etc.

Joe knew that I played and understood baseball, albeit on a miniscule level compared to him. We often dove into conversations on the talkback about what he wanted to see live or replayed. (Announcers could speak to me in the production truck on "talk-back" by hitting a button that killed their mikes on the air, but not to me. The announcer's voice would be on a separate speaker in the production truck. It's also called a "cough button" in case they need to clear their throat or speak to each other off air.)

One game, I noticed the third baseman was playing too deep for what I deemed a bunting or sacrifice situation. I pressed the button on the console to notify Joe. He immediately repeated my observation on the air. On the next pitch, the batter bunted down the third-base line for a base hit.

Joe thanked me, which was immensely satisfying. Respect from the talent is what you strive to achieve. Hopefully you've earned it before you work together, but gaining his admiration remains one of my fondest career memories. He later wrote a letter to NBC Sports, recommending me to produce the Olympics. A marvelous gesture from a marvelous person.

The Reds and Astros legend passed away on October 11, 2020, at the age of seventy-seven.

———

In 1994, Drake asked me to produce ESPN's World Cup draw show, which announced each team's opponents and venue destinations. Since the draw was held in Las Vegas, the telecast required glitz, of course. I worked with Dick Clark Productions to weave the entertainment portion into the actual draw. The event featured performances by Vanessa Williams and Stevie Wonder, whom I met afterwards. When I thanked Stevie for his fantastic musical contribution, he was exceptionally gracious.

I also produced World Cup soccer in the Cotton Bowl in Dallas and the Citrus Bowl in Orlando in 1994. The two Cotton Bowl matches included Germany vs. South Korea (with legendary player Jürgen Klinsmann on June 27, 1974) and Spain vs. South Korea (on June 17, 1994). After the June 17 match, I stepped into our production trailer and noticed everyone was engrossed with the television. They weren't watching World Cup soccer, however. It was a car chase in Los Angeles. Not just any car chase, but one involving a white Ford Bronco driven by Al Cowlings. His passenger was O. J. Simpson.

Earlier in the day, the NFL star was charged with the brutal murder of his ex-wife, Nicole Brown Simpson, and her friend, Ronald Goldman. Beyond our production crew, it also captured the attention of the nation. Cowlings called 9-1-1 as he drove the getaway car and claimed that Simpson was armed with a gun pointed to his head. O. J. demanded that Cowlings drive him to his estate in Brentwood, or he would kill himself. That led to a slow-speed chase that ended at Simpson's home. After an hour or so, both men surrendered to police.

The Knicks were playing the Rockets in the NBA Finals that night. New York won game five, 91–84, led by Patrick Ewing's 25 points and 12 rebounds. The series went to seven games before the Rockets prevailed. NBC Sports, which carried the series, was not too pleased with the O. J. interruption. With a 9 p.m. Eastern time start, the car chase cut into most of the game. Police caught up with the Bronco as the NBA game was starting.

Bob Costas recently described how NBC Sports chief Dick Ebersol asked him to interrupt the telecast with sporadic updates on the spectacle so they wouldn't have to preempt the game. O. J., who was a former commentator for NBC Sports and a friend of Costas, later told Costas that he tried to call him during the chase, but a person in the NBC control room thought it was a prank and hung up. Costas confirmed that when he visited O. J. in prison. The chase and capture lasted more than three hours, longer than the game itself.

While I was establishing myself at ESPN, I continued to produce and direct events for HSE.

Circa 1999, I was asked to interview for the ESPN coordinating producer job for both MLB and college baseball. Another offer was for coordinating producer of college basketball. (ESPN did not have NBA then.) It was flattering, but like the CBS opportunity, I declined it due to family considerations and the fact that I had a good job in Dallas–Fort Worth. I was honored to be considered for those esteemed roles.

ESPN gave me the opportunity to collaborate with gifted announcers and production personnel such as Mike Patrick, Suzy Kolber, Beth Mowins, Bob Ley, Chris Berman, Bonnie Bernstein, Robin Roberts, Brad Nessler, Bill Raftery, Reggie Miller, Summer Sanders, Michele Tafoya, Charley Steiner, Tim Brando, Gary Thorne, Dave Campbell, Bob Carpenter, Chris Berman, Dave Ryan, Dick Vitale, Jim Valvano, Larry Conley, and Jay Bilas. I also sat alongside skilled directors including Marc Payton, Jimmie Moore, Doug Holmes, Scott Johnson, Ken Dennis, Mike Schwab, Ken Fouts, and Chris Lincoln.

Dick Vitale always impressed me with his enthusiasm, dedication, love of the game, and most importantly, his heart off the court. He surprised people with personal notes and gifts and sometimes provided financial support to those in need. One day when we were at Louisiana State University, head coach Dale Brown asked Dick to speak to his team and some family members after practice. Without any preparation, he gave one of the most inspirational speeches I ever heard. That's Dickie V.

Few people remember that Dick was head coach of the Detroit Pistons from 1978 to 1979. During that season, he coached my future boss and good friend, UCLA all-American Roy Hamilton. Roy was a broadcast associate for CBS Sports when we met. I worked with him on the 1986 NBA playoffs when Ralph Sampson and Hakeem Olajuwon, a.k.a. the "Twin Towers," were with the Rockets. Our paths crossed again at the World Basketball Championships in Toronto in 1994, when Dream Team II defeated Russia, 137–91. Years later, we both worked for Fox Sports Net. Roy has been one of my biggest allies and friends in the business. He was responsible for hiring me for most of my national gigs there: *Sunday Night Fights*, *ACC Sunday Night Hoops*, college football and basketball, and the Nike Hoop Summit. Thanks, Roy.

I also cherished the ESPN games I did with Jim Valvano, head coach of the 1983 NCAA champion North Carolina State. Many remember the classic clip of him running around the court looking for someone to hug after the Wolfpack won the title in a major upset of the Houston Cougars. Others were moved by his emotional, inspirational speech—"Don't give up. Don't ever give up"—at the 1993 ESPY Awards. Valvano died of cancer at forty-seven, less than two months later.

Prior to an ESPN college basketball telecast in Austin that I was producing, I picked Valvano up at the airport. He was arriving from Los Angeles, where the previous night he had appeared on *The Tonight Show* with Johnny Carson. His engaging personality made him a frequent guest. We drove to the Barton Creek Resort, where legendary University of Texas media relations director Bill Little and his Longhorn staff treated us to dinner. At the adjacent table was retired Texas Longhorns head coach Darrell Royal. Jimmy V and Royal exchanged greetings.

The next evening, Texas basketball head coach Tom Penders invited us to a club and restaurant on 6th Street in Austin. I was merely included because I was the producer, but the entire conversation was between Penders and Valvano. I was the proverbial fly on the wall. I felt fortunate to listen to them rekindle their friendship and trade stories. The camaraderie between coaches is special.

————

Here's a tease I wrote and produced for the Little League World Series regional games on ESPN on August 7, 1998:

**Little League World Series**

When you open a treasure chest of youth, the spirit of baseball casts a magical trance. Collecting cards, placing them on spokes, and dreaming about becoming a big-league star.

For many kids and their parents, realizing that dream begins with a plastic ball and bat, then on to tee-ball, and soon, it's on to Little League. It is here they begin to show all-star potential, and it's here where a trip to Williamsport, Pennsylvania is their ultimate goal.

While the likes of Seaver, Sheffield, Key and Ripken Jr. have indelibly stamped their Little League legacies, others are beginning to dazzle us today. Few will reach the big leagues, but for now, reaching Williamsport and the World Series championship casts an even brighter spotlight. A win in tonight's regional championship makes that dream a reality.

# CHAPTER 17

## *Three-Plus Decades with the Cotton Bowl Classic*

*When I moved to Dallas,* the annual Cotton Bowl Classic football game was already in its third decade. Historically played on New Year's Day, it was (and still is) one of the premier events held in our area. That made it an incredible honor to be asked by its new head of marketing, Rick Baker, to oversee the production of the 1989 jumbotron show in the historic yet dated Cotton Bowl Stadium. There was one slight issue, however. The venue did not have a jumbotron or any type of "tron."

We did our homework and found a few companies that provided portable large screens for special events like auto racing, parades, and soccer. Large electronic screens simply were not prevalent then. Few stadiums offered them. Texas Stadium, home of the Dallas Cowboys, had a monochrome highlight board, but its video quality was poor, and it was not suitably large for an outdoor stadium. So we enlisted a Pennsylvania company that delivered a temporary screen and set it up near the east endzone. Providing a signal or video to the screen was challenging, because there was no control room.

I hired a regional vendor, Earl Miller Productions, to provide cameras, replay machines, and crew in a small mobile television truck. I produced and directed the show. We imported the network feed from the main broadcaster, CBS, and supplemented it with our own cameras on the field and one up top. Additionally, I was hired to provide a ninety-minute stadium pregame show to entertain the fans with background on the game. I showed a twenty-five-minute highlight reel from a previous year's game that had a connection to one of the competing teams that year. Rick Baker later asked me to produce the official sixty-minute highlight video that documented the game. This meant I was overseeing three major productions: the pregame show, the actual game in the stadium, and the documentary.

My first game was the 1990 classic between eighth-ranked Tennessee (coached by Johnny Majors) and tenth-ranked Arkansas (coached by Ken Hatfield). Jim Nantz and Pat Haden broadcast the game for CBS. Tennessee triumphed in the contest, toppling Arkansas 31–27, highlighted by Volunteer tailback Chuck Webb's 250 rushing yards.

Afterwards, I edited the video tapes into an NFL Films-style highlight video and wrote a script to send to Nantz to record at a studio in his hometown in Connecticut. No internet files in those days. He recorded his narration on reel-to-reel, then overnighted it to me. I added classical music to the mix, and we were good to go. Nantz was a pro and a pleasure to work with. We spoke many times on the phone to make sure we were on the same page with the script and inflections. Our video won first place at the World-Fest Houston international video festival. I credited him for that. I was pleased and humbled to read what he said about me in a story written by *Dallas Jewish Life* sports editor Dave Sorter.

Steinfeld "is very thorough; well-organized," said Nantz. "He is a maniac about detail and has very high standards, which suits my style. It's always neat to see the end product. He was left with some not-memorable games. I remember when Miami throttled Texas [46–3 in the 1991 Cotton Bowl] and he came up with a spectacular video. That's the mark of a top-notch producer."

Nantz and I collaborated on the highlight video for the following three seasons until NBC took over in 1993.

The Cotton Bowl was one of the first major events to have a title sponsor. That tradition has continued since then:

1989 to 1995: Mobil Cotton Bowl Classic
1996 to 2014: Southwestern Bell, SBC, and then AT&T
2014 to present: Goodyear

Many networks have carried the Cotton Bowl. Beginning in the 1950s, the rights bounced from NBC to CBS to NBC to CBS to Fox to ESPN, where it remains as of this writing.

In 2010, the game moved from the Cotton Bowl to the Dallas Cowboys' new stadium in Arlington. For those who grew up with the venerable Cotton Bowl, the change was bittersweet. The event had become so big, the old press box could no longer accommodate the media and marketing demands. Dallas Cowboys owner Jerry Jones actually played in the 1965 Cotton Bowl when his Razor-backs defeated Nebraska, 10–7, so the classic is dear to his heart.

AT&T Stadium, the new venue, provides far better visibil-ity and marketing opportunities for sponsor engagement. It also boasts a state-of-the-art television production control room and (what was then) the largest video screen at a stadium in the nation. The center-hung scoreboard, offering crisp 4K video output, looks impressive. I had a general idea what the jumbotron would look like when I toured the stadium during its construction, but the final product—stretching 53 yards horizontally between the two 20-yard lines—surpassed my expectations. The videoboard is so large we employ two game cameras: one on each side of the sta-dium so fans watching the game on each side could see the teams and ball going in the correct direction.

Shout-out to the Dallas Cowboys for allowing me to enter their control room each year to oversee our Cotton Bowl productions.

My Cotton Bowl affiliation has allowed me to collaborate with many talented people linked to the sponsors, including Goodyear, AT&T, and The Marketing Arm (an agency that works with Goodyear). I work closely with each school's media relations directors, video producers, and athletic department staff to make sure we execute branding and video properly on the scoreboards, videoboards, and monitors throughout AT&T Stadium.

Preparation takes months. I have monthly, then weekly, meetings with the Cotton Bowl staff and with major sponsors to guarantee every detail is addressed. I stay in touch with chief marketing officer Michael Konradi and Rick Baker all year, touching base in the spring and summer until we rev up around September.

As Rick Baker, the president and chief executive officer of the Goodyear Cotton Bowl, recently told me, "You do a terrific job producing our philosophy and making it come to life. The Cotton Bowl is very fortunate to have you on our team."

I appreciate that his Cotton Bowl staff have entrusted me with the annual responsibility for their game, especially when it's a playoff semifinal. I look forward to the upcoming expanded college football playoffs and the Goodyear Cotton Bowl's revered and respected position on the sports landscape.

# CHAPTER 18

## *Now Batting: Steinfeld, Tobolowsky, Bodzin, Donosky . . . and Mantle?*

*I was born in Jersey City, New Jersey* in 1955 and lived in nearby Rutherford until we moved to Dallas on June 5, 1965, when I was nine years old. It was quite a culture shock. In New Jersey, I walked across the street from our apartment to Washington Elementary School to play stickball, wiffleball, and regular baseball. That's what we did every day, weather permitting, including the hot summer months.

We played organized Little League, or as my age group was called—even in New Jersey—the "Texas League." We also collected Topps baseball cards with the hard pink gum inside. We all hoped to find a Mickey Mantle, Roger Maris, or any New York Yankee baseball card in our random packs, which we bought at Stio's Drugstore on Union Avenue. Occasionally, my father brought home a pack or two. My grandfather, Barney Israel, who lived in North Bergen, took my brother and me to Yankee Stadium to attend day games, Bat Day, or even Old-Timer's Day. Each visit to the baseball mecca was a thrill.

I loved taking the bus from my grandparents' apartment in North Bergen to the Port Authority in Manhattan, then onto the subway to Yankee Stadium. Those memories are etched in my mind: subway riders wearing their Yankee caps and Yankee Stadium signs in the subway station as we disembarked the train. Walking up those steep stairs from the tracks to street level felt momentous and piqued our anticipation. From the ground level, we saw the stadium through the elevated tracks on one side, Manny's Baseball Land and other souvenir stores on the other, and the smell of hot pretzels and hot chestnuts roasting on an open fire. What an atmosphere.

After entering through the vomitory and walking in the stadium, our eyes would be treated to the lush green grass, the white façade on top of the stadium, and the perfectly manicured infield. The visuals were extra impressive and beautiful, because in the early 1960s all we could see on WPIX 11 television—at least in my living room—were black and white pictures.

I was a big Yankees fan and remained so when we moved to Texas in 1965. Dallas did not even have a big league team then.

Fast-forward to 1970 middle school, namely Benjamin Franklin Jr. High School in North Dallas. I played on the school baseball team along with my best friends Ted Tobolowsky, Mark Bodzin, and my Hebrew school buddy, Robert Donosky. I also played on the Jewish Community Center teams with those three. Robert's dad coached our team many times at the JCC, then known as Julius Schepps Community Center.

Many classmates played on my junior high school team, including one whose father was a legendary Yankee: Mickey Mantle. My teammate's name was David Mantle. Mickey was originally from Oklahoma, but he bought a house in North Dallas and lived across the street from the synagogue my family belonged to, Shearith Israel. Mickey's sons, including David, went to public school. David looked just like his father, except he had red hair. It was always a novel treat to read the batting order lineup and see "Steinfeld, Mantle, Tobolowsky, Donosky," etc.

David had a natural swing like his dad but unfortunately did not inherit his father's speed.

"Is your dad ever going to come to one of our games?" I once asked. He said he didn't know. It was nice that his mom occasionally attended, but we were disappointed that the Yankee slugger never graced us with his presence. Or did he?

Imagine "The Mick" watching and cheering on your team! Decades later, a year before Mickey died, HBO produced a documentary and asked him if he had any regrets in his life. He shared how he shied away from being in public but later realized how much it would have meant for fans and families in his hometown to meet him, and, conversely, for him get to know them.

"He couldn't come to our games, because people would bother him. He would have to sit in the car and watch the games. Sometimes we didn't even know he was there," said his son, Danny Mantle.

Indeed, The Mick did watch us play. We just didn't know it.

On that same special, Mickey told Bob Costas that he wrote a letter to his dad, who had been deceased since 1951. He confessed how sorry he was for not being there for his kids, like his dad was for him. His words reminded me that I needed to tell my kids that I love them.

On August 13, 1995, I attended Mantle's funeral at a North Dallas church on the corner of Inwood Road and Northwest Highway. I could not get inside for the ceremony, but was able to get a funeral program pamphlet that I still have today. I watched and listened just outside the church. I saw the pallbearers, who included Whitey Ford and Yogi Berra. Bob Costas gave an impressive, articulate, and heartfelt eulogy. I went as a fan, but more so out of respect for my classmate and teammate, David Mantle. I met up with David at our Hillcrest High School forty-year reunion in 2014 to relive old memories.

Today, I have a pristine New York Yankees navy blue and white pinstripe wool baseball cap, signed by Mickey Mantle and Whitey Ford. It is authenticated by a certificate signed by Mickey E. Mantle, David H. Mantle, and Dan M. Mantle from Four M Enterprises, Ltd. It's one of my favorite collectibles and holds tremendous personal meaning for me.

# CHAPTER 19

# *Managing a College Football Telecast on One Leg*

**When a prime-time game** is scheduled for national TV—in this case, on Fox Sports Net—I have time early on gameday for a workout. When we produce games in Norman, Oklahoma, our crew usually stays at the Marriott Postal Hotel. It was also called the NCED Hotel and Conference Center (National Center for Employee Development), where post office employees stayed while training at a building across the parking lot. The rooms were stamp-sized, even smaller than the ones at most New York City hotels. Yet it was a quality site (operated by Marriott), with excellent food options, entertainment and workout facilities, an outdoor running track, obstacle course, tennis courts, indoor golf driving range, ping pong, volleyball, basketball, and a weight room. It was five minutes from the stadium, so we took advantage of the amenities.

On gameday, September 27, 2008, I woke up, went downstairs for a workout with weights, ran on the outdoor trail, and then hit the gym to shoot baskets. After our director, Phil Mollica, started shooting with me, a couple of production technicians challenged us to a game of two-on-two. Phil and I accepted the invitation and emerged victorious. At 10:00 a.m., as we were about to head upstairs, two of our camera operators saw us and were disappointed we didn't tell them we were hooping it up.

They persuaded us to play one more game to 10 points. Although they were not avid hoopsters, we didn't want to disappoint them. "Game on," we agreed.

The game started, and Phil and I had things under control. As I was about to shoot an outside jumper, both opponents went for the block, yet they were out of control. I was sure that I would be fouled. As I shot, both of them slammed into my right leg—one from each side —causing my leg to snap. I fell to the ground and said, "I believe you broke my leg."

"How can you be certain?" one of them countered.

"Didn't you hear it snap?" I asked.

The guys were sorry. Phil, however, wanted me to get up and complete the game. Yes, he was kidding. They helped me to the bleachers and offered to take me to the hospital. I had a better idea. I asked them to help me to my room so I could shower and then go to the Switzer Center on campus, where the Sooners locker room was located in the north end zone of Gaylord Family Stadium. I hoped the team's medical staff, who handle orthopedic-type injuries all the time, might be around to help me, especially since I was set to produce their nationally televised game against TCU mere hours later.

As I arrived at the Switzer Center about noon, the complex was virtually empty. It was still six hours before kickoff. Oklahoma coach Bob Stoops spotted me limping into the locker room, shook his head and said, "What did you do to yourself since I saw you yesterday?"

"I'm pretty sure I broke my leg playing basketball at the hotel," I told him.

"Follow me, if you can," Stoops said. He introduced me to head trainer Scott Anderson, who examined my leg and concurred with my assessment. He wrapped my leg, gave me a walking boot and crutches, and asked me to return at 3 p.m. when the team's head orthopedic doctor could examine me further and take X-rays.

I remained determined to produce the game. One of our crew's runners made a makeshift wheelchair and pushed me around the stadium complex to the Fox production truck, where I kept my leg elevated. At 3 p.m., I was wheeled back to the locker room, where the entire Sooner team was now inside. They must have wondered what the heck I was doing there with the game approaching. The doctor was punctual and gladly helped me. We went into a small adjoining room where he X-rayed my right leg. He confirmed that I had fractured my fibula but did not seem overly concerned because it was a clean break. Although he did not think I needed surgery, he recommended I see my orthopedist in Dallas. He offered me painkillers to get through the evening but said it might make me feel a bit loopy. I turned it down, knowing that I would be producing a national telecast. Instead I asked for extra-strength Advil.

I can't thank the Oklahoma athletic department enough for their cooperation, expertise, and concern. I wrote to Oklahoma athletic director Joe Castiglione to tell him how much I appreciated their hospitality and care.

When 6 p.m. rolled around, I was sitting inside the front row of the production truck again with my broken right leg. I was relieved to make it through the game. The only issue I now had was getting back to the hotel and driving my car for three hours back to Dallas. I could not push on the gas or brake with my right foot, but fortunately I could use the paddles on the steering wheel to engage the pedal for more power as needed. Unbelievably, during my 190-mile drive on Interstate 35, there was only one traffic light from Norman to my home in North Dallas. That meant I could use cruise control most of the time to accelerate or decelerate.

I arrived home safely Sunday morning. Thank you again, Sooner Nation, for helping me. The Sooners were satisfied as well, winning the game 35–10, due to the arm of Heisman Trophy winner Sam Bradford.

# CHAPTER 20

# *The* Best Damn Fight *Night at the Playboy Mansion*

*For about 10 years,* various vice presidents of production for Fox Sports Net, including Arthur Smith, Bill Borson, Roy Hamilton, Gary Garcia, Doug Levy, and the late Doug Sellars, hired me to produce a weekly series of championship boxing events titled *Sunday Night Fights,* and later *Best Damn Fight Night,* with George Greenberg in charge of production. It aired late spring to late fall until college basketball's *ACC Sunday Night Hoops* took over the time slot—which I also produced.

That boxing package gave me the chance to produce a sport that endures intrinsic issues yet holds its own in the history of sports television. It's been one of the all-time best attractions for pay-per-view, and it helped establish that genre as a prolific money earner for both boxing and sports television. In this case, we provided a weekly two-hour live package of championship bouts and undercards promoted by Goossen, Goossen-Tutor, or Top Rank. The prominent names we televised included Thomas "Hitman" Hearns, Tim Witherspoon, Greg Page, Hector Camacho Jr., David Reid, Hasim Rahman, James Toney, Olympic gold medalist Andre Ward, Riddick Bowe, Vassily Jirov, Lance Whitaker, and Holly Holm.

We had a few special shows: the 2007 return of Evander Holyfield at the new American Airlines Center in Dallas; a show

One of our guests during our "live" boxing show at the Playboy Mansion in Los Angeles in 2017 was one of *The Girls Next Door* stars, Bridget Marquardt.

at San Antonio's Alamodome; and a boxing card at a famous venue known for scenarios other than boxing—the Playboy Mansion in Holmby Hills, California. Yes, that Playboy Mansion, in the sunset days of Hugh Hefner and his *Girls Next Door* trio of Holly Madison, Kendra Wilkinson, and Bridget Marquardt, who were in attendance.

Our announcers were Barry Tompkins, Rich Marotta, former WBA Lightweight champ Sean O'Grady, host Chris Rose, and reporters Rodney Peete (former NFL quarterback), Rob Dibble (an MLB All-Star pitcher and 1990 World Series champion), and Leeann Tweeden.

We presented two main events and some undercards if we needed to fill. The opening fight on our live card was an eight-round super middleweight bout between Andre Dirrell and Kenny Kost. The headliner was a ten-round Continental Americas heavyweight

My wife Sarah and daughter Elaine at the post-fight party at the Play-boy Mansion in Los Angeles in 2017.

championship bout between Tony "The Tiger" Thompson and Timur Ibragimov. These weren't sexy championship battles, but quality, professional, television-worthy matchups. Our hope was that each fight would go the distance so we would not have to fill with those undercard bouts. We also had contingencies with plenty of celebrities to interview, as needed.

On February 16, 2007, we opened the show with a dramatic shot in front of the Playboy Mansion, welcoming viewers to this exclusive party. Only a few select people were invited, including our viewers on *The Best Damn Sports Show Period*. Sitting next to me in the production truck was Emmy-winning director Craig Janoff, who worked ABC Sports events such as *Monday Night Football*, the World Series, MLB All-Star Game, Kentucky Derby, Belmont Stakes, Preakness Stakes, and Super Bowls. I've never worked with a more detailed, hands-on director than Craig. I've seen him up in the rafters surveying camera angles and making sure he was satisfied with the lighting.

We ran a feature on Hugh Hefner's love of sports and boxing and had Leeann Tweeden interview him alongside Holly, Bridget, and Kendra, the stars of the E! network series *The Girls Next Door*. We showed other celebrities arriving, then spotlighted Grammy nominee Brian McKnight singing the national anthem. About twenty minutes into the show, our ringside announcers, Barry and Rich, previewed the fight. I had Sean O'Grady backstage to interview Tony Thompson, who had just arrived for his main event later in the evening.

But Thompson had a problem. Someone snuck backstage and stole his size 16 boxing shoes. Although such mammoth-sized footwear isn't usually sitting around in an emergency, one of our producers, Matt Schnider, had a pair of size 15 Jordan basketball shoes and loaned them to Thompson for the fight. Thompson retained his title by unanimous decision and partly attributed his win to the clutch assistance from our esteemed crew member.

In the comain event, 2004 Olympic bronze medalist Andre Dirrell won an eight-round unanimous decision over Kenny Kost, knocking him down in rounds one and six. Both fights went the distance, allowing the show to time out well. Afterwards, everyone partied at the Playboy Mansion. My wife, Sarah, and daughter, Elaine, flew in for the evening to experience the atmosphere and celebrities at the exclusive, intimate event.

## Sunday Night Fights

Each Sunday from spring through fall, we featured top boxers. Many were in the twilight of their careers, others were just beginning. We saw Mia St. John, Laila Ali (Muhammad Ali's daughter), Terence Crawford, Robert "The Ghost" Guerrero, 2004 Olympic gold medalist light heavyweight Andre Ward, Riddick Bowe, Hasim Rahman, and James Toney.

Unfortunately, boxing can be brutal. We witnessed one tragedy that could have been prevented. On September 12, our show originated from Harrah's casino in Kansas City, Kansas, across the river from Kansas City, Missouri. The main event was a twelve-round North American Boxing Federation Championship featuring Kabary Salem and Randie Carver.

Carver was repeatedly headbutted in the early rounds by Salem—who was not penalized—then knocked out in the tenth round after taking a right-left combination to the head. He tried four times to get up but could not. The paramedics in the ring worked on him for twenty minutes before taking him to the hospital, apparently unconscious.

Our reporter, Sean O'Grady, had pleaded with the referee to stop the fight. He could see that Carver was done and had no way to defend himself.

Carver died two days later after emergency brain surgery. He was only twenty-four years old.

When incidents like that happen on live television, you hope and pray for the best, since you don't know the ultimate outcome. Astute journalists understand that you shouldn't speculate or guess while in the midst of such grave moments. You recap what transpired, report facts, and provide information from the experts and officials at the venue.

## Fairway Robbery in Vegas

On a lighter note, on July 7, 2001, we were in Las Vegas a day before our Fox Sports Net *Sunday Night Fights* telecast main event featuring 1996 Olympic gold medalist David Reid. I had time to go to the TPC at the Canyons Golf Course (now called TPC Las Vegas) to play a round on an excellent layout in the desert mountains overlooking the Vegas strip.

I was paired with three strangers who were serious golfers, which was virtually a prerequisite if you wanted to undertake a difficult course that featured many greens surrounded by canyons.

On this beautiful morning, I hit a nice drive on a par five. As my ball raced down the fairway, a pack of coyote pups ran out from the desert, chased my ball, and played with it a few seconds. One pup then picked it up in its mouth and raced off with his siblings. I've lost golf balls before, but that disappearance topped it all.

We could not believe what we witnessed. Everyone had a big laugh . . . except me. How was I going to get the ball back? I was hoping the pup might drop it as he retreated into the desert, but no luck. The coyotes just vanished.

I drove my cart to the area I last saw the wild canines. A PGA marshal was monitoring the hole. "Yeah, I saw that," he said. "Quite amusing."

"Well, funny yes," I chuckled, "but they stole my ball. Now what do I do?"

"The pups do that with their mom about once or twice a week," he explained. "They have some fun. The rule states that you should put a new ball where you suspect your original one lay, with no penalty."

I submitted that tale to a contest sponsored by American Airlines' *American Way Magazine*. My story, titled "At Least They Didn't Gnaw Your 9-Iron," was published in its March 1, 2002, edition, with original artwork.

Combining work and pleasure, as I did with my oddball golf anecdote, is yet another perk of my chosen career. Sometimes you end up with a memorable story like that.

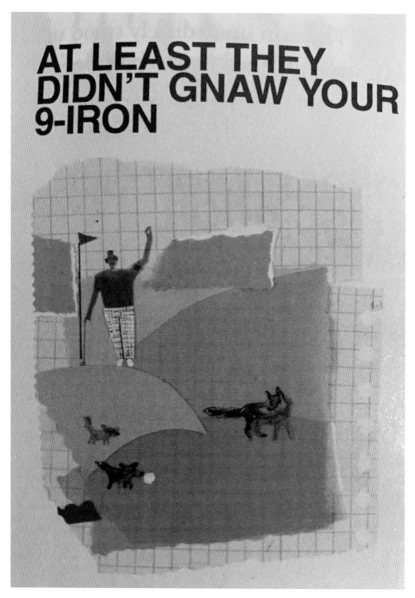

Artwork in *American Way* magazine that accompanied the article about my golf experience in Las Vegas with coyote pups.

# CHAPTER 21

## Prime Network/Fox Sports Net: 1995 to 2020

*In 1994, several regional sports networks,* including Home Sports Entertainment in Houston and Dallas, were acquired by Liberty Media. This changed HSE and the other regionals' names to Prime Sports. I was asked to develop the logo and animation package, so I contacted the NBC graphic designers I worked with at the 1992 Olympics in Barcelona. We created a logo with the word "Prime" and a pennant flowing in the middle.

Nothing really changed in our southwest region, since we operated Prime as a regional network with the Texas Rangers, Dallas Mavericks, and Southwest Conference college events.

Then, in 1996, Liberty Media sold its entire group of regional channels (except for the ones that were locally owned) to Fox Sports, which rebranded them as Fox Sports Net. There was national programming, but each regional had a geographic schedule and moniker. The one in Texas, called Fox Sports SW, covered Texas, Oklahoma, Arkansas, and parts of Louisiana.

With the panache of the Fox Sports name and a budget to produce national shows that aired on all FSN regionals, opportunities now arose to produce national college football games, boxing, and national college basketball. I was one of the lead FSN national producers, as well as on the Fox Sports SW regional level.

One week, I produced a Dallas Cowboys press conference show on a Monday, two San Antonio Spurs games during the week, a national college football game on Saturday, and an Evander Holyfield fight in Dallas the next Monday. For me, the week was just routine.

In March 1993, for example, this was my itinerary during a two-week span:

*Monday*: Prepare for upcoming shows in my HSE office.

*Tuesday*: Travel to San Antonio to produce Mavericks–Spurs game on HSE.

*Wednesday*: Return to Dallas to direct the Trail Blazers–Mavericks game on HSE.

*Thursday*: Direct two SWC women's basketball tournament semifinal games for HSE.

*Friday*: Direct four SWC men's basketball quarterfinal games for HSE.

*Saturday*: Direct the SWC women's championship game for HSE.

*Sunday*: Produce the SWC men's championship game for ESPN. After the game on Sunday, fly to ESPN headquarters in Bristol, Connecticut for a MLB seminar the next morning.

*Tuesday*: Return to Dallas to prepare for upcoming games.

*Wednesday*: Fly to Los Angeles to produce and direct the Spurs–Lakers game for KSAT in San Antonio.

*Thursday*: Return to Dallas to prep for ESPN's MLB game.

*Friday*: Fly to Florida to produce the Pirates–Twins exhibition game on ESPN.

## Our Entertaining Reporter Jim Knox

Along the way, I produced thousands of events for the FSN network, both nationally and regionally. During my years handling college football for Fox Sports Net and FS1, our sideline reporter was often an entertaining guy named Jim Knox.

"Knoxy" lived in Dallas most of that time, so we traveled together for many games. He also was the reporter on Texas Rangers home dates, which meant he sometimes worked two games on the same day, in two different towns or states. Kickoff time for Big 12 football games was usually 11:00 a.m. As soon as the football game was off the air, around 2:15 p.m., Knoxy was ready to rock and roll to the nearest airport to fly home. Few destinations offered nonstops on Saturday afternoons, but since we lived in Dallas, we could get a flight to DFW or Love Field between 3:00 and 4:30 p.m. I didn't enjoy frantically rushing to the airport, but Knoxy was desperate to make those flights, whether or not he had a game. That meant him driving the rental car around stalled traffic and past parking lot attendants directing traffic. Knoxy always had the car strategically parked. For a while, we relied on the school or police to escort us off campus, past the throng of people and cars, but after a couple years, that perk evaporated.

Occasionally, I asked Knoxy to tape a pretease. This fifteen-second on-camera creative open helped tee up the game before our actual preproduced animated intro. Most of the time, those bits were humorous. Occasionally, they turned dangerous. Here are a few of his highlights:

## October 2, 2010: Georgia vs. Colorado

One of the greatest college sports mascot traditions is the running of Ralphie the Buffalo when the Colorado football team takes the field in Boulder. Knoxy wanted to join Ralphie on her late morning jaunt around the field, so we cleared it with the school and Ralphie's handlers. Or so we thought. Knoxy planned to start near the gate where Ralphie begins her run, then follow her around the field, if he could keep up. Everything began perfectly.

"We head downstairs," said play-by-play announcer Joel Meyers, "to one of the great traditions in college football with Jim Knox, Knoxy."

"All right, Joel, here we go again, I am running with Ralphie. They say Ralphie has a four flat in the 40," said Knoxy, who ran down the far sideline, parallel to Ralphie. Suddenly, at the 20-yard line, Ralphie and her handlers veered right, straight at Knoxy, who took a hard turn and was already out of breath. "We're going to turn it around, and here we go down the stretch. Come on Ralphie, bring it on baby!"

Knoxy was now fifteen yards away from a stampeding five-hundred-pound buffalo. He believed he was going to beat Ralphie to her pen, but as he glanced back to see how safe he was, he didn't notice a handler wearing a black cowboy hat and eyeing him down. At the 45-yard line, Knoxy was knocked to the ground by the cowboy. You could hear the collision.

"What happened?" Knoxy wondered. "I got clipped at the 50! Where's the penalty flag?"

Ralphie concluded her run and beat Knoxy.

"That was legal," Meyers insisted. "I'm sorry. That was not a block in the back."

Fellow commentator Joel Klatt, who was just beginning his career and is now Fox's top college football analyst, chuckled, "That was not a block in the back." Meyers agreed, "That was textbook, as he lowered his shoulder."

I instructed our director Kenny Miller to show the field-angle replay of the collision.

"You can see he's completely in front of Knox," said Meyers.

Klatt smartly used the telestrator to draw a circle around the cowboy, adding, "He's lining him up. He's lining him up right here. It's a legal hit. Facemasks in front, that's what they say. Good force. That's unbelievable."

"Is Knoxy in the infirmary or out of the infirmary?" Meyers asked.

"You okay, Knoxy?" said Klatt.

Knoxy disputed their interpretation. "They needed to throw a flag on that, Joel. Definitely a flag. He came out of nowhere and clipped me twice. I love this game." Klatt could be heard laughing in the background.

What made it extra funny was that it was captured live, including Klatt's ad-lib decision to telestrate the cowboy who clipped our reporter. Knoxy later recalled the incident when the *Columbia Missourian* newspaper wrote a feature on him.

"The guys (in the production truck) are dying laughing, the guys in the booth are dying laughing. All I'm thinking is, I have to get up to interview the coach. I don't have time to lay here and play hurt."

We laugh about it even today. It's also on YouTube, where it has nearly 200,000 views.

Knoxy is an entertainer. When you're producing a telecast, you're in show business, and show business is entertainment. Which explains his other amusing exploits.

At Missouri, he rode a Harley-Davidson motorcycle onto the field intended for singer-songwriter Sheryl Crow, the homecoming parade marshal. The nine-time Grammy winner told him it was too cold, but she was happy to hear he enjoyed the ride.

Other times he was tossed up and down on a sofa by tailgaters at Kansas State, was a passenger on the horse-drawn Sooner Schooner as it took the field in Oklahoma, and opened the show sitting atop a float at the Oklahoma State homecoming parade in Stillwater.

## Knoxy's "Unique" Sideline Angle

Despite those funny stories, Knoxy could flip the switch to straight news reporter. Harry Plumer of the *Columbia Missourian* chronicled this in a November 16, 2011 story titled, "Fox Sports Jim Knox Brings Unique Aspects to Sideline Reporting." An excerpt:

A few hours before gametime in beautiful Boulder, Colorado.

"He doesn't always want to do just the easy, normal way," Knox's producer Robert Steinfeld said. "He does do good reporting when he needs to do it, but he's trying to add some color to the game, and that makes it a little bit different. He's also got a little bit of daredevil in him."

Both of those sides of Knox were easy to see during the first quarter of Saturday's Missouri-Baylor game in Waco.

During the pregame, hundreds of Baylor freshmen lined up in the south end zone of Floyd Casey Stadium and then sprinted to the other end of the field to create a human tunnel for the team to enter the field. At risk of getting trampled by the mass of humanity, Knox lined up at the front, and led the charge while yelling into his microphone. It created a unique pregame scene for Fox Sports, one that Knox says added a lot to the overall telecast.

"It's much more than just X's and O's coming at you," Knox said. "It's entertainment."

Minutes after the run, Baylor superstar (and future Heisman Trophy-winning quarterback) Robert Griffin III limps off the field with an apparent injury. Knox rushes his camera crew near where Griffin is sitting on the Baylor bench and hurriedly sets up a live shot. After he gets the go-ahead from the producer [me] in the truck, Knox closes his eyes, tries unsuccessfully to fix what the Texas wind has done to his hair and wipes his face with his hand.

Then, boom, he's back on national telecast. Now he's the guy trying to give insight on the potential Heisman Trophy candidate's condition for the rest of the game. He handles both in stride.

Most of the above anecdotes were lighthearted, but some represented serious teaching moments for aspiring producers and talent. At a Pac-10 college football game I was producing for Fox Sports Net on November 7, 2009, Cal tailback Jahvid Best, a preseason Heisman Trophy candidate, hurdled over Oregon State safety Cameron Collins on a 7-yard TD run. He was hit by a second defender in midair and landed on the back of his head in the end zone, resulting in his helmet flying off. He briefly lost consciousness. Paramedics and team officials came to his aid and removed his jersey as they attended to him.

Both Cal and Oregon State players were on their knees hoping and praying for a sign of good news. In these moments, you want to see fans and players from both sides expressing goodwill. It's also when a producer needs to alert the network's executive producer and coordinating producer about the situation, while providing guidance and support.

We remained patient in the truck. The announcers were reminded never to speculate on the player's status or make any statement about his condition other than what we could obviously observe, or if we received official word from the school. Taking our time, we replayed what happened, without being dramatic. We respectfully showed what transpired, mindful that family and relatives might be watching. If it's too gruesome, we could even opt not to replay it. If deemed palatable, perhaps show it once. Wait for official word from the school media relations director or team doctors. There are also HIPAA rules—the Health Insurance Portability and Accountability Act—to follow about releasing the private injury status of amateur players. Sideline reporters often see firsthand what is happening, but again, must not speculate on the injury. Reporters and announcers in the booth should wait until we receive official word.

The running back was taken off the field on a stretcher, wearing an oxygen mask, then rushed to an emergency room. At least one family member was present on the field as fans shouted, "Jahvid . . . Jahvid."

At the hospital, it was determined that he suffered a concussion. He was released the next day and appeared on the sideline that next weekend at Cal's game against Arizona, where he was named honorary team captain. He did not play the rest of the season.

In 2010, Best entered the NFL draft and was chosen by the Detroit Lions with the thirtieth pick in the first round. He played for the Lions from 2010 to 2012.

## Life Can Be a Kick When You (Almost) Realize a Dream

Growing up in Dallas in the mid 1960s and '70s, I loved walking across the street to the Jewish Community Center athletic field to kick field goals and punts. I emulated the kicking style of New York Giants placekicker Pete Gogolak, a former soccer player who was one of the first to kick field goals soccer-style. He had a long career, first with Buffalo from 1964 to 1965, then from 1966 to 1974 with New York, where he earned a spot in the Giants' Ring of Honor.

I also loved to punt the football around the field. I had a strong leg, possibly from walking up and down our apartment stairs in New Jersey and Dallas. That also added velocity to my baseball throws, as I used my legs to generate momentum and power. The problem was that there was nowhere for me to display my kicking abilities. My parents did not allow me to play tackle football. Not until my BBYO (B'nai B'rith Youth Organization) days in my mid-to-late teens was there an opportunity to play flag football. We didn't kick field goals and rarely punted, but nonetheless, I enjoyed kicking.

When I graduated Hillcrest High School and went on to the University of Texas in Austin, I still wanted to kick. I was not good enough to make an organized team, much less in college, yet I still dreamed. Fortunately, Memorial Stadium in Austin was open to the public when the Longhorns were not practicing or playing, and no other events were being held. I seized the opportunity to bring my football and punt it up and down the artificial turf field. The field was long and extra wide due to the track that surrounded it. And the south end zone was deep, unlike today's massive new addition.

As a member of *The Daily Texan* sports staff beginning in 1974, I found myself covering Longhorn practices and scrimmages and also writing features. One of my first features was, of course, about the kicking game. I interviewed the two placekickers, Billy "Sure" Schott and Mike Dean.

In 1976, I was awed by freshman placekicker and punter Russell Erxleben, a future consensus three-time, first-team all-American who set the record for the longest field goal in NCAA history: a 67-yard boot, using a tee, against Rice in 1977.

Every time I watched him kick field goals conventional style (straight on), kickoffs, or punts, I was impressed with his leg strength. The ball rocketed off his foot like a knuckleball and didn't begin to spiral until it was halfway up to its apogee. His kickoffs and field goals were the same, with the ball flying through the air until it began to flip end-over-end halfway up.

I copied his punting style and eventually could punt so well that students and locals using the track often asked if I punted for the team. Despite the compliment, I figured they must not have seen a college football game. If they had, then they would have known my range was about 45 yards, while Erxleben's and the average collegiate punter's kick would soar 60 to 70 yards (minus the 15 yards from the line of scrimmage to where the punter kicked the ball).

Twenty years later, I still enjoyed punting. So when our Fox Sports Net football crew was in College Station for a Texas A&M game, I was at Kyle Field late on that Friday—right before the Aggies' walk-through. Usually, the announcers and I watched the practice and talked to players and coaches. Our expert commentator that day was Bucky Richardson, the former Texas A&M quarterback and 1988 Cotton Bowl Classic MVP in the Aggies' win over Notre Dame.

I was on the turf with a football in hands and in my workout gear. How could I pass up the opportunity to relive my Longhorn days and punt the ball around the field? On a clear, ninety-degree day with a light wind, Bucky sat in the shade of the giant press box and watched me kick. I trust he was impressed with my "athletic" ability.

I soon noticed someone walking out of the Aggies' locker room. It looked like a graduate assistant or coach. He watched me kick for a while and then was nice enough to ask if I'd like to kick the ball his way. He'd catch it and then pass it back to me.

"Sure," I said, punting the ball his way. He looked tall, around six foot two, and threw it 40 yards to me like he was a former quarterback. He said I punted it pretty well.

"Is it okay if I punt it back to you?" he asked five minutes later.

"Fine," I said. What I didn't know was that the ball was about to soar 30 yards over my head, high or higher than Erxleben's punts. Wow, that was exceptional for a coach, I thought. As I retrieved the ball, I looked at Bucky Richardson and shook my head with amazement.

"You know who that is, don't you?" said Bucky, matter of factly.

"Hmm, no," I replied. "Should I?"

"That's Shane Lechler," he said. Lechler was a senior punter on the team.

What an opportunity for me to kick with one of the greatest punters of all time! Lechler, a three-time, first-team All-Big 12 selection (1997 to 1999), held the longest career punting average in NCAA history (44.7 yds), was first-team AP All-American in 1999, and played for the Raiders from 2000 to 2012 and the Texans from 2013 to 2017. He became a six-time, first-team all-pro selection and was named to the NFL's all-decade teams of the 2000s and 2010s, as well as the NFL's 100th Anniversary Team.

"So you're Shane Lechler?" I respectfully said. "Thanks for letting me know."

He laughed.

I introduced myself and mentioned that I was producing his game the next day. I told him that it was my dream to punt on the field before a college game. I always loved watching the kickers warm up. He then offered me a chance to realize my dream—one that I couldn't accept—but it was generous of him to offer.

"Would you like to come to Waco next week if you're not working and join me out on the field before the game to warm up and punt with the team? I'm sure [head coach R. C. Slocum] would let you do it."

Texas A&M mascot Reveille VIII, 2010.

Not only did I have another game that week, I added, "I'm not sure how my Longhorn buddies would like me putting on an Aggies jersey."

"The offer stands," he told me.

Thank you, Shane.

## Dodge National Athletic Awards Show Benefiting the March of Dimes

I was proud when Fox Sports Net VP of Production Gary Garcia asked me to produce the Dodge National Athletic Awards Show, which benefited the March of Dimes. Organized with the charity's leaders in Detroit, the annual show was held, appropriately, at the Fox Theatre in downtown. The venue, now listed on the National Register of Historic Places, opened in 1928 as a flagship and largest movie palace for the Fox Theatre chain. It seated five thousand patrons and was fully restored in 1988. It was one of five Fox showcase theatres built then; the others were in Brooklyn, Atlanta, St. Louis, and San Francisco. More recently, it hosted the two-night primary debate for the 2020 Democratic presidential nominees.

After filming the ceremony, Fox Sports Net would nationally air it weeks later on its regional sports networks. My job was to see the big picture, format the show, make a production schedule, logistically keep it moving, and serve as liaison between the March of Dimes, sponsors, network, set designers, and our production personnel. I even contributed ideas for celebrity honorees and helped enlist a few. One of my finest honors was coming on stage—sporting my tuxedo—in front of thousands of guests, patrons, sponsors, and honorees. Like a warmup act, I explained the show and asked for the audience's help in making it an event. After my warmup, I returned to the production truck behind the theatre, but the crew locked me out. They were either embarrassed at my on-stage act, or were toying with me. I believe it was a combination of the two. Eventually they unlocked the truck so I could produce the show.

FSN's fine production people made the event remarkable, including host James Brown (borrowed from CBS Sports), director Anthony Giordano, and feature producer Loy Maxon. During my stint producing the show, these were a few of the iconic sports honorees:

- Carl Lewis—nine-time Olympic gold medalist in track and field (including four consecutive times in the long jump)
- Bob Stoops—head coach, Oklahoma Sooners (2000 national championship, ten-time Big 12 champion)
- Bob Lanier—eight-time NBA All-Star and chairman of the NBA's "Stay in School" program, later renamed "Read to Achieve"

Oklahoma football Head Coach Bob Stoops *(center)* and NASCAR driver Bill Elliott *(right)* at 2001 Dodge National Athletic Awards.

- Roger Clemens—seven-time MLB Cy Young Award winner
- Bill Elliott—two-time Daytona 500 winner who was named one of NASCAR's fifty greatest drivers
- Sean Elliott—San Antonio Spurs champion
- Jackie Joyner-Kersee—three-time Olympic gold medalist in the heptathlon and long jump

## Bayou Bowl All-Star Game

In 2004, I produced the Bayou Bowl, an annual high school all-star football game between top recently graduated seniors from Texas and Louisiana. It was played at Stallworth Stadium in Baytown, Texas, twenty-six miles east of Houston. Texas won, 18–15.

Fox Theatre, Detroit. Dodge National Athletic Awards host venue.

The game's offensive MVP was Texas Tech-bound Danny Amendola of the Woodlands, Texas. The future NFL receiver had a 48-yard punt return and threw an 18-yard end-around touchdown pass to Terrence Nunn of Cypress Falls in the first quarter.

Let's go back to one of the producer's jobs: coordinating with the game officials and the "red hat" (the person on the sideline on headsets with me, who cues the game officials when to start the game, when to go to break, and when to play afterwards).

After running our opening segment with the announcers, we went to the first prekick commercial break. Via headset, I notified our red hat that we were in break and that I would tell him when to cue the game official to hand the ball to the kicker to start the game. That was the red hat's only job, to ensure the officials knew when we were ready to begin. We had established a cueing system to prevent any communication issues. Even then, if our red hat needed to get the referee's attention, he could step on the field. The officials would whistle all play dead, and the game would stop if someone other than the twenty-two players and officials set foot on the field.

For some reason, beyond any comprehension, the kicker placed the ball on the tee. Anticipating that the kickoff was imminent and that we may miss it on television, I pleaded with our red hat to not let them kick. I was bewildered that he failed to go on the field, because we had not yet completed the commercial break.

"Don't let them kick!" I pleaded. "Go out on the field. Don't let them start."

But to no avail. The game began. Or did it?

Our production truck was parked below the press box. I took off my headset, asked director Adam Hinsdale to man the fort, and ran full speed to the stadium gate and onto the field before the first series of downs began. I don't know how I raced there so fast, but I did. Since we had a pregame meeting with the game officials, they were familiar with me. I explained to the referee that we missed the kick and requested that they rekick. To be fair, these game officials were not used to televised games, despite our pregame meeting.

The referee looked confused. How could I be on the field if I was supposed to be producing the game in the truck? I was relieved that he granted our request and made them rekick. We were lucky that the original kickoff did not end up being returned for a touchdown. And since it was only an exhibition all-star game, did it really matter if we started again?

So, that's what a producer does when faced with adverse situations. You think fast.

## ACC Sunday Night Hoops

During the early 2000s, I was assigned a new plum package of prime-time Sunday night ACC basketball games. It fit perfectly into my schedule, as the games occurred after the college football season and during the same time slot as *Sunday Night Fights*, which went on hiatus then. *ACC Sunday Night Hoops* featured storied matchups, with NCAA champion teams such as Duke, North Carolina, North Carolina State, Maryland, and Virginia, and head coaches such as Mike Krzyzewski (Duke), Roy Williams (North Carolina), Leonard Hamilton (Florida State), Herb Sendek (North Carolina State), Gary Williams (Maryland), Skip Prosser (Wake Forest), and Seth Greenberg (Virginia Tech). What a learning session I received while observing their practices and getting to know them on a personal basis.

Our gifted production crew remained virtually constant through the years, including Tim Brando, Dan Bonner, Mike Gminski, reporters Jenn Hildreth and Charles Davis, director Lonnie Dale, and associate director Jil Gossard-Cook, who is now a wonderful, award-winning producer for the Atlanta Hawks.

One year, our boss suggested adding retired ACC legends to our announcing team each week. We spotlighted North Carolina first-team all-American guard Kenny Smith; Clemson academic all-American point guard Bobby Conrad (who became a US attorney general); and David "Skywalker" Thompson, a three-time, first-team all-American and three-time ACC Player of the Year from North Carolina State. Thompson, the number one overall pick by both the ABA Virginia Squires and NBA Atlanta Hawks, eventually signed with the Denver Nuggets. He finished runner-up to Julius Erving in the first-ever slam dunk competition held at the 1976 ABA All-Star Game in Denver and was named MVP.

Thompson's uncanny leaping ability and snazzy slam dunks prompted the nickname "Skywalker." Now, long after playing in his last NBA game for the Seattle Supersonics and in his late forties, he was working with us. At the morning shootaround, while we waited for North Carolina State to begin practice, we shot the breeze with him. Although he was sharply dressed in slacks and street shoes, he said he could still dunk the ball. Was he going to attempt to slam it? We did not want to see him injure himself, but without warming up, he stepped on the court and with just one leap, jammed it. I will never forget that moment. We were in awe. No stretching, no sneakers, no shorts, just 6' 4" David Thompson doing his Skywalker thing right in front of us, two decades after he last played.

Among the coaches I've known, Mike Krzyzewski was both intelligent and impressive to watch. He always took time before or after practice to ask how we were and talk about whatever topic was important to him. Coach K would present us with topics on his agenda at the moment and what he'd like us to convey during the telecast. He had a focused audience listening to his every word—us.

## FSN Big 12 Football Crew Bowling Tournaments

Our Fox Sports Net national Big 12 football package carried stellar games and telecasts through the years. Since our on-air talent and a core crew of technicians traveled together, I thought it would be fun to host an annual bowling tournament on the Friday night before a game each season, after we completed our set day. When

Sideline reporter Laura McKeeman on our FSN football crew in 2012.

I reminisce about the days with those colleagues, they always refer back to our bowling events.

I usually booked the bowling tournaments in smaller towns where I could reserve the lanes. Everyone looked forward to the hijinks and competition. The first classic took place before a game in Stillwater, Oklahoma. The closest bowling alley was in Perry, twenty-five miles away, about one mile east of I-35. I wasn't expecting much, but when we arrived at Strikes! Family Fun Center, we were impressed that it offered neat lanes and the latest computer scoring. One crew member threw the ball so hard, it jumped from his lane to the next and got a strike. Naturally, we counted it.

We also played in Lincoln, Nebraska; at Iowa State in Ames, Iowa; and at the KSU Bowling Lanes in Manhattan, Kansas. These fun social activities helped us establish chemistry and rapport.

In March 2023, play-by-play announcer Mike Morgan reminded me he still has his trophy in his office, with a photo of his winning team. It included our reporter Laura McKeeman, now Laura Rutledge, of ESPN/ABC. When Laura was a newcomer with us, she was the reigning 2012 Miss Florida.

Another future ESPN/ABC talent who was working her way up the proverbial ladder was Michelle Beadle. As an intern for the San Antonio Spurs and a reporter on the team's Coyote Clubhouse show, she possessed a natural on-air ability and a rapport with the people she interviewed. One season on FSN football, she served as the Fox Box score bug operator before making her big jump to TNN, CBS, Yes Network, various entertainment shows, ESPN, and NBC Sports.

# CHAPTER 22

# A Cannon Triggers a Night of "Drench" Warfare

**On November 4, 1994,** during Home Sports Entertainment's (HSE) pregame show on opening night of the basketball season, smoke from a pyrotechnics show triggered a water cannon on the concourse level, soaking fans, players, coaches, and members of the Spurs' ownership group. The deluge of water—which reached all the way onto the east side of the court—blasted at pressures as high as 2,900 gallons per minute for four minutes, according to Alamodome director Mike Abington.

The game between the Golden State Warriors and the San Antonio Spurs was delayed fifty-one minutes. Fans were forced from their seats and scrambled to the arena's corridors, away from the torrent of water. No injuries were reported, although one cameraperson was helped up after he was hit by the rushing stream of water.

Spurs longtime season ticket holder Lee Smith told Epicbuzzer. com, "The water was pushing us. We were forced down the aisle. This will be the most memorable game. We were laughing all the way down."

Spurs All Star David Robinson recalled the night during an interview with MySA. "I do remember the water cannon night. That was almost a surreal experience. Ya know, you never expect something like that to happen. . . . It was comical, really. You can't help but laugh. We were all like this is crazy."

It was startling yet hilarious to see Warriors head coach Don Nelson and his staff waiting it out at the floor-level concession stand to grab a bite. Afterwards, he joined Warriors TV, which had to fill the entire delay.

That was the first of two water situations I encountered during NBA games. The second occurred in New Orleans twenty-four years later.

On February 7, 2018, I was producing a Pacers vs. Pelicans game on a stormy day in New Orleans. During warmups, one player noticed water on the court and saw a stream of drops raining down from the roof. The water formed a puddle near the foul line. The game was delayed while Smoothie King Center's maintenance crew tried to patch the leak. It was no easy task, since accessing that spot on the arena's ceiling proved to be difficult and dangerous.

I immediately informed the Fox Sports SW studio producer that we needed support from the pregame show talent in Irving, Texas. I also alerted our executive producer. The NBA league office was aware, too. As the water dripped onto the court, workers devised a makeshift plan to attach a large tarp to the ceiling to capture the leak. The NBA game officials, coaches, team representatives, and arena personnel occasionally checked the court conditions. So did I, leaving the truck a few times to see what was happening.

Not knowing how long this would last, our announcers threw it back to the studio for fill programming (which included text crawls alerting viewers of the delay). Periodically, viewers were returned to the Smoothie King Center for updates. We rarely had anything new to report, since the information from the team and building personnel was sparse. The team declined to give us any official word and instead directed us to the arena's representatives.

After two hours, Pacers head coach Nate McMillian said, "The guys basically didn't want to play this game under those conditions. The players didn't want to risk injury in the event the makeshift fix didn't hold up for the duration of the game. All it takes is one spot for a player to slip on. Mentally, guys really wouldn't have been able to go out there and play."

The Pelicans' dance team and mascot provided entertainment for almost two hours, but when the decision to postpone was announced, many fans booed. I believe they voiced their displeasure because it took nearly two hours to reach that decision.

The team provided this official statement:

"The New Orleans Pelicans announced that tonight's game against the Indiana Pacers has been postponed by the NBA due to a leak in the roof at the Smoothie King Center. SMG officials worked diligently to address the matter, but the NBA determined to postpone the game out of an abundance of caution for players' safety."

Despite not having a game to televise, we did provide news coverage with reports and interviews with arena officials. Our crew worked a normal full day/evening, as it was close to 9 p.m. when the game was called. The league rescheduled the contest for March 21, which we televised under perfectly dry conditions.

# CHAPTER 23

## *WNBA and the Dallas Wings*

*In July 2015,* the Tulsa Shock of the WNBA announced it would relocate to Dallas and become the Dallas Wings. The team would play at College Park Center, a three-year-old, seven-thousand-seat arena on the campus of the University of Texas at Arlington. (The franchise, founded in 1998 as the Detroit Shock, won three WNBA titles before moving to Tulsa for the 2010 season.)

The Wings' inaugural campaign in Dallas featured an 11–23 record under head coach Fred Williams and leading scorer Skylar Diggins-Smith, the former Notre Dame star. Home telecasts aired on a local UHF station with the action called by Ron Thulin, an excellent, veteran play-by-play announcer, and analyst Raegan Pebley, head coach of TCU women's basketball.

During that initial season, Ron asked for my professional opinion of their production. After watching a few telecasts and attending one game in person to see how the crew prepared and produced the show, I reported back to him and the team.

I provided a litany of recommendations to improve the productions. These were well-received by the team's GM Greg Bibb, Chief Marketing Officer Nicole Smith, Media Relations Director Bianca Gamez, and Thulin.

Months later, after Bibb integrated some of my ideas (along with Thulin's), I was offered a chance to produce the games for

2017. I accepted the role and brought the Wings' telecasts up to speed, making them worthy of airing on Fox Sports SW. We also gave up-and-coming director Eric Delley the chance to work an entire package of games.

Producing their games has been rewarding, especially on Kids' Days each summer, when the team plays at noon to encourage campers to attend. For this special event, thousands of children don matching-colored T-shirts so they do not get lost. This inspired me to capitalize on the theme and invite kids to star in our opening segment, instead of the real announcers. We've done it three times (except for 2020 and 2021, due to COVID-19 protocols).

"A special tip of the hat to our executive producer Bob Steinfeld for his commitment and dedication to producing a best-of-class show," said Bibb, the Wings' president and CEO. "Thank you, Bob."

## Kids' Day Opening Segment, July 2018

Set to animation and music, Fox Sports SW depicted campers arriving outside the arena.

Kid announcer "J" launched our telecast with, "Buses arriving from all over the metroplex with thousands of campers ready to watch today's game between the New York Liberty and Dallas Wings at College Park Center."

The kids, who ranged in age from eight to fourteen, looked cute as they sat in front of the production truck monitors wearing Fox Sports and Dallas Wings t-shirts.

"Hi, I am J along with my friend E. We're here to watch the Dallas Wings play today, but we wanted to tour the Fox TV truck first."

"Next thing we know," E continued, "they handed us microphones and asked us to record an open just like the real announcers."

"Well, uh, I think we got this E," J said unconvincingly, as she nodded yes. "It might be Kids' Day, but the focus should be on the veterans. For the Wings, Skylar Diggins-Smith is having her best

WNBA season. Her scoring is up, and she's having a ball playing with Liz Cambage. I'd just like to see her minutes decrease a bit. Long season."

E added, "For the Liberty, you have to fear Tina Charles. The former MVP scored 34 points when they played the Wings in May. Hopefully the Wings will match her strong presence inside."

"I think we might have a future in broadcasting," J told her, "but for now, I am actually excited to watch the game. We better get inside."

"Exactly," E agreed. "So let's toss it inside to Ron Thulin and Christa Gerlach, who's calling today's action."

The two adorable kids then high-fived each other, acknowledging they did a splendid job!

We recorded Kids' Day segments two additional times, including in 2022 with drama students from a Fort Worth private school. Here's how they did:

## Aces vs. Wings: June 15, 2022

We crowned each of the children with an official sports broadcaster title: producer "A"; director "C"; graphics associate producer "E"; play-by-play "G"; and expert analyst "H."

G: "Welcome to camp day at College Park Center, where the young, emerging Dallas Wings host the first-place Las Vegas Aces. Now, let's check out the Bally Sports SW production truck as we get ready for today's game."

A: "We have a lot of great storylines today. I hope you did your homework, Mr. Director."

C: "Well, yes, Ms. Producer. I started reading your rundown after camp and videogames. But next time would it be possible to actually spell out the words? I'm not really good with acronyms and emojis. Like, what does P-I-T-M-D mean?"

A: "That stands for 'push in tighter, Mr. Director.' As the drama unfolds, you need to direct your camera ops to use their glass."

C: "Got you. Hey, Clara, what's that on your graphics monitor? You texting again in the truck?"

The monitor showed the letters L-S-T-S.

E: "Hey, sorry, just trying to tell you 'Let's start the show!'"

A: "You're right, let's start. G and H, can you hear me? Or do I need to come out there and get you ready myself?" (G and H are ignoring her.) "Hey, if you guys don't stop fooling around, we'll miss the tip. So, let's do this. Three . . . two . . . one . . ."

The WNBA opening animation then keyed into a shot of the arena.

G: "From College Park Center in Arlington, Texas, it's a special camp day show as the Dallas Wings host the Las Vegas Aces on Bally Sports Southwest. Hello everyone, I'm 'G,' with my classmate and friend 'H.' I don't believe you know too much about basketball, but your mother does, right?"

She feigned being offended.

H: "Hey! Yes, my mom, the head coach of the TCU women's basketball team, tried to offer suggestions, but as the analyst today I *did* my homework. Arike Ogunbowale is their leading scorer, but I've been very impressed with the play of Allisha Gray, who came into camp in the best shape of her career, and her stats prove it. That doesn't surprise me. She was the 2017 WNBA Rookie of the Year."

G: "That's impressive. Are you sure that didn't come from your mom?"

H (shaking her head): "Please!"

G: "So, what about the first place Las Vegas Aces?"

H: "Well, glad you asked, 'G.' The Aces feature a very talented squad with a lot of depth. But I especially like shooting guard Kelsey Plum. You know, she is the all-time leading scorer in college basketball history, so it's not surprising she can pour in the points. And that's what she did against the Wings on June 5, tying her career high with 32 points. Controlling her will be key for Dallas today."

G: "It will be a great game today on Bally Sports Southwest, so when we come back we'll hand over the mikes to the 'old folks,' Ron Thulin and Raegan Pebley. Or will we?"

———————

In 2023, I concluded my seventh year producing the Wings. Team President Greg Bibb signed me to be executive producer for both the Wings and their sister franchise in the National Lacrosse League, the Panther City Lacrosse Club, which played out of Dickies Arena in Fort Worth during the winter when the Wings' season is dormant.

Our WNBA budget and equipment is less than an NBA team's minimum, so our telecasts don't have all the bells and whistles, such as multiple replay operators.

We do have a reporter, which I love to integrate into our shows. Up-and-coming talent appreciate the chance to learn from our production team and get on-camera experience with national exposure on WNBA League Pass, Amazon, and CBS Sports. During year one, I hired two reporters and split their assignments.

One was Jada Butts, a former basketball player for Raegan and TCU. The other was Alexa Shaw, a TCU broadcast journalism student who worked for head coach Gary Patterson's football program. Both did well, but Alexa really stood out. She was a natural, just like Michelle Beadle when she started her career with the San Antonio Spurs.

Alexa worked all the games during her second year. Early in her third year—soon after graduating from TCU—she was hired by NBC Washington regional sports channel to host a studio show. One year later, she was NBC's studio host at the Olympics.

Next, we hired Katie Engleson from Bally Sports SW for one campaign. After COVID-19 hit, we did not use any reporter for two seasons.

In 2022, we resumed full productions at home and enlisted Maggie Hale, a raw young freshman reporter recommended by Mike Martin, her broadcast journalism professor at TCU. I first worked with her on Panther City lacrosse games before I thought she was ready for WNBA.

We also employed Jen Hale—no relation to Maggie—who had been my colleague with the New Orleans Pelicans for six years. Jen is a sideline reporter for Fox's NFL games and shows., including then *Skip & Shannon: Undisputed* on FS1.

In 2023, ShaVonne Herndon, from Houston, took over the reporter role. Her love and knowledge of basketball, and especially the WNBA, made her an instant success on our telecasts.

That same year, former University of Texas basketball great Fran Harris filled in for Raegan Pebley when she had other commitments. Fran was a star on the UT Longhorns national championship in 1986 and has developed an impressive career in the business world and in broadcasting. In addition to pitching her sports drink company on ABC's *Shark Tank*, she has appeared as a host and interior designer on HGTV, provides play-by-play and expert commentary on ESPN, and helps organize grass roots basketball endeavors in our hometown Dallas.

Among our newest players that season was 2019 WNBA All-Star Diamond DeShields, who won an WNBA title with the Chicago Sky in 2022. Diamond is the daughter of former MLB second baseman Delino DeShields and the younger sister of former Texas Rangers outfielder Delino DeShields Jr.

In 2019, while playing professionally in the WNBA offseason in Turkey, she suffered a back injury. An MRI revealed a tumor in her spine, which posed a risk of paralysis. After surgery, she struggled to recover mentally and physically, uncertain if she would ever play again. She persevered, however. As she mentioned during her introductory press conference, her father offered her the best advice: "You are in control, so be in control."

That's a lesson to which we all should subscribe.

But Diamond never played for the Wings that first season, due to a preseason knee injury.

My most enjoyable season proved to be 2023, because the team finished as the number four seed and earned homecourt advantage in the first round of the playoffs. They defeated the Atlanta Dream three games to none, then faced the top-seeded, defending champion Las Vegas Aces. But the Aces, coached by Naismith Memorial Basketball Hall of Fame head coach Becky Hammon and led by superstar talent such as former WNBA MVP and 2023 WNBA Defensive Player of the Year A'ja Wilson, were too much to handle. The Wings were swept in three games, yet they came close to winning the final one in Arlington.

The Wings exceeded GM Greg Bibb's realistic goal of hosting the first round. Much of that success stemmed from new head coach Latricia Trammell, who established a positive, family-like culture on and off the court. Wings forward Satou Sabally and guard Arike Ogunbowale were named to the WNBA All-Star Game, while Sabally was named Associated Press and WNBA Most Improved Player and was selected to the All-WNBA First Team.

ESPN/Disney had exclusive rights to Wings' playoff games, but I was fortunate to be asked by the league to work those games with the best seat in the house as the court administrator/time-out coordinator. More on that role in an upcoming chapter.

In 2024, our expert analyst Raegan Pebley accepted an offer to become the general manager of the Los Angeles Sparks. We not only lost an excellent broadcaster, but a person we all admired and respected. We wished her the best with the Sparks—except when they were playing our Wings.

To replace her, I suggested we first ask our Wings Ambassador and Naismith Memorial Hall of Famer Nancy Lieberman if she'd

Our original Dallas Wings broadcast team on Fox Sports SW. *Front row:* Ron Thulin (PBP); Raegan Pebley (analyst); and Alexa Shaw (reporter). *Back row:* John Jagou (assistant producer); Yours Truly (producer); and Eric Delley (director).

like to do a few games. As you know, I am friends with "Lady Magic," and I thought she'd be a great addition if available. Wings COO Amber Cox made it happen. I then offered selected games to Hall of Famer Sheryl Swoopes. She really wanted to be back in the WNBA after an illustrious career as one of the greatest players ever with the four-time WNBA champion Houston Comets (1997–2000). We booked her for seven home games. As mentioned, I hired Fran Harris to rejoin our shows for an increased number of games. Harris was named to the Southwest Conference All-Decade Team and was SWC Player of the Year in 1984–85. Coincidentally, she was a teammate of Swoopes on the Houston Comets 1997 WNBA Championship team. She later played for the Utah Starzz.

# ESPN and Lifetime Cover the WNBA's Infancy

My tenure with the Dallas Wings was not my first foray into the WNBA. In fact, I have been involved with the league since its inception.

In 1997, while freelancing for various networks, ESPN invited me to produce the inaugural season of the WNBA on Lifetime Television and ESPN. I thought that helping launch a new league would be a unique challenge. I had two announce crews. For Lifetime, Michele Tafoya handled play-by-play. Analysts were: Reggie Miller, an active Indiana Pacers all-star (who was later named to the NBA 75th Anniversary Team and the hall of fame); 1990s University of Connecticut star Meghan Pattyson; and swimmer Summer Sanders, a two-time Olympic gold medalist, who was early in her broadcast career.

On ESPN telecasts, Robin Roberts provided play-by-play, while UConn women's basketball head coach Geno Auriemma offered analysis.

While in Sacramento that inaugural year, young ESPN director Mike Schwab and I attended a Monarchs' practice and afterwards played a two-on-two game against a couple of Monarchs. I was in my early forties and in good shape, jogging regularly and playing hoops a couple times each week. I thought I could compete. Schwabby was younger and could play, too. One player was Corrisa Yasen, a 6-foot rookie guard from Purdue University, where she was named female athlete of the year in her junior and senior seasons and was the Big Ten Athlete of the Year. Additionally, she won the NCAA heptathlon title in 1996.

Yasen and a frontcourt player challenged us to play two-on-two, and we accepted. It was a back and forth contest to ten baskets, but ultimately we won. The real question was, did we win, or did they let us win? It appeared we won legitimately, until Reggie Miller, watching from the sidelines, said he would take the place of the taller player and run it again with Yasen. Suddenly, Yasen flashed her pedigree and was instantly much better. Schwabby recently told me that Reggie complimented him that day, saying he "played defense well," before Reggie drove and dunked over his head. Otherwise, Reggie just kept feeding the ball to Yasen, who schooled us—and me—every chance she had. We met our match and thanked the Monarch players for letting us "win" the first game. It was also a blast playing against Reggie.

Our productions went smoothly. After the season ended, Lifetime's executive producer congratulated us and commended our efforts. Weeks later, unfortunately, he said that despite our fine work, his boss wanted the next year's production truck to solely use women in above-line positions: producer, director, associate director, associate producer, and production assistants. Although that made sense, it put several people out of work . . . including me.

As a freelancer, I had little recourse. During the subsequent months and years, many ESPN personnel said, "I heard you were suing ESPN for reverse discrimination." That was never true.

If your boss says you are being replaced due to your gender, it might appear to qualify as a legal transgression. Yet I simply did not want to pursue it. The climate then was unlike today, where we witness a proliferation of lawsuits in network television. If I did pursue litigation, it might have been professional suicide. Both then and now, I remain a proponent of women's rights, equality, and fairness. I've covered women's sports with the same zest and energy as any game, no matter the gender. Yes, it was hard to accept being replaced in that manner. Mentally, I felt really down. Was doing freelance the right road? Despite decisions beyond my control, I maintained my confidence. Many years later, I was back in the WNBA and thriving, producing games on various networks.

## WNBA Commissioner's Cup Championships

The WNBA also gave me opportunities to produce major events for the league. This included a CBS national game between the

Washington Mystics and Dallas Wings in 2021, with play-by-play announcer Lisa Byington and analyst Lisa Leslie, who ESPN.com named the fifth greatest WNBA player of all time in 2021. That widely viewed broadcast was fantastic, because Byington was able to set up Leslie to discuss being a team leader. I made sure we had flashback vignettes from Leslie's career, including video from 2002 when she became the first WNBA player to dunk.

In the 2021 inaugural Commissioner's Cup championship between the Seattle Storm and Connecticut Sun in Phoenix (again with the two Lisas, plus reporter Anne Marie Anderson), the circumstances were unique. Five days earlier, Seattle's Breanna Stewart, Sue Bird, and Jewell Lloyd helped the United States win its seventh consecutive Olympic gold medal. Now they were in Arizona playing for another championship and money. They showed no signs of jet lag.

Our production incorporated next-generation tracking technology. Players wore sensors that provided data, such as how fast they sprinted or how often they jumped. For all sports, this new state-of-the-art tracking represents a quantum leap in how fans view telecasts, how oddsmakers create betting lines, and even how player agents and franchises negotiate salaries.

Moreover, optical tracking technology generated three-dimensional immersive highlights that we sprinkled throughout the Amazon Prime telecast. Rush Media had several trucks at the Footprint Center to combine that technology with our camera and replay sources.

The Storm trio carried their team to a resounding 79–57 victory, leading by 28 points heading into the fourth quarter. Storm players earned in excess of thirty thousand dollars each, while Sun players earned ten thousand dollars each, according to the league's postgame story.

*"First time I worked with Bob it was for the WNBA's inaugural Commissioner's Cup game. Few people in the business will outwork Bob. In fact, I think he blends the suggestions and observations of*

*a grizzled vet in the business with the enthusiasm of a rookie doing this job for the first time."*

— LISA BYINGTON, Milwaukee Bucks (NBA) and Chicago Sky (WNBA) play-by-play; CBS March Madness play-by-play

In 2022, I returned to my role producing the Commissioner's Cup championship, this time as the Las Vegas Aces battled the Chicago Sky. The league hired Yes Network's play-by-play Michael Grady; Naismith Basketball hall of famer Dawn Staley, head coach of South Carolina and Team USA; former DePaul hoops star and Yes Network commentator Sarah Kustok; plus reporter Zora Stephenson, who worked on Milwaukee Bucks and Yes Network telecasts.

The matchup featured the defending WNBA champion Chicago Sky, led by all stars Candace Parker and Courtney Vandersloot, versus the surging Las Vegas Aces, whose own bevy of stars included A'ja Wilson, Kelsey Plum, Chelsea Gray, and Jackie Young. Parker played magnificently in front of her hometown fans at Chicago's

2021 WNBA Commissioner's Cup Championship Production Team. *Left to right:* Hall of Famer Lisa Leslie (commentator); Anne Marie Anderson (sideline); me (Producer); and Lisa Byington (PBP).

2022 WNBA Commissioner's Cup Championship Production Team.
*Left to right:* Sarah Kustok (commentator); Michael Grady (PBP); me
(producer); Hall of Famer Dawn Staley (commentator); Zora Stephenson (reporter).

Wintrust Arena, amassing 20 points and 14 rebounds, but it wasn't enough to hold off the strong Aces squad, who won 93–83. Plum led the way with 24 points, while MVP Gray added 19.

Our production truck, provided by Ross Production Services, was parked outside the venue, where I was positioned next to our director, graphics coordinator, and associate director. We produced many vignettes—also called "bumpers," which are sandwiched between commercials—that spelled out the league's initiatives. This not only rewarded players, but provided an additional pool of money for charitable and civic organizations.

## CBS National Telecast

On June 20, 2023, I produced a CBS national telecast between the Seattle Storm and Dallas Wings at College Park Center. Although I was employed by Rush Media—the production company that packaged the event for the NBA—I still worked with CBS's New York production personnel, including coordinating producer Todd Keryc and game supervising producer Jawn Morales. As I handled the game for the esteemed "Tiffany Network," I reflected on that moment from the 1980s when I turned down CBS's wonderful offer to join their staff full-time in New York.

This time, I collaborated with basketball legend Sheryl Swoopes. The four-time WNBA champion was a six-time WNBA All-Star, three-time Olympic gold medalist, 1993 NCAA champion at Texas Tech, and a 2016 Naismith Memorial Basketball Hall of Fame inductee.

It's not too often that an analyst possesses that many accolades, so when you produce a game like that, you make sure you showcase her resume. That's why I procured video of her historic Houston Comets game from July 27, 1999, when she became the first WNBA player to ever record a triple-double: 14 points, 15 rebounds, and 10 assists.

Our associate producer, John Jagou, created a smart-looking animated graphic that highlighted Swoopes's achievements. Our reporter, Morgan Ragan, who regularly works for the Sacramento Kings, teed up the graphic and the triple-double footage before we showed Sheryl at the table with play-by-play announcer Pat Boylan.

I smiled when it appeared that Sheryl was touched by the gesture. The arena's public address announcer, John Liddle, proudly acknowledged her to the College Park Center fans.

We later showed Sheryl's Houston Comets 1997 WNBA championship team photo and a 1996 Team USA poster (signed by every team member), which was hung in my daughter's bedroom. It was a gift to me from USA Basketball for producing Team USA games. I took a picture of it and used it on the air.

CBS National Telecast Broadcast Crew for Seattle Storm vs. Dallas Wings June 20, 2023. *Left to right:* Hall of Famer Sheryl Swoopes (commentator); Morgan Ragan (reporter); Pat Boylan (PBP); and me (producer).

## Caitlin Clark's First-Ever Professional Basketball Game

As I began preparations for the 2024 season, I noticed that our single Wings preseason home game, May 3, was going to be against the Indiana Fever, which held the first overall pick in the April 15 WNBA Draft. The presumptive first pick would be Iowa's Caitlin Clark, who was being hailed as the best collegiate player since Connecticut's Diana Taurasi in 2004. Taurasi is the WNBA's all-time leading scorer and recognized as the best player in league history.

Now, we've never televised a preseason game; in fact, we had already announced our regular season television schedule, but I touched base with COO Amber Cox and suggested that we do so. It would be a fantastic opportunity to promote our ticket sales (though our season tickets were already sold out for the first time), show off our team and personalities, and market "our" product while we had national eyeballs wanting to see Caitlin's first professional game. How would she do against the best players in the world? The game, originally scheduled for 11:30 a.m., was moved to primetime, 7 p.m., and voilà, our game was added to the schedule. Now, all we needed was for the Fever to select Clark and that she would play in the game. I have to hand it to our president and CEO Greg Bibb for having the foresight to schedule the game with Indiana months before she decided to forgo her final season of eligibility at Iowa—which of course she did to live her dream to play in the WNBA.

The game was picked up by WNBA League Pass and Bally Sports SW Extra regionally, but when the NBA Dallas Mavericks and NHL Dallas Stars playoffs series extended and suddenly were scheduled that same evening, along with the Texas Rangers, Bally Sports SW had to move our game to BallySports.com and its app. Still, WNBA League Pass gave the game national distribution.

I spent many weeks prepping for that historic telecast—Caitlin's first-ever professional game, but since we were a Wings telecast, we would focus most storylines on our team, not Caitlin Clark's Indiana Fever. I arrived at College Park Center at 9:30 a.m. to attend the Wings shootaround practice at 10:00 a.m. followed by Indiana's at 11:00 a.m. Most of our announcers were there, too. Those shootarounds are a great way to see how teams will play against their opponent that night. The coaches go over scouting reports (opponent's tendencies, strengths and weaknesses) and how they will execute against that in this game. It helps to attend those shootarounds so we can learn what the players are learning. You can also speak to players afterwards.

When it was time for Indiana to practice, there were at least twenty-five camera crews on the side of the court for the first fifteen minutes until Indiana's Director of Media Relations asked everyone to leave so the team could practice privately for forty-five minutes, and then they would reopen for coach and then player interviews. It was the most reporters and cameras I'd ever seen at a WNBA shootaround in Arlington. When Caitlin Clark stepped up to the microphone, reporters asked her questions for about fifteen minutes, which is long for a shootaround. It showed the enormous impact the rookie was already having on the league. I was standing immediately to Clark's right. When the opportunity allowed, I said, "Caitlin, I know you are very proud of your passing ability. How much are looking forward to serving it up to the 'bigs' like Aliyah Boston? How's that been in practice this week?"

She smiled, then spoke about how great it's been and how she was looking forward to it in tonight's game.

After the interview, I went to the production truck, parked in the loading dock, and met with our crew to get the truck's equipment loaded up with elements for the show, including highlights, graphics, music, and animations.

The day was going well. I held our production meeting at 4:00 p.m. with announcers Ron Thulin and Sheryl Swoopes and reporter ShaVonne Herndon, plus our director Scott Dailey, associate producer John Jagou, stage manager Knisha Godfrey (a TCU Horned Frogs basketball player), and intern Aaliyah Moore (a Texas Longhorn basketball player), who would be shadowing Herndon that evening.

The meeting was going smoothly. I reviewed our production schedule, storylines, and goals for the evening, and then at 4:20 p.m. I received a text from my daughter, Elaine, that my mother-in-law, Lola Esquenazi, who was in hospice care, had just passed away. I had visited her at the hospice in North Dallas before heading to the shootarounds that morning. I knew the situation was grave when I left to head to Arlington, so I had a plan B standing by in case I could not produce the game—John Jagou would step up.

The game was only two and a half hours from tip. The show was ready to go. We had a set plan. Everyone knew the schedule and what to do. Even my Run of Show (format with specific instructions/storylines) was specific. I felt I needed to be with Sarah and the rest of the family. I had worked so hard to get that historic show ready, but G-d had a different plan. When leaving the building, I reached my wife by phone. She said I should stay to produce the game, but my heart was saying to be with her. On top of that, it was our forty-third anniversary. When I arrived at the hospice and saw my family and Sarah's brothers, I knew I had made the right decision.

As far as the game, Caitlin Clark scored 21 points and looked great, but Arike Ogunbowale hit a game-winning 3-pointer with a few seconds left to win it. Clark took a desperation 3 as time expired, but the ball hit the side of the backboard. The Wings won 79-76 in front of a sold-out preseason game crowd.

In life there's happiness and sadness. There are good times, bad times, and times to reflect. I experienced so many emotions in one day. In the end, my family counted the most. I appreciated the understanding from the Wings family, league associates, our production crew and announcers.

# The Caitlin Clark Effect: Dazzling Record-Setting Performance vs Wings

There's no doubt the popularity in the WNBA surged following the selection of Caitlin Clark by the Indiana Fever with its #1 pick in the 2024 WNBA draft. The impact was not only felt in Indianapolis but throughout the league, as most teams decided to move her games to larger venues due to never-before-seen ticket demand. TV ratings followed her from college too, which resulted in a new, increased eleven-year media rights deal, beginning in the 2025–2026 season, with The Walt Disney Company, NBCUniversal, and Amazon, with the anticipated addition of other networks.

So, on July 17, 2024, when the deal was reported by national media sources, Clark was in Arlington, Texas, at sold-out College Park Center to play the Dallas Wings in a nationally televised game on ESPN. The WNBA hired me to work as Court Administrator / Time Out Coordinator (more on that role in Chapter 26).

And Clark shone. She put on a thrilling performance scoring 24 points and set a WNBA record dishing out 19 assists, surpassing the 18 by Chicago's Courtney Vandersloot in 2020. Clark dazzled the fans, and me, with behind-the-back dribbles and passes. While most fans are familiar with her uncanny long-range shooting ability "from the logo" as many call it, she's equally as dangerous distributing the ball. She has the talent and vision like the greatest passers of all time, such as the NBA Lakers' Magic Johnson and WNBA all-time greats Tina Penicheiro and Sue Bird (the league's all-time assist leader). As defenders collapsed, each of those stars had the talent to pass the ball not where you "are" but where you "will be." And Clark did that time after time in this game. But even that record-setting performance was not enough as the Wings' Arike Ogunbowale hit a dagger, off-balance three pointer (just before the shot clock expired) with 44.6 seconds left in the game, basically sealing the victory.

In my role, I sat near midcourt at the scorer's table and witnessed one of the greatest rookie performances in WNBA history and a much-needed win for the Dallas Wings.

# CHAPTER 24

## *"Lady Magic," Nancy Lieberman*

***When you think of the premier players*** and contributors in American women's basketball history, names come to mind like Sue Bird, Diana Taurasi, Candace Parker, Maya Moore, A'ja Wilson, Breanna Stewart, Tina Thompson, Sheryl Swoopes, Tamika Catchings, Ann Meyers, Cynthia Cooper, and Cheryl Miller. One player, however, who became a personal and professional friend of mine was Nancy "Lady Magic" Lieberman.

At Old Dominion, Nancy became the first two-time winner of the Wade Trophy presented to the nation's top women's basketball player. She led the school to consecutive Association for Intercollegiate Athletics for Women national championships in 1979 and 1980. She was a three-time Kodak All-American. On November 5, 2022, Old Dominion unveiled a six-foot bronze statue of her. She is the first person to be immortalized on its campus. Additionally, a portion of the campus's 43rd Street was dedicated "Nancy Lieberman Pass."

She represented the United States on the 1975 Pan American team when she was only seventeen years old and a senior at Far Rockaway High School in Queens, New York. In 1976, she was a member of the first-ever USA women's Olympic team that won the silver medal in Montreal.

Nancy was the number one overall pick in the Women's Pro Basketball League (WBL) for the Dallas Diamonds in 1981 and was named Rookie of the Year, averaging 26.3 points per game. After playing for the Los Angeles Lakers' summer pro league team in 1981, she returned to the Dallas Diamonds of the Women's American Basketball Association in 1984, averaging 27 points per game, earning league MVP honors, and leading the team to the WABA championship.

In 1986, she played for Springfield in the men's United States Basketball League (USBL). Later, she joined the Washington Generals, the not-so-fortunate regular opponent of the iconic, world traveling Harlem Globetrotters.

At thirty-nine years old in 1997, she suited up for the Phoenix Mercury for the inaugural season of the WNBA. In 2008, at fifty years old, she signed a seven-day contract and played one game with the Detroit Shock, becoming the oldest player in league history.

The basketball lifer was hired as general manager and head coach of the WNBA's Detroit Shock in 1998. During her three seasons, Detroit became the first expansion team to make the playoffs.

Nancy then worked in the NBA G League as coach and assistant GM of the Texas Legends, guiding them to the playoffs in her first season. Later she moved into a front-office position while joining Fox Sports as analyst for NBA games.

In 2015, she became only the second female assistant coach in NBA history, joining the Sacramento Kings.

When she became a studio commentator for my New Orleans Pelicans telecasts, the pregame show occasionally originated from New Orleans. When that happened, I made sure to have her join us on headset for a quarter to provide her perspective.

Coaching remained in her blood, however, prompting her to accept an offer from Ice Cube. The actor, rapper, songwriter, and filmmaker, who founded the BIG3 League, asked Nancy to serve as the first female head coach of a men's professional team. She guided the Power to the 2018 title and was named Coach of the Year, another first for women.

Oh—and the prestigious Nancy Lieberman Award is presented annually by the Naismith Basketball Hall of Fame to the nation's top point guard in women's Division 1 hoops.

Nancy's achievements have been recognized by her peers. She was inducted into the Naismith Memorial Basketball Hall of Fame, the Women's Basketball Hall of Fame, the Nassau County (New York) Sports Hall of Fame, the St. Louis Jewish Sports Hall of Fame, and the Virginia Sports Hall of Fame.

June 23, 2022 marked the historic fiftieth anniversary of the passage of Title IX, the federal civil rights legislation credited with bringing gender equity to education and sports. As producer of the WNBA Dallas Wings, I felt that would be a fitting night to spotlight Nancy. Who better to talk about Title IX than a person whose life and career were positively affected by that law? When the Wings faced the Indiana Fever in Arlington, Texas, I invited her to join Ron Thulin and Raegan Pebley on headsets during the game, which was carried nationally on CBS Sports Network and WNBA League Pass, plus regionally on Bally Sports SW.

I asked Nancy to record an opening tease script that I wrote. Although she was bopping in and out of town for hall of fame responsibilities and coaching BIG3, she found a few hours for me to visit her home, just ten minutes from mine in Dallas. The following text scrolled on screen before Nancy began speaking:

*No person in the United States shall, on the basis of sex, be excluded from participation in, be denied benefits of, or be subjected to discrimination under any educational program or activity receiving federal financial assistance.*

Nancy then delivered her powerful message:

Despite wide-ranging goals, Title IX is most famous for its impact on expanding opportunities for women and girls in

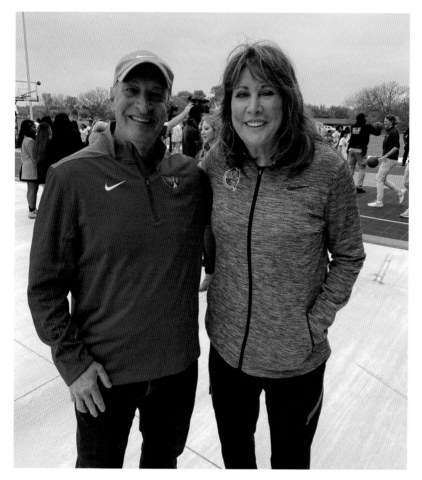

I joined Naismith Memorial Basketball Hall of Famer Nancy Lieberman at the dedication of one her Dream Courts in Dallas in 2023.

sports. In 1971–1972, just under 300,000 girls participated in high school sports. By 2018–19, it blossomed into 3.4 million, an 11-time increase.

Hi, I'm Nancy Lieberman. I'm thankful for Title IX, the positive impact it had on me, and for those playing in tonight's WNBA game between the Indiana Fever and Dallas Wings. Enjoy the show!

On the same evening of the anniversary of Title IX, I did a little research and discovered that three of the rookie guards playing in our game were 2022 Nancy Lieberman Award nominees: Indiana Fever's Kayla Pointer (LSU) and Destanni Henderson (South Carolina); and the Dallas Wings' Veronica Burton (Northwestern).

Nancy was thrilled to hear that and wanted to meet and take photos with them. The Wings provided her front-row seats, and she enjoyed the evening from many perspectives. The WNBA and CBS appreciated our efforts to honor this female sports icon.

My first time working with Nancy dates way back to her Dallas Diamonds days when we teamed up on collegiate basketball games for HSE and ESPN. In 2011, we also collaborated on the Dallas Mavericks' championship parade telecast. This was a seminal moment in the history of the city of Dallas, and it was significant to me as producer, since I began my NBA career with the Mavericks in 1980.

It is hard to find anyone with more combined basketball and broadcast knowledge than Nancy.

While she understands what it takes to get a show on the air, and how to get a team to play together and win a championship, her virtues extend far beyond that. She constantly gives back to the community with her Nancy Lieberman Charities, which has donated more than $25 million to underserved communities nationwide since 1980.

Her "Dream Court" initiative has led to the construction of more than 120 courts paired with educational programs. Ninety high school seniors have been sent to college, and more than 5.1 million students a year benefit from her charity efforts. Nancy, who received the Dr. Martin Luther King Civil Rights Award in Memphis, Tennessee, on January 16, 2023, remains dedicated to expanding and ensuring that educational and sports opportunities exist for economically disadvantaged youth. Approximately 85 percent of the students she supports via basketball camps, Dream Courts, college scholarships, and school supplies programs are from low-to-moderate-income families.

In 2013, Nancy teamed up with comedian, actor, and film director Billy Crystal to unveil a Dream Court in Crystal's Long Island hometown of Long Beach, New York. This boosted the recovery efforts from Superstorm Sandy. In 2022, she joined with Vanessa Bryant to open three Kobe and Gigi Dream Courts in Anaheim, California, and in Kobe's hometown of Lower Marion, Pennsylvania.

The day before her statue was unveiled at Old Dominion, Nancy Lieberman Charities and Pepsi Stronger Together dedicated a Dream Court at East Ocean View Recreation Center in Norfolk, Virginia. It was the 116th Dream Court donated by her charity in underserved neighborhoods.

Nancy's son, T. J. Cline, a professional basketball player himself, follows his mother's footsteps as a community activist. Cline, the 2017 Atlantic 10 Player of the Year for the Richmond Spiders and AP Honorable Mention All-American, helps her teach kids about leadership skills, basketball fundamentals, drug and alcohol awareness, handling peer pressure, and getting a good education.

Just get Nancy started on any of these topics, and you'll need to buzzer her off the court.

On February 11, 2023, Nancy again broke barriers by earning an award traditionally presented to outstanding individuals in the NFL community who devote their time to community issues and the welfare of humanity. The Humanitarian Awards, bestowed during Super Bowl week, usually honor a team owner, coach, general manager, current player, and/or retired player.

The Humanitarian Awards were held at the twenty-sixth annual Leigh Steinberg Super Bowl Party. Organizers lauded Nancy as "a visionary who's not only broken the mold for what it means to be an athlete, but for someone who has also developed strategies to address some of the world's most challenging inequities in business, sports, social justice, diversity, and inclusion within the entertainment industry."

Nancy has a warm heart, as well. After I suffered a heart attack during a flight to New Orleans and had successful quadruple bypass surgery, few people outside my family checked up on me more than her. She frequently phoned to see how I was and if she could do anything to help. Just hearing her voice and knowing how much she cared meant a lot. Lady Magic, a hall of famer who is constantly on the run and being pulled in myriad directions every day, somehow still found time to call me. Thank you, Nancy, for your care and friendship.

# CHAPTER 25
## *Superstars Surpassing My Expectations*

*Although I've met many superstar athletes* and broadcasters, a few truly exceeded my expectations and perceptions. I already held each in high regard, based on reputation and the quality of their athletic or journalistic achievements. Yet when I first encountered members of this group, I walked away amazed. Sports history is littered with tales of fans who were disappointed when they finally saw their hero face-to-face and were crushed to discover that their real-life persona was anything but heroic. Let me present five superstars who represent just the opposite:

1. **David Robinson of the San Antonio Spurs**
   Whenever I spoke to "The Admiral" or worked with him during my years with the Spurs, I was always impressed with the engaging way he carried himself. His parents were in the military, so his upbringing was quite disciplined. The Naval Academy graduate was friendly, and he respected that you had a job to do. He never put himself in a position to fail. He was also a big influence in San Antonio, where he helped to establish the Carver Academy and his foundation.

2. **Cal Ripken Jr.**
   The Baltimore Orioles icon is as A-list a sports star as there is. As I wrote earlier in this book, I collaborated with

him on the Cal Ripken World Series and got to know him fairly well. He was tall for a shortstop at 6 foot 4. For a superstar comparison, pitcher Nolan Ryan is 6 foot 2, shortstop Derek Jeter is 6 foot 3, outfielder Barry Bonds is 6 foot 2, outfielder Mike Trout is 6 foot 2, and shortstop Corey Seager is 6 foot 4. According to Baseball Scouter, the average big league shortstop is 6 foot. Whenever I was with Cal, I could sense his love of the game and his family's legacy within the sport. Cal was warm, friendly, and always engaged during our meetings and planning sessions. I felt like I was with a good friend.

3. **Robin Roberts**

The ESPN broadcaster was part of the telecasts I produced for the WNBA's inaugural season in 1997 (along with Geno Auriemma, head coach of UConn women's basketball team). Working with Robin, I felt like she was a close friend, even though it was the first time we collaborated. Her sincerity and drive to succeed made her a zero-maintenance colleague. I marveled at the work she did in her home state of Mississippi and at Southeastern Louisiana University, where she graduated cum laude in 1983 and played basketball. More impressive was the courageous way she fought and beat myelodysplastic syndrome, a form of blood cancer. Her chronicle of her illness, which aired on ABC's *Good Morning America*, earned her the Peabody Award in 2012.

In November 2023, officials at Southeastern Louisiana University broke ground on the Robin Roberts Broadcast Media Center and the $40 million renovation of D. Vickers Hall. The center will add thirty-three thousand square feet to the academic building and include three broadcast media studios with a newsroom, film studio, and multimedia studio. The project on the Southeastern campus will be paid by Capital Outlay funds and a partnership donation from Roberts herself.

"I am so incredibly proud . . . to know that this broadcast center is going to attract students from all over the country and the world," Roberts told the crowd in attendance. "But more importantly, to know that we're going to allow them to have big dreams . . . and have those dreams come true."

4. **Bob Costas**

You hold certain people in high regard, yet only a few surpass your expectations. This NBC sportscasting legend was one of them. If you missed the chapter about my interactions with Bob at the Barcelona Olympics and in the United States, give it a read.

5. **Merle Harmon—Announcer Texas Rangers Baseball 1982–89**

When I think of the nicest, most respectful, humble, professional, and kindest announcers I've worked with, it would be hard to top play-by-play talent Merle Harmon. By the time I had the privilege to produce his games on Home Sports Entertainment he was in the twilight of his illustrious broadcasting career. And what an amazing life he led in and outside the booth.

He served in the United States Navy in the Pacific in World War II, then went on to earn his degree in radio and television broadcasting and marketing from the University of Denver in 1949. He cut his teeth in broadcasting that same year calling minor league baseball in Topeka, Kansas, and eventually landed a job as the first-ever voice of the University of Kansas radio network. Fortunately, a job opened up in nearby Kansas City as the voice of the MLB Athletics, which had relocated from Philadelphia. In 1961, ABC Sports tapped him to anchor studio shows and do play-by-play on college football games on weekends in New York, so he began to commute from Kansas.

Harmon also worked MLB games for the network with broadcast partner Jackie Robinson, the first African American to play in MLB in the modern era. He eventually worked for the Milwaukee Braves, Minnesota Twins, and Milwaukee Brewers, where he teamed up with former MLB catcher and colorful personality Bob Uecker.

"His dedication to family and broadcasting were second to none, and I will always be grateful for the latitude and direction he gave to me as I was entering the profession," Uecker said in a press release by the Milwaukee Brewers in 2009.

While in Milwaukee he established a chain of retail stores selling licensed sports merchandise called Merle Harmon's Fan Fair. I was a minority partner in one of those stores in Texas.

Harmon also became the voice of the New York Jets for nine seasons, which included their run to the Super Bowl in 1968 and the famed Heidi Game against the Oakland Raiders, when viewers on the east coast failed to see the dramatic conclusion when NBC switched those viewers to the television film *Heidi* before the game ended. Fortunately, Harmon's radio call was unaffected, though Jets fans probably would not have preferred to hear the Raiders score two late touchdowns to win.

In the early 1980's he called regional NFL, MLB, and college basketball for NBC Sports, Southwest Conference football for Raycom Sports, and then concluded his career working in Arlington calling Texas Rangers games that I produced or directed, which included Nolan Ryan's 5,000[th] strikeout game August 22, 1989.

"If the event warrants," Harmon told writer Maxwell Kates for the Society of American Baseball Research (SABR), "let the crowd and TV director take over to capture the emotion."

I directed that game (David Handler produced) and that's what Harmon did after Ryan struck out Rickey Henderson for the 5,000$^{th}$ strikeout—silence except for the reaction of the fans and players.

On July 1, 1987, Harmon was the first voice heard on New York's WFAN Radio, his recorded call of the NY Jets winning Super Bowl III.

What a career he had in the booth, but what a heart he had off of it. He volunteered at many nonprofit agencies including soup kitchens, food banks, and his church in Grand Prairie, Texas. I recall one story when a large group of campers were planning to stay at his church, but the air conditioning broke. He arranged for the contingent of kids to come to his home in Arlington to swim, eat, and cool down.

He always sent a nice letter to my family during the holidays and another after the season to me. I still have some of those personalized letters.

One of his sons, Bruce, became one of the best sports camera operators in the nation. He began on our Rangers crew and worked his way up to the national level with many of the major networks, including ABC at the 2024 NBA Finals.

I remember visiting Merle in an Arlington hospital as his health was failing due to pneumonia. I wanted to let him know how much I appreciated working together and that I was praying for his recovery. On April 15, 2009, he passed away at eighty-two.

I always receive sentiments of overwhelming respect and admiration for Merle Harmon when people discover that we worked together. It's great when your working associates are like family. Merle certainly made you feel that way.

I wish someday the National Baseball Hall of Fame

would honor Merle with the Ford C. Frick Award for his major contributions to baseball and his respect for the game, just like his former broadcasting partner Bob Uecker, who received it in 2003.

# CHAPTER 26

# NBA: The Best Seat in the House

*Having produced NBA games* for forty years, I've developed quite a few good and lasting relationships, many with league representatives. As with any business, the hierarchy changes. That puts new faces in charge of the broadcasting and other roles, all of which made me grateful to stay in touch with the league after I concluded my role with the New Orleans Pelicans. Since I had been commuting from Dallas to New Orleans, it was only a matter of time before the team wanted a producer who lived nearby. Once that transpired, I still wanted to be associated with the league to utilize my knowledge of the game and my broadcasting production experience.

I contacted Paul Benedict, the NBA's senior vice president of broadcasting, to pursue a position as a "CA/TOC," or court administrator/time-out coordinator. This was a key gig on national telecasts in my southwest region and other cities. Numerous CA/TOCs, including my good friend and former ESPN coordinating producer Brian Sherriffe, has done this job for years. Brian handles the Los Angeles Lakers and Clippers and works many other cities out West, such as Denver, Portland, and Las Vegas (WNBA).

In 2018, NBA Director of Broadcasting Dana Jones asked me to join the league in that capacity, mostly for national games in Dallas. She understood I was still a freelance producer, so if an assignment arose at the last minute, she was willing to find a replacement for me. That sounded practical. While this gig was distinctively different from producing, it shared similar working conditions: I'd be watching a game closely and listening to a bunch of people on different channels on the headset who often talked to me simultaneously, each with important questions or information.

On one channel, I'd be listening to the NBA replay center in Secaucus, New Jersey; on another was the NBA broadcast operations center; on a third channel was the associate director in the network production truck (or studio) televising the game; a fourth channel carried the announcers; and a fifth channel let me speak directly to an NBA technician, in case we had any problem at the remote. One of my responsibilities was to keenly monitor whether the officiating crew needed a replay review, such as when a foul merited two or three free throws.

When there was a pending review, I'd immediately inform the NBA replay center about its nature. If either coach challenged a call, I'd alert the replay center and the network while switching on the green challenge light. To allow the crew chief to review the play, I'd spin or raise the monitor around so they could watch the video while donning headsets to communicate to the replay center.

In Dallas, my seat is in the front row, near center court. A small table area holds the monitors and my audio console. Sitting directly to my left are scoreboard and clock operators, and to my right is the public address announcer.

Some people say I have the best job in the house. Indeed, it's an excellent assignment, and you must know the rules and the players and possess an instinct for what's happening before a call is made. Although you never speculate, it gives you an advantage if you've seen it before.

Preparation for the two-and-a-half-hour job begins days in advance, when you contact each team's media relations director to inform them of the show, confirm which players or coaches will be miked up, and see if anything special is planned of which the league should be aware. I communicate with the network producer and associate director to see who they will request for interviews and if they are planning anything unique for the broadcast. Finally, I contact both local broadcast producers (if they are doing the game) to apprise them of the national time-out format, tipoff time, and anything out of the ordinary.

Four hours before tipoff, the league calls the CA/TOCs working that night's national games (normally a doubleheader) to review what we've learned from the aforementioned people and to communicate anything they want us to concentrate on or find out.

I arrive at the venue three hours before tip and review my checklist. I inspect the arena for proper advertising signage, because the NBA's national telecasts have protocols for signage on the basket stanchions, floor, backboards, and sideline ad boards. It's also my duty to contact the local ad board operator to review the rotating ad board signs that change every three minutes on dead balls.

In Dallas, I cue the ninety-nine-minute countdown clock. About seventy minutes before the game, I head to the NBA officials' locker room to introduce myself as the CA/TOC, identify the network and announcers broadcasting the game, provide the names of any players/coaches who will be miked up, and share instructions from the league. Sometimes, the crew chief or other crew officials will advise me of something to look out for.

Back on the floor, I stay in touch with the associate director to be sure he or she is ready for tip and hear how accurately the team operations crew is executing the timing of the tip, anthem, lineups, and lights out/up. Once the lights come back on after the home introductions, I cue a ninety-second countdown clock. As soon as that clock hits zero, the network AD (associate director) and I make sure they are ready for the opening tip.

When I get the signal from the production truck, I cue the crew chief—making sure my hand is raised and I'm in their direct line of sight—and we're off and running. I always designate the exact tip time to include in my postgame report to the league.

All those logistics take place before the contest even starts.

On February 4, 2022, a Philadelphia 76ers–Dallas Mavericks game on ESPN was delayed forty-four minutes during the first quarter when Mavericks superstar guard Luka Doncic told the officiating crew one rim looked crooked. I quickly alerted the network production truck, the league office, and replay center. Crew chief Courtney Kirkland stopped the game and sent the teams to their benches to assess the situation.

Mavericks 7-foot-4 center Boban Marjanovic tried unsuccessfully to yank the rim level. Arena personnel brought out a ladder to straighten the rim, but when they checked it with a level, it caused the backboard to lean. Minutes later, they replaced the entire hoop, backboard, and stanchion, which had to be wheeled out once the old one was removed. No one knew how long it would take, because many wires had to be pulled to the clock, photography equipment, and more. The officials also needed to provide the teams with five minutes of warmup time once the new equipment was set up. I kept in constant communication with arena personnel, the officiating crew, media relations directors, broadcasters, league, and network.

It's beneficial for everyone to know that a league representative is there in person to help facilitate and communicate what is transpiring. After the game, of course, I documented the crooked rim in my report.

On February 11, 2020, during a Nuggets–Mavericks telecast on ESPN, we received notice that the league was suspending games due to COVID-19. Our game concluded, but the rest of the season was in limbo "until further notice." We had little notion about the pandemic the nation would soon face.

# CHAPTER 27

## *Moderating Sportswriter Joe Posnanski's Book Event*

*In the summer of 2023,* Rachelle Weiss Crane at the Dallas Aaron Family Jewish Community Center asked me to moderate a BookFest event on October 26, 2023—my birthday, incidentally—when New York Times bestselling baseball author Joe Posnanski would be in Dallas on his national book tour to promote *Why We Love Baseball: A History in 50 Moments*. She contacted me because of my knowledge and love of baseball and to promote my book event in 2024. I was flattered and agreed to participate.

I had never moderated an event like this, yet I felt up for the challenge. To prepare, I scoured the internet for expert tips. Many were obvious, like properly introducing the guests and actually reading the book. Another was to end the session with a "lightning round" of quick and/or unique questions, which I did.

I watched Joe's appearance on *CBS Morning Show*, as well as an interview he did with baseball writers and stats gurus in Denver. I listened to his podcasts with Michael Schur—the ex-*Saturday Night Live* producer and cocreator of NBC's *Parks and Recreation*—and subscribed to Joe's blog.

I wanted to get to know Joe personally, so I phoned him to introduce myself and explain that I had a lively show planned. What he didn't know was that I was going to present video

Joe Posnanski's Dallas Jewish BookFest event for his new book *Why We Love Baseball.*

from some of his "50 Moments" and surprise him with personal appearances by former Texas Rangers named in his book and in his blog.

Here's an excerpt from what he wrote on his blog (which can be found at joeblogs.joeposnanski.com) the day after the BookFest:

## What a Crazy Event in Dallas!

Well, that was wild. We did a "Why We Love Baseball" event on Thursday night at the Aaron JCC in Dallas, and it turned out to be quite a bit more emotional than I expected. I was told by the moderator, longtime television producer Robert Steinfeld, that there would be surprises. He was not lying.

So, right away, I got the sense that this night would be different. Robert [is] an ultra-successful sports television producer who has done many incredible things, and he had laid out an entire run of show for this night. And he wanted to surprise me. So early on, he had me tell one of my favorite stories, my Jim Kern story, which I will share again here.

Jim Kern was a power reliever for Cleveland in the 1970s, when I was a kid. At one of my first games at Cleveland Municipal Stadium, I saw a few Cleveland players signing autographs for some other kid, so I rushed over with a few scraps of paper and a pencil and tried to get in on the action. I'm going to guess this was 1975 or 1976. I was probably 8 or 9, and I had never gotten an autograph before.

I was effectively boxed out by the other kids—I was really small—and slowly it began to occur to me that the players were leaving. Jim Kern was the last one signing, and I was desperate to get his autograph. He said: "Sorry guys, I gotta go," and I began bawling. It's not my proudest moment, but there you go. Jim saw me crying and rushed back, quickly scrawled his name on one of my pieces of scrap paper and raced off.

And with that, I was the single happiest kid on planet Earth, and I rushed back to the seat to show my Dad the autograph and . . . well, what do you think? I couldn't even find it. You don't have people sign autographs in PENCIL, and he had rushed through, and the autograph was so light that you couldn't even see it.

Maybe 30 years later, I wrote about this story. And not long after, a friend handed me a baseball autographed by Jim Kern. And the ball read:

As you might imagine, that became one of my absolute prize possessions. But, as many of you might know, the story doesn't end there, because a few years ago, our dog, Westley, got hold of that baseball. And, well . . .

Yeah. So, anyway, I told that story again. And suddenly,

Robert says something like: "Well, Joe, we have a surprise for you."

And Jim Kern stands up and walks over and hands me an autographed baseball. And on it, he writes:

You will notice the ellipses. Well, on the other side he wrote:

I mean . . . what is even happening?

Then we began talking about the book, the funny moments, the ball bouncing high off of José Canseco's head, the four consecutive fouls balls that David Hulse hit into the Angels dugout that one day, and then there was a question from the audience.

"Joe," the question went, "do you think that David Hulse hit those four foul balls into the dugout on purpose?"

And the question came from: David Hulse. Yeah.*

*My answer was: "I mean, David Hulse was famous for his bat control, so OF COURSE he hit the foul balls on purpose."

There was a lot of other cool stuff like that: Thank you, Robert.

Jim Kern's participation came about after I read Joe's blog and book. Why not invite "The Amazing Emu" to the event, I thought? I had worked with Kern twenty-five to thirty years earlier as our expert analyst on college and minor league baseball games on HSE but had not spoken to him since. When I contacted Kern, he said he lived in Granbury, about ninety minutes away in traffic. I thought it would be a thrilling surprise to present Joe with a new baseball to replace the chewed up one. Kern said he had an old American League ball he would sign.

Somehow, the 6-foot-5 pitcher was able to walk by Joe without being recognized fifteen minutes before the event began. I ran a few funny clips from Emu talking about playing in the minors and another about pitching for the Rangers. After Joe told his story, we showed the chewed up baseball on screen. I soon introduced Kern like it was an episode of *This is Your Life* (an NBC show that ran from 1952 to 1961 that surprised guests with flashbacks of their lives and appearances by colleagues, family, and friends). Kern walked up to the stage and presented the ball. A heartwarming moment.

I reached David Hulse via broadcaster Tom Grieve, who confirmed that Hulse still lived near Dallas. Tom, a former Ranger, GM, and Emmy-winning broadcaster, is a terrific guy.

"Is this David 'The Incredible' Hulse?" I asked when I phoned him. It sure was. He already knew about Joe's book because while being interviewed on Dallas sports radio station The Ticket days earlier, the interviewer mentioned that the book detailed how he fouled off four pitches in the Angels dugout. I asked him to surprise Joe by being in the audience. I thought it would be a fun surprise. He enthusiastically agreed. I was elated that he and Kern attended. Rachelle was also excited, so she emailed them a formal invitation to underscore they were special guests.

The show, as well as its lightning round, turned out spectacularly. Joe and the audience were surprised. Kern and Hulse played along perfectly. Special thanks to everyone who hung around afterwards to sign autographs and receive a signed copy of Joe's *Why We Love Baseball.*

# CHAPTER 28

## *Producing the 2022 Battle 4 Atlantis College Hoops Tourney*

**As I wrote earlier,** I produced the WNBA Commissioner's Cup Championship game in Chicago on July 26, 2022. The production was packaged by Ross Production Services of Connecticut, hired by the NBA to provide remote mobile services and technical crew. The league asked me to produce the game, which aired on Amazon Prime. It went very well and was my first time working for Ross Production Services and its coordinating producer Jay Levy (who previously held that position with ESPN, overseeing college basketball). I had a lot in common with Jay, who eventually hired me to produce college football games which aired on CBSSN and ESPN in 2022 and 2023. Ross was expanding its footprint as a packager and getting more assignments from various networks and leagues, including ESPN.

Months later, Jay asked me to do a big college basketball tournament during the Thanksgiving holiday in Nassau, Bahamas, at Atlantis resort. The eight-team "Battle 4 Atlantis" required two production crews each doing two games a day for three consecutive days. With my vast experience, he wanted me to work with ESPN talent Jon Sciambi and Jimmy Dykes. I had worked with Jimmy numerous times twenty years ago at ESPN, so I looked forward to teaming up with him again. It was my first time working with Jon, who calls the Chicago Cubs' television package. Notably, Jon had just been named the ESPN radio voice of the 2023 World Series.

Not too often do you get a chance to produce a game in "paradise." In this case, it literally was paradise, namely Paradise Island, where the November temperature was in the low eighties and the sun shone every day we were there. Here's how I prepared.

First step, I researched the event and our production plans. Jay set up a call with me and the other producer to discuss telecast times, number of cameras, tournament contacts, and the production support we'd receive from ESPN. This included edit time to produce flashbacks of the 2021 Battle 4 Atlantis Championship, highlight packages on the star players, and more. Then I studied the teams and began a graphics list to send to our graphics associate producer.

While reading Tennessee's schedule, I noticed that the Volunteers were playing an exhibition the next day in Frisco, Texas. Their opponent was Gonzaga, one of the nation's top teams. Since that was just ten minutes from my home in North Dallas, I asked Tennessee media relations director Tom Satkowiak for a media pass. It was an ideal opportunity to scout the Volunteers and to meet coach Barnes and the players. It also helped establish a relationship with Satkowiak and the team.

Studying eight teams required far more preparation than a single contest between two clubs. I read game notes and scoured TV schedules to see when those teams played on ESPN or CBS. I subscribe to ESPN Plus, which is essential to catching games unavailable on the main networks. Hearing local announcers give you inside information is tremendously helpful.

I requested Jon and Jimmy's perspective on possible storylines. Jimmy mentioned that they previously shot some fun pieces with Sebastian the Sea Lion and the trained dolphins at the Atlantis. The difference this time was that we did not have the ESPN budget for our camera crew . . . until I asked for it.

Kansas head coach Bill Self had been suspended for the opening four games of the season, so our initial Atlantis telecast marked his first game back. His return was newsworthy, so I asked Jay Levy if we could get an ENG (electronic news gathering) crew on set-day. My reasoning was that we'd be remiss if we did not have sound from Coach Self addressing his suspension. ESPN would want that, as would viewers.

We could also use that camera to shoot Jimmy with Sebastian the Sea Lion and interviews with players and coaches. Our camera operator could bank some day and evening scenes to roll into the show. We'd get our money's worth.

ESPN approved our request, but the problem was that we could not find an ENG crew. Jay tried but had no luck. I took it on my own to find a local crew, which was not easy on that island. I Googled television production photographers and found a company called Jiggy Productions, which shot commercials and shows. Kyle Thornton of Jiggy—which had done prior assignments at the Battle 4 Atlantis—replied to my email and promised they could help. So less than twenty-four hours before the shoot, we hired Jiggy.

Julian, the camera operator, met me at 7:15 Tuesday morning at Dolphin Cay at the Atlantis. I had already set up the shoot with the resort. Its marine mammal specialist promised that Sebastian and the dolphins would do whatever Jimmy Dykes wanted.

It was amusing to see Sebastian and his trainer respond to Jimmy via flopping, footwork, and more. We aired their vignettes throughout the three telecast days. One of those pieces was sent to the producer of the Maui Invitational basketball tournament, where ESPN commentator Jay Bilas was working. On Monday night, as the Maui tourney promoted our games, Jay said that he was sure Jimmy Dykes would have fun with Sebastian the "seal." Jimmy soon texted Jay to correct him.

"Sebastian would be offended that you called him a *seal*," wrote Jimmy, noting that the seal is the sea lion's archrival when they play mammal games. To surprise Jay, Jimmy set up a piece with Sebastian telling him what Jay called him. Sebastian, a.k.a. "Sebo," responded with a loud noise, sounding highly offended. We sent the piece to the producer of the Maui Invitational to surprise Jay on their show that evening.

By 8:30 a.m., we were done with Sebo and the dolphins. Later, at the Imperial Arena's makeshift locker room, we interviewed Kansas's Bill Self, freshman sensation Gradey Dick, returning star Jalen Wilson, and others. We recorded great sound to use all week. I especially liked coach Self's bite about how excruciating it was to sit out the first four games. I asked our director Logan McDonald to send those bites to ESPN in Bristol, so perhaps SportsCenter could use it to promote our game.

The productions went smoothly, thanks to Ross Productions' outstanding technical staff. Instead of an on-site production truck, we had a "flypack" production. That meant that all the equipment was flown in from the United States in self-contained, protective cases. The hotel allowed Ross engineers to convert a storage room into a control room with the equipment. It was amazing.

Our most exciting game turned out to be the semifinal. Kansas led Wisconsin for most of the game, but Tyler Wahl and the Badgers made a run in the second half to take a lead before the Jayhawks' Kevin McCullar Jr. hit a three-pointer in the closing seconds to send it to overtime. We had excellent replays to show how the play came to fruition. Zach Clemence was falling out of bounds trying to save the ball, but he knew exactly where McCullar would be positioned, so he was able to get him the ball for the game-tying shot.

Overtime boiled down to the final seconds, with Wisconsin leading 68–67. Sophomore Bobby Pettiford, a 6-foot-1 guard, flew in from what seemed like midcourt to grab an errant three-point shot by Clemence and somehow make a twisting reverse layup with 0.2 seconds remaining, for a 69–68 Kansas victory.

The crowd went wild, but as producer, you must be aware of the situation. We still needed to announce the player of the game, highlight the bracket, and most importantly, show the replays of the unbelievable ending. Meanwhile, our associate director Gretchen Schackelford was cautioning me that ESPN wanted us to wrap it up quickly to launch the next game at another site. My challenge was to satisfy both the viewer and network. Those at home wanted to see what happened and how the play developed. The network also wanted us to do that, but quickly. I'm not sure everyone was happy at that point, but we did a good job to satisfy both. It's a fine line.

In the title game, Kansas played Tennessee. The Volunteers, whom I considered my national dark horse team after seeing them beat Gonzaga, prevailed 64–50. During that game, we showed a piece the Tennessee team provided us of players Jonas Aidoo and Jahmai Mashack cavorting on the Atlantis resort slides and other attractions. All that merriment was well received by the network and our viewers.

# CHAPTER 29

## *Hopelessly Devoted to Olivia Newton-John*

*Any one of my friends and fraternity brothers* at AEPi in Austin from 1974 to 1977 would find it remiss if I didn't dedicate one chapter to Olivia Newton-John. If you saw my frat room, you would have shared some people's opinion that I was a bit obsessed with her. Ample evidence would have proven that beyond a shadow of doubt. Yes, millions of fans and I found her attractive, but from the start, I was a really big fan of her singing and music.

It took a while for others to acknowledge her talent. She won the 1973 most promising female vocalist award by the Academy of Country Music; ten American Music Awards; ten Billboard Awards; 1974 Female Vocalist of the Year by the Country Music Association Awards; four Grammy Awards (from her eight nominations); four People's Choice Awards; two Golden Globe nominations; plus a 1999 Daytime Emmy Award.

Beyond her music, she was honored for her humanitarian work for breast cancer research by the Red Cross; Cadillac Concept; the Kimmel Center; and she was named Officer of the Order of Australia for "service to the entertainment industry as a singer and actor, and to the community through organizations supporting breast cancer treatment, education, training and research and the environment." She was also an advocate for animal rights and environmental causes.

*My University of Texas AEPi fraternity room, 1975.*

Olivia Newton-John lent her name to the Cancer Wellness & Research Centre in Australia. She championed the vision to build a world-class hospital that supports patients in body, mind, and spirit. Her fundraising helped raise more than $17 million. She was also associated with the Olivia Newton-John Cancer Research Institute in Melbourne.

Unfortunately, Olivia passed away from breast cancer in August 2022.

My wife and I had the honor to see her in concert many times in Dallas, Oklahoma, and Las Vegas, where we once met her backstage at the Flamingo Hotel on May 29, 2014. I showed her a photograph of me in my AEPi frat room at the University of Texas in 1975. She signed it.

In 1976, I convinced the editor of the arts section of *The Daily Texan* (the University of Texas student newspaper) to allow one of their sportswriters (me) to travel to Houston to review Olivia Newton-John's concert at the Houston Livestock and Rodeo. It was one of her first prominent concerts in the United States. I kept a

*Sarah and I went to Las Vegas to see and meet Olivia after her perfor-
mance at the Flamingo. We had seen her perform many times in the
Dallas area, but it was the first time we had the pleasure to meet her,
which I enjoyed.*

copy of the review for my stringbook. Shoutout to AEPi fraternity
buddy Ron Feldman, who "begrudgingly" (just kidding) tagged
along for the trip.

On March 3, 1976, I jotted a handwritten note next to the
article: "This is my favorite story that I have written so far as a
journalist. I am going to send her a copy." Here's my review:

### Olivia Shines in Astrodome Performance; Vocalist Shedding Stereotyped Image
*By Bob Steinfeld*
*Texan Staff Writer*

Think of Olivia and you have to think of the perky, bright
and beautiful superstar, Olivia Newton-John. In concert at the
Houston Livestock Show and Rodeo last weekend, she finally

showed that she is shedding her country-stereotyped-unserious image brought on by her first hit songs.

Olivia was the highlight of the two and a half hours of bronc-busting and steer wrestling at the Astrodome. The sharp, high-voiced singer performed before 42,000 people Saturday night and 25,000 Sunday afternoon.

She put on two shows Saturday and two Sunday. To attract a crowd to the rodeo, she performed as halftime entertainment for more than an hour. It was the best halftime show I have ever seen. And for sure the most beautiful.

A revolving stage was rolled out to the middle of the dirt-covered Astrodome floor, which put her at least 100 feet from the surrounding crowd.

Although she admitted it's hard to reach an audience so far away, she got the hesitant audience clapping and singing to "The River's Too Wide." She seemed at home before her largest crowd ever.

Then she asked the crowd, "Has anyone ever heard of Willie Nelson?" It seemed kind of strange coming from the mouth of the English-born singer. But the crowd responded with overwhelming assurance.

Right away, most of the people thought Nelson would appear on stage, but he didn't. Olivia said, "He couldn't be with us today, but I'm going to sing you one of his songs."

It was "Blue Eyes Crying in the Rain," recorded by Nelson last year. And honestly, she sang it better than Willie did. Her sweet voice and sensual expressions seemed to fit into the lyrics more so than the bearded Nelson did on his record.

Then she sang her new release, written for her by the Bee Gees, "Come On Over." It didn't impress me, but she says it will be the first hit off her next album by the same name. The song was released last week and the album will be released this week.

Olivia's manager, Lee Kramer, said, "Olivia has seven gold records already and in a couple of months she should have nine."

In the future, look for Liv on the cover of Redbook, on an ABC television special and on the movie screen. The vivacious 26-year-old has entered a film career. "I have looked at a lot of scripts, but I haven't found anything that relates to the way I feel," the singer said candidly. "So, you see, I'm not going to do a film just to be doing it."

Saturday night, she was scurried across the dirt floor by jeep to the stage. Her silk green pant suit, which sparkled from the spotlight reflection, only enhanced her radiant beauty.

Sunday, she appeared same fashion, but her outfit was completely different. She was in a more relaxed mode, sporting a nylon shiny-red, but buttoned-up shirt and patched blue jeans. She seemed more at ease handling the large, but mostly unresponsive crowd. The audience, mostly composed of cowboys, hesitated before the smart young singer tactfully told everyone to join in.

As she sang "I Honestly Love You" Saturday night, a few fans scampered onto the dirt floor and headed for the stage. One almost made it, but was grabbed by policemen who tried to guard the lovely star.

Sunday, things were under control and the only time the crowd went berserk was when Olivia made a lap around the perimeter of the Astrodome in the jeep. It brought her fans, young and old, to the steel retaining bars.

As a reminder of the concert, Olivia bought a horse from the livestock show to send to her Malibu, California, home.

Newton-John sang most of her hits, "Please Mr. Please," "Let Me Be There," "Is There Anybody Out There Who Can Shine?" and "If You Love Me, Let Me Know." The element of consistency made the performance come alive. Her songs sounded just like the recordings, which I am sure was just like the crowd wanted them to be.

Olivia has left her stereotyped spot as just a "country girl" born in England, though raised in Australia, and winner

245

of the Best Country Female Vocalist Award image. She has become a diversified superstar able to challenge any material confronting her.

And when she sang The Hollies' "He Ain't Heavy, He's My Brother" from her album "Clearly Love," it typified her ability to make love and emotion exist in song.

# CHAPTER 30

## *It's a Wrap*

*Before bidding adieu,* and calling it a "wrap" as we do in the entertainment business, I will leave you with lessons I've learned along the way working in sports television. Many can be employed in other fields or endeavors in the pursuit of a quality career and personal life.

1. Be good at what you do and work hard. In this small profession, there is always someone wanting your job and willing to do the work. The openings for NBA and MLB producers are rare. Never be complacent. Give it your best shot every time.

2. Be passionate. Determine which job you like best, whether it's producing, directing, announcing, writing, or on the technical side as camera operator, technical director, audio tech, video tech, or within operations. Whichever intrigues and fascinates you and seems like fun (not work) is what you should pursue, at least initially.

3. The experience and understanding you absorb in each phase of our business will help your career in the long run. For example, if you start out in production, it will help you if you ultimately choose to pursue an on-camera position, because you will understand technically how to approach

your story. Being on the same page with your producer and director will be key to your success.

4. Don't ever take your job for granted. Don't complain that you have too much work, because there are plenty of qualified people who need work. If you feel overworked, turn down a few jobs and take a breather. That will allow others to get an opportunity and give you a chance to recharge.

5. Surround yourself with the best people, and let them do their jobs. You pay them for their judgement as well as their expertise.

6. Be punctual and expect others to be.

7. Set expectations instead of rules, as former Duke and Team USA head coach Mike Krzyzewski professes.

8. Come prepared. Don't just show up and start thinking about your show. Organization and a game plan are essential for your production team's success.

9. Read the information (formats, rundowns, checklists, copy, etc.) that is sent to you by all producers. It will answer most questions you have in advance of a show, and it will provide you time to validate the information is correct. If the scheduling or equipment is not right, contact the person who sent you the book ASAP.

10. As a producer, keep your eye on the big picture.

11. Listen to your announcers and crew members. Encourage input and participation.

12. Follow up storylines with quantified graphics and visual recaps. Viewers have more interest in the players and teams when you develop their stories and backgrounds, so do your homework.

13. Recap, because viewers rarely stick around for the entire ride.

14. Have fun.

15. Most importantly, learn how to temper your attitude and work better with the crew, as I have had to do. I came

from the old school networks, where many producers and directors were extremely aggressive and intense on the air. They were more cordial off the air, but that's the way I thought all shows were managed. When I began working in local and regional settings, that attitude did not fly. It took me a while to understand that. I also had to manage my temper and mature. I've evolved over the years. I know there's still an element of ABC Sports' high standard that remains ingrained in me.

If you reflect back on your childhood you can also learn to reach inside your soul to put things in perspective. Remember what it was like when you went on road trips with your parents? It was the journey along the way that became embedded in your memory: those individual stories, unexpected joys, or even unfortunate times that you can appreciate or even laugh at today.

Thank you to everyone who's been a part of these wonderful times and more in the future, because I still have the honor and privilege to say, "3 . . . 2 . . . 1 . . . We're on the air!"

So, "Dominate where you can."

# Producer Preparation Schedule for College Football and the Celebrity Guest List for *Tailgate Party*

## Prepping the Week: Producing a Big 12 College Football Telecast

Monday

- Watch press conferences from the schools and/or conference that week.
- Recontact media relations directors for each school.
- Touch base with talent on storylines.
- Get final edit information to associate director and/or production assistants in studio for player highlight packages, flashbacks, and other roll-ins.
- Confirm crew is set and verify if additional support personnel is needed.
- Set up Zoom meetings with head coaches and coordinators for later in the week, or schedule in-person meetings Friday (or sometimes both).
- Read school game notes.

## Tuesday

- Conference call with network executive producer and/or coordinating producer, talent, and above-line personnel to review last week's show. Discuss format, script, sponsor, or other refinements for this weekend's telecast.
- Confirm conference timeout coordinator (red hat to cue commercial breaks).
- Begin work on formats.
- Review research sent by network.
- Initiate contact with next week's game media relations directors.

## Wednesday

- Review production schedule with tech manager and operations producer.
- Formulate open rundowns.
- Review sponsored elements.

## Thursday

- Approve production elements for open and in-game, such as player packages and flashbacks.
- Flesh out storylines with talent.
- Send "Steiny Pack" with rundowns and copy so production and talent can preview.
- Travel to game (or sometimes wait until early Friday morning).

## Friday

- Go to stadium for set day. (This is when the production truck arrives at venue. The crew erects cameras, runs audio lines to booth, and we prepare graphics and elements in the truck. This "set day" allows us time to get ready so the next day we are ready for the show. It also allows our crew to iron out problems or issues that might arise with equipment or at the venue.)
- Meet with media relation directors.

- Watch home team practice (walk-through).
- Watch scouting/coaches video with our analyst.
- Crew loads in graphics and sets up camera and announce booth.
- Visit with home coach after walk-through/practice.
- Production meeting with talent and above-line production personnel.

## Saturday

- Check audio and cameras.
- Director camera meeting.
- Producer replay ops meeting.
- Graphics and video playback elements review with talent.
- Rehearse the open. Either record the open or do it live.
- Oh yeah—produce the game.

## Sunday

- Review the game at home.
- Start it all over again on Monday.

# The Final Guest List of *Tailgate Party* in 1989:

Lee Trevino, golf legend

George W. Bush, Texas Rangers owner and future president of the United States

Derrick Johnson, turkey bowler

Jeff Torborg, Chicago White Sox manager

Dave Lopez, Dodgers all-star

The San Diego Chicken, famed San Diego Padres mascot

Jeff Cesario, comedian

Mark McGwire, Oakland A's all-star

Dave "Travelin" Davlin, basketball juggler

Rick Honeycutt, Oakland A's pitcher

Uwe Blab (and his pet bird, Buster Blab), Dallas Mavericks center

Tony LaRussa, Oakland A's manager

Bruce Lietzke, pro golfer

Ray Palacios, Kansas City Royals catcher, who stuffed a baseball in
    his mouth
Cathy Rigby, Olympic gymnast and actress
Bryan Harvey, California Angels pitcher
Rafael Palmeiro, Texas Rangers first baseman
Randy White, Dallas Mavericks forward
Gary Cogill, movie critic
Charley Pride, country singer and Negro League all-star
Steve Timmons, US Olympic volleyball star
Karch Karaly, US Olympic volleyball star
Tim McKyer, San Francisco 49ers cornerback
Dallas Cowboys Cheerleaders
Bobby Bragan, MLB player and manager
The Star Flyers Trick Frisbee Team
Michael Carter, Olympic medalist and San Francisco 49ers nose tackle
Sharon Hargrove, author of *Safe at Home: A Baseball Wife's Story*
Jim Kern, Texas Rangers and Cleveland Indians pitcher
Tom Candiotti, Cleveland Indians pitcher
Jim Sundberg, Texas Rangers all-star catcher
Joe Carter, Cleveland Indians outfielder
Merle Harmon, Texas Rangers announcer
Herb Score, Cleveland Indians all-star pitcher and broadcaster
Gene Stallings, college and NFL head coach
Herschel Walker, Dallas Cowboys running back
Mexican Olympic Bobsled Team
James Donaldson, Dallas Mavericks center
Donnie Gay, eight-time world champion bull rider
Tony Dorsett, Dallas Cowboys running back
Jim Lefebvre, Seattle Mariners manager
Ron Hudson, world's fastest cop
Durwood Merrill, Major League Baseball umpire
Vic Voltaggio, Major League Baseball umpire
Harold Reynolds, Seattle Mariners all-star
Drew Pearson, Dallas Cowboys receiver
Dan Reeves, Denver Broncos head coach
Mike Greenwell, Boston Red Sox all-star outfielder

Captain Greg Dubrile, shark hunter
Tom House, Texas Rangers pitching coach and Atlanta Braves pitcher
Forrest Gregg, NFL hall of famer and SMU head coach
Mike Calbot, golf trick-shot artist
Phil Rizzuto, New York Yankees shortstop and broadcaster
Spud Webb, Atlanta Hawks' slam dunk champion
Tim Brown, Los Angeles Raiders receiver and Heisman Trophy winner
Bill Chaffin, attempted record of most free throws in ten minutes
Karl Malone, Utah Jazz all-star
Dave Righetti, New York Yankees all-star pitcher
Jay Johnstone, New York Yankees broadcaster
Rolando Blackman, Dallas Mavericks all-star
Jim Wynn, Houston Astros outfielder
Bob Aspromonte, Houston Astros third baseman
Mickey Rivers, Texas Rangers all-star
Orlando Cepeda, San Francisco Giants and St. Louis
    Cardinals all-star
Bob Whitcomb, bowling ball juggler
Joe Garagiola, MLB catcher and broadcaster
Ralph Branca, Brooklyn Dodgers pitcher
Bobby Valentine, Texas Rangers manager
Mary Valentine, Branca's daughter and Bobby's wife
Ernie Harwell, Detroit Tigers hall of fame announcer
Steve Busby, Kansas City Royals pitcher and Texas Rangers broadcaster
Lawrence "Herkie" Herkimer, inventor of pompoms
Meadowlark Lemon, Harlem Globetrotter
Lou Whitaker, Detroit Tigers all-star
Ashrita Furman, Guinness record holder for most Guinness World
    Records
Frank Tanana, Detroit Tigers and California Angels pitcher
Cliff Harris, Dallas Cowboys safety
Conni Gordon, world's fastest painter
Dave Stewart, Oakland A's pitcher
Lanny Wadkins, pro golfer
Terry Bradshaw, Pittsburgh Steelers hall of fame quarterback
Spanky McFarland, actor in the 1930s *Our Gang* Little Rascals films

# APPENDIX 2

# *"The Evolution of Golf in Texas" and "New NBA Rivalry for Texans"*

**The Evolution of Golf in Texas**
*By Robert Steinfeld*
*A Feature from Summer 2008*
*Written for Direct Energy Grand Slam*
*Read by President George H. W. Bush*

The royal and ancient game of golf rooted itself in Texas history in the 1860s. San Antonio, Dallas, and the coastal resort island Galveston were early centers of activity. Exhibitions by prominent British and American golfers helped popularize the game in the early 1900s. Two members of Britain's great triumvirate, Harry Vardon and Ted Ray, made several stops in Texas.

Tom Kite is well aware of Vardon's legacy. In 1981 and '82, Kite won the Vardon Trophy for the PGA Tour's lowest scoring average.

By the 1920s, oil was flying in Texas and so were those little white balls. Golf courses and clubs, bankrolled by petroleum resources, began a boom throughout the state.

National attention was being diverted from the northeast to the southwest, and in 1922, the first Texas Open was held in San Antonio's Brackenridge Park. The $5,000 first prize was the largest at that time in professional golf.

The biggest milestone in Texas golf history came in 1927 when the National Professional Golfers Association championship was the first major golf event held in the state and was won by Walter Hagen.

From the 1930s to the mid '50s, the first batch of Texan golfing greats were beginning to write their names in Lone Star history. In 1945, Byron Nelson won 18 tournaments—including 11 in a row—a record that still stands today. The Byron Nelson Classic is played each year in the Dallas area.

Fellow Fort Worth native Ben Hogan rose to prominence during the same era. In 1949, an automobile accident in west Texas almost took his life, but determined as he was, he won five of the six tournaments he entered, three of them majors: the Masters; U.S. Open; and the only British Open he entered. He's endeared today by members at one of the state's golf course treasures, the Colonial Country Club in Fort Worth, the first Texas venue to host a United States Open in 1941.

Houston area golfers were establishing their credentials as well during the '50s and '60s, with the likes of Jimmie Demaret, Jack Burke Jr., and Dave Marr. During this time, Lone Star collegiate golf was developing a national reputation. From 1949 to 1952, North Texas State in Denton, coached by Fred Cobb, stunned the long-established northeast schools by winning the NCAA men's golf championship. Future pro Don January led the charge.

Fellow Dallasite Lee Trevino began carving his name in Texas golf lore during the '40s and '50s, playing on local public links, including Hardee's "pitch and putt," a nine-hole, par three course where he once shot a course-record 35 for 18 holes! He began playing on the PGA tour in 1967 and went on to win 29 times, including six majors.

From 1956 to '85, the University of Houston and coach Dave Williams established one of the greatest and successful golf programs in state history, winning 16 NCAA championships. Just a few former Cougars from that era: Homero Blancas, Bill Rogers, Bruce Lietzke, John Mahaffey, Steve Elkington, and Fred Couples.

The University of Texas also established success in the late '60s through today, beginning with legendary coach Harvey Penick, who helped Tom Kite and Ben Crenshaw in the Austin area on their way to their great careers at UT.

Following in Kite and Crenshaw's footsteps at UT in the '80s and '90s were future U.S. Open champion Mark Brooks and future British Open champion Justin Leonard.

———

In researching this book and perusing my old University of Texas *The Daily Texan* stringbook, I came across the following story from August 1, 1976, which showed my interest in the NBA and the San Antonio Spurs, thirteen years before I began producing their games. Please note what I wrote about the NBA considering implementing the three-point line and my view of the NBA's minimum salary (which now stands at $1.1 million).

### New NBA Rivalry for Texans

*By Bob Steinfeld*
*Texan Staff Writer*
*August 1976*

Houston and Dallas always have had a bitter sports rivalry, but now Texas' third largest city will become a bitter foe for the NBA Houston Rockets.

The San Antonio Spurs, one of the four former ABA teams which will join the NBA next year, hope to develop one of the fiercest sports rivalries in the state with the Rockets.

*[Author's note: The Dallas Mavericks did not enter the NBA until 1980]*

"It'll be an outstanding rivalry, and we're looking forward to playing in Houston," Spurs' general manager John Begzos said.

"There should be no attendance problem, because we have had tremendous crowds against them in preseason games."

While the Spurs will become a new addition to the league, some of the old ABA traits will not. The ABA red-white-and-blue basketball has been discontinued, as well as the exciting three-point shot.

"But the three-point line may come back," Begzos said. "The general managers voted it in, but the coaches said forget it."

Other axed ABA trademarks are three teams: Virginia Squires, Spirits of St. Louis and Kentucky Colonels. The other four former ABA teams—New York Nets, Denver Nuggets, Indiana Pacers and Spurs—have been dispersed into three of the four NBA divisions.

The Spurs will join Atlanta, Cleveland, Houston, New Orleans and Washington in the Central Division of the Eastern Conference, while the Nets will tangle with Boston, Buffalo, New York Knicks and Philadelphia in the Atlantic Division.

In the Western Conference, the Nuggets and Pacers will compete with Chicago, Detroit, Kansas City and Milwaukee for the Midwest title while the Pacific Conference remains intact. Golden State, Los Angeles, Phoenix, Portland and Seattle round out the Western Conference.

The playoff system will remain the same with the best four teams in each conference competing. At the end of the regular 82-game season, conference leaders will receive a bye into the second round while the other three teams battle to remain alive in the playoffs.

To keep the players happy during and after the long season, Begzos said the minimum NBA salary has been raised from $20,000 to $30,000. He also said, "to look for veteran salaries to rise."

The Spurs added a veteran to their roster through the ABA dispersal draft when they picked up former Kentucky Colonel Louie Dampier for $20,000. Dampier will complement George Gervin and James Silas in the Spurs' backcourt.